WHY STATES MATTER

WHY STATES MATTER
An Introduction to State Politics

Gary Moncrief and Peverill Squire

ROWMAN & LITTLEFIELD PUBLISHERS, INC.
Lanham • Boulder • New York • Toronto • Plymouth, UK

Published by Rowman & Littlefield Publishers, Inc.
A wholly owned subsidiary of Rowman & Littlefield
4501 Forbes Boulevard, Suite 200, Lanham, Maryland 20706
www.rowman.com

10 Thornbury Road, Plymouth PL6 7PP, United Kingdom

British Library Cataloguing in Publication Information Available

Library of Congress Cataloging-in-Publication Data

Moncrief, Gary F.
 Why states matter : an introduction to state politics / Gary Moncrief and Peverill Squire.
   pages cm
 Includes bibliographical references and index.
 ISBN 978-0-7425-7037-5 (cloth : alk. paper) — ISBN 978-0-7425-7038-2 (pbk. : alk.
paper) — ISBN 978-0-7425-7039-9 (ebook) 1. State governments—United States.
I. Squire, Peverill. II. Title.
 JK2408.M64 2013
 320.473—dc23

                                                                    2013018701

∞™ The paper used in this publication meets the minimum requirements of American National Standard for Information Sciences—Permanence of Paper for Printed Library Materials, ANSI/NISO Z39.48-1992.

Printed in the United States of America

To Heidi and Janet

Contents

Preface

In June 2013, as this book was being sent to the printer for production, *Governing Magazine* published an article titled "Could Gay Marriage, Marijuana and Guns Lead to a Fragmented United States of America?" The theme of the article—that gridlock in Washington, D.C. and partisan realignment in the states is creating the conditions for a policy renaissance in state government—is precisely the theme of this book. It is, we contend, the main reason why states matter today more than at any time in at least the past two generations. But we also argue that states have always been a crucial part of the American political system. This, too, is an important theme of the book.

The proposition that states increasingly matter was highlighted by two U.S. Supreme Court decisions announced in late June 2013. From an ideological perspective, one decision (striking down a key aspect of the Voting Rights Act, originally passed by Congress in 1965) was hailed by conservatives while the other decision (striking down the Defense of Marriage Act passed by Congress in 1996) was hailed by liberals. For the purposes of the argument we make in the book, however, the key thing is that both these decisions could be interpreted as limiting the power of the national government in favor of greater state policy discretion, again emphasizing the notion that the states matter.

At virtually the same time that the U.S. Supreme Court was handing down these landmark decisions, another political spectacle captured the attention of many Americans. An effort to pass a strict anti-abortion measure in the Texas Senate was derailed by filibuster mounted by a lone state senator. Most state legislative chambers do not allow filibusters but a few do, using rules that are different from those employed in the U.S. Senate. The presiding officer handling the filibuster in the Texas Senate was not a senator, but rather the state's lieutenant governor, who is empowered by the Texas Constitution to play that role. Most lieutenant governors around the country do not enjoy similar power. The filibuster was streamed live, so that Texans around the state could watch (as could political scientists in Boise, Idaho, and Columbia, Missouri). With many eyes watching, the legislature had to hew closely to its rules. Many, but not all, state legislatures stream their sessions. This incident demonstrated another theme of our book: Each state has its own governing rules and structures, making them different from each other, and from the federal government. And, of course, the reality that abortion laws can vary dramatically by state reinforces our earlier theme.

The next several years will bear witness to the important role of the states, as they make important decisions about how to implement the Affordable Health Care Act, how to address critical state and local infrastructure needs, and how to balance social responsibility against fiscal responsibility. As we emphasize in the book, the decisions made by state legislators, state governors, state judges, and state bureaucrats impact the daily lives of every American in ways that are both obvious and subtle. This reality will only become more apparent in the coming years.

Together or separately, we have been involved in the creation of about a dozen books, almost all of which focus on some aspect of state legislatures, and almost all of which were written almost exclusively for an academic audience. This book is a bit different. Its subject matter takes us well-beyond the institution of the legislature and into broader areas of federalism, policy making, American institutional development, electoral systems, and fiscal policy. Moreover, we wrote it with a somewhat broader audience in mind—a book that can be used in a variety of courses and, we hope, might find a more general audience. We have tried to explain why states matter, why budgets and electoral systems matter, and why states are more capable of governing today. We have tried to explain the different views of federalism, and we have tried to do all this in an objective and balanced manner.

For these reasons, this was a difficult book to write. The relationship between the federal government and the states has been the subject of passionate political debate and political action over the past few years, making the subject, for us, something of a moving target. But, although we were each sidetracked by other projects along the way, we continued to come back to this one because we think it is a critically important story to tell. Through all this, the staff at Rowman & Littlefield was remarkably patient. And yet, once we completed the manuscript, the staff moved with considerable speed to get the book to print. We owe special thanks to Jon Sisk, Elaine McGarraugh, and Benjamin Verdi for shepherding the manuscript from inception to completion.

As always, there are many to thank as a project such as this is completed. We thank all those representatives of state organizations who graciously consented to interviews. We appreciate the support and encouragement of our colleagues at Boise State University and the University of Missouri. Moncrief especially wishes to acknowledge the immense benefit of a semester on sabbatical leave that greatly facilitated the completion of the manuscript. And we wish to recognize the patience, encouragement, and understanding of our spouses, Heidi and Janet.

1

Making a Case for the States

JUST OFF INTERSTATE 35, near exit 235, close by Danny Edward's Boulevard BBQ Restaurant, you will find a well-kept, two-story home on Barber Avenue in Kansas City, Kansas. There is a fence separating the property from that of the neighbor's a few feet to the east. The fence line is also the state line, because the neighbor lives on W. 32nd Street in Kansas City, Missouri. The residents of these two houses can literally converse with one another across the back fence, but they live in different states.

In what ways does this seemingly small fact matter? As table 1.1 makes clear, it matters in many ways. These two people, who live less than twenty yards from each other, pay different state income tax rates. They pay a different sales tax and they pay that tax on different items. The Kansan pays much higher taxes on beer, tobacco, and gasoline. He also pays more for a license to hunt or fish, and probably pays more to register his automobile. However, he pays a little less to send his daughter to the University of Kansas than his neighbor has to spend to send her son to the University of Missouri.

If the Kansan is found in possession of more than 1.2 ounces of marijuana, he can be charged with a misdemeanor (up to one year in jail). Walk across the street into Missouri, he can be charged with a felony (up to seven years in prison). The traffic laws are different for these two individuals; whether you have to wear a motorcycle helmet, whether you can text while driving a car, and the maximum speed at which you can drive are different. The maximum speed limit in Missouri is lower than in Kansas; since you can text while driving in Missouri, apparently lawmakers think you should at least drive a little slower. In terms of

TABLE 1.1
Kansas City, KS, versus Kansas City, MO, 2012

	Kansas	Missouri
State Income Taxes		
Rate Range	3.5% to 6.45%	1.5% to 6.0%
Number of Brackets	3	10
Low Bracket	$15,000	$1,000
Highest Bracket	$30,001	$9,001
Federal Taxes Deductible?	No	Yes
State Corporate Tax Rate	4.0%	6.25%
Federal Taxes Deductible?	No	Yes
State Sales Tax Rate	6.3%	4.225%
Applied to Food?	No	Yes (1.225%)
State Gas Tax	$.26 per gallon	$.173 per gallon
Tobacco Tax	$.79 per pack	$.17 per pack
Beer Tax	$.18 per gallon	$.06 per gallon
Sales Tax Also Applied?	No	Yes
Medicaid Eligibility Limit	150% of federal poverty rate	185% of federal poverty rate
Child Health Insurance Program (CHIP) Eligibility Limit for Family of three	$44, 101	$55,590
Resident Tuition at Flagship State University	$8,790	$9,272
Speed Limits, Maximum Posted		
Rural Interstates	75 MPH	70 MPH
Urban Interstates	75 MPH	60 MPH
State Marijuana Laws	Possession of any amount (first offense) is a misdemeanor, punishable by one year in jail and a $2,500 fine.	Possession of thirty-five grams or less is a misdemeanor, punishable by one year in jail and a $1,000 fine. Possession of thirty-five grams to thirty-five kg is a felony, punishable by seven years in prison and a $5,000 fine.
Deer Hunting License	$37.50 (general resident, firearm, any white-tailed or mule deer)	$17 (resident, firearm, any deer)
Fishing License	$20.50 (resident)	$12 (resident)
Motor Vehicle Fees		
Registration	$35–$45	$18.50 to $51.25 (depending on horsepower) + $3.50 processing fee
Title	$10	$8.50 + $2.50 processing fee + state and local sales tax
Motorcycle Helmet Law	Covers riders aged seventeen and younger	Covers all riders
Texting and Driving	Prohibited for all drivers	Allowed for drivers over twenty-one years of age

social services, one may be eligible for Medicaid while the other may not. The same is true for state-administered health insurance for their children.

These are but a few examples of how states matter. When it comes to voting, taxes, environmental regulations, social services, education, criminal justice, political parties, property rights, gun control, marriage and divorce, and just about anything else other than national defense, the state in which you reside makes a difference. That idea—that states matter—is the fundamental concept behind this book. So much attention is paid by the media to the national government and what the president and Congress are doing—or not doing—that it is easy to lose sight of the fact that states are different and their policies are different and these differences have a real, direct effect on the lives of their citizens. Despite a long-term trend toward centralization of power at the national level, the states still have considerable latitude in many policy areas—more so than most people may realize.

The Kansas City case is just one of many examples of communities, separated by a half-mile or less, in different states with important policy positions: Fargo, North Dakota, and Moorhead, Minnesota; Piedmont, West Virginia, and Westernport, Maryland; Cincinnati, Ohio, and Covington, Kentucky; Ardmore, Alabama, and Ardmore, Tennessee.

Perhaps no more dramatic example of neighbors in two different policy worlds would be the people of Lewiston, Idaho, and Clarkston, Washington. Only the width of the Snake River—three hundred yards—separates those who live in a state (Washington) where the citizens have legal access to medical and recreational use of marijuana, state-recognized same-sex marriage, assisted suicide for the terminally ill, and labor union–friendly laws from a state (Idaho) with none of those policies.[1] States, it seems, do matter. Despite the obvious expansion in the power of the national government, states still play a critical role in our federal system. Indeed, as governments the states are more active today than ever. As makers of policy, states are more important than the national government on some issues, and ahead of the national government on some others. And, as the national government struggles to find its way through the morass of hyperpartisanship and budget deficits, the role of the states as problem-solvers has increased.

The Historical Context

To claim that states matter today does not require us to argue that they matter in quite the same way as in the past. It would be foolish to believe that states hold the same position, relative to the national government, that they did in 1790.

We think it foolish to even argue that states *should* hold precisely the same position as they did in 1790; after all, hardly anything in the world is as it was in 1790. The role of all governments was much smaller in those days; there were few large cities, virtually no public education,[2] public health, or public welfare, and very few public roads. Industrialization had not yet occurred on any significant scale. The vast majority of labor and commerce in the United States was associated with farming and maritime trade. Many people died of diseases that today are controllable. The average life span was about forty-five years, compared to about seventy-eight years today. The infant mortality rate (well below 1 percent today) was as high as 15 percent in 1790.

The first US Census, conducted in 1790, indicated the total population of the thirteen states was 3.9 million, which is barely more than 1 percent of the population of the United States today. Of that 3.9 million, the largest urban area was New York City with a population of 33,131.[3] Today, there are more than one thousand cities in the United States with a population greater than New York City in 1790.[4]

Of the 3.9 million people counted in the 1790 census, almost seven hundred thousand were slaves. Clearly, the economy was much different than today, as were the views about one human being owning as property another human being. The usual estimate is that about 90 percent of the workforce was employed in agriculture in 1790, while today less than 2 percent is thusly employed.

Obviously, the nature of society was very different. The population was relatively small, residing almost entirely on small farms and homesteads, with considerably less interaction or interdependence among people than we find today. The role of government—all governments, regardless of national, state, or local level—was very limited. As one observer notes, "[L]ife itself was far less complicated than it is today; and government did not do very many things and frequently did not do them well. . . . Those days are no more, and it is wholly unrealistic to expect they will ever return."[5]

Moreover, the relationship between these levels of government was very different. Scholars often characterize the original relationship between the states and federal government as "dual federalism"—by which they mean the national and state governments tended to operate in separate policy spheres. For the most part, however, neither sphere was very large.

From the founding it was unclear exactly what the relationship between the national and state governments ought to be. The Articles of Confederation—the first system under which the country operated—gave the states the upper hand. But that system failed, leaving open the question of how the different levels of government were to relate. When the Constitution was adopted, there was still considerable uncertainty. There were those, like Alexander Hamilton, who argued forcefully for a nationalist perspective—contending that the primary constituents of the new system were the people, and that it was "the people" as a collection of individuals who were sovereign grantors of authority to the new government. Under this view, the national government would hold a preeminent position. A second view was that the federal system was agreed to by the states themselves, not individuals. In this view, the states were the sovereign grantors of authority to the new government, and as such retained the ultimate sovereignty themselves. Proponents of this view saw the federal system as an agreement—a compact—of sovereign states. Obviously, this tug between two views—the nationalist and the compact—is still with us today. In 2010, governors or legislatures in several states invoked the "compact theory" as they argued that states had the constitutional authority to reject the newly enacted federal health-care law. These claims were largely unsuccessful, but they highlight the fact that such arguments have been central to some of the most historic moments in the country's history.

James Madison, one of the key architects of the new system, essentially argued that both the nationalist and the compact theories were correct—or at least they were partially and equally correct. Madison described the system as a "compound republic." As Martha Derthick notes, "It is a pity that Madison's term *compound republic* did not survive in our political language for it conveys the complicated and ambiguous intent of the framing generation and helps to make comprehensible what otherwise is bewildering to the modern citizenry."[6]

Madison's compound republic was a system that "sought to assemble majorities of two different kinds: one composed of individual voters, the other, of the states as distinct political societies."[7] The individual voters, by forming an "association of people, under a constitution of government, uniting their power" provide the nationalist perspective.[8] The states, as "distinct political societies" forming together, provide the compact perspective.

We will explore the various interpretations and mutations of federalism in greater detail in chapter 2. For now, it is enough to note that whatever the "proper" federal relationship was at the time the Constitution was ratified, it has changed substantially over our history. Certainly, the Civil War resulted in a different version of federalism than that which had existed previously.

But the most dramatic changes in the federal relationship occurred in the twentieth century. The expansive role undertaken by the national government during the Great Depression of the 1930s and Civil Rights era of the 1960s are particularly important in redefining the nature of American federalism. The changes do not end there; an activist US Supreme Court and US Congress continued to push the limits in redefining the acceptable reach of national power through most of the century.[9]

If the national government was usurping some policy-making roles traditionally left to the states and their localities, it was largely due to the states' intractability in exercising their responsibilities, and inability to meet the needs of their citizens. Most states were unwilling or unable to devise modern revenue systems until forced to do so by the economic collapse wrought by the Great Depression. And when states did change, it was often too little, too late to have a meaningful effect, leaving the national government's "New Deal" programs to carry the burden.

As former North Carolina governor Terry Sanford wrote in 1967, "Out of the ordeal of the depression came damaging blows to the states. From the viewpoint of the efficacy of state government, the states lost their confidence, and the people their faith in the states; the news media became cynical, the political scientists neglectful, and the critics became harsh."[10] Borne of this era was a dramatic expansion of federal aid to the states, the phenomenon known as "fiscal federalism." Between 1930 and 1980, fiscal federalism was central to redefining the relationship between the states and national government.

Furthermore, many states had neglected to redistrict their legislatures for years, leaving rural interests with inordinate political power in some legislatures. State officials were poorly paid, poorly staffed, and poorly rated. In the most hyperbolic muckraking tradition, one journalist wrote in mid-century that "State government is the tawdriest, most incompetent, and most stultifying unit of the nation's political structure. In state government are to be found in their most extreme and vicious forms all the worst evils of misrule in the country."[11] Among the evils of state governments he specifically identified "low-grade and corrupt Legislatures."[12]

Meanwhile, under the revived rubric of "State's Rights," government officials of the southern states resisted a national desire to end segregation and ensure civil rights for racial minorities, especially African Americans. It was an ugly time, pitting citizen against citizen, and the national government against some of the state governments. As one historian put it, "By the 1950s and 1960s, the only time state action made headlines was when a racist governor stood in the schoolhouse door."[13]

It is easy to dismiss the bulk of the twentieth century as a "lost era" for the states. But some argue that, despite the obvious shortcomings of the states, they were sometimes doing modernizing, innovative work at various times during the century.[14] One can make that case for some states during the Progressive Era, early in the twentieth century. And one can certainly make that case for most states during the last quarter of the twentieth century.

Starting with the "reapportionment revolution" of the 1960s and 1970s, and facilitated by reformist-minded groups like the Citizen's Conference on State Legislatures, The National Conference of State Legislative Leaders, the Eagleton Institute of Politics at Rutgers University, the Ford Foundation, Carnegie Corporation, and the Twentieth-Century Fund, state governments were pressed to modernize and develop their institutional and policy-making capacities.[15] Some of this story is told in greater detail in chapter 4. For now, it is worth noting that state governments generally—and state legislatures in particular—became much more capable policy making institutions during the modernizing period often known as "legislative professionalization" in the 1960s and 1970s.

To put it simply, out of all this turmoil, state governments were pushed to become much more capable governing partners in the federal system today. This may not often be recognized by the media or even by members of Congress (many of whom are themselves former state legislators but seem to forget this as soon as they get inside the Beltway). But apparently the general public recognizes it, on some fundamental level, as evidenced by the fact that surveys consistently demonstrate a higher level of trust for state government than national government. A recent Pew Research Center poll indicated that far more people (51 percent to 33 percent) held a favorable view of their state government compared to the federal government, and the gap has been increasing over time.[16] Furthermore, on questions about "honesty in government," "addressing people's needs," "careful with the people's money," and "is generally efficient," the states consistently receive higher marks than the federal government.

Red States, Blue States, Big Sorts

Red state, blue state is part of today's political lexicon. It developed from the desire in the visual media (print and electronic) for a simple way to show how states were voting in the presidential election. Why? Because the presidential election is determined by the Electoral College and the vote units in the Electoral College are the states. If presidential elections were not decided in blocs of state units, no one would have conceived of red and blue states. If you think about it, it is really rather silly to talk about a state that votes 51 percent or 52 percent or 53 percent for the Democratic candidate as Blue and a state that votes 51 percent or 52 percent or 53 percent for the Republican candidate as Red. It is only because of the winner-take-all nature of American electoral politics—especially presidential election politics—that the red/blue dichotomy works at all.[17] And even then, it works in a rather superficial way that masks the political complexity of the states.

On another dimension, the "red state, blue state" characterization actually works fairly well for some states. The reason is that most states are not evenly divided politically; instead of a 51-49 partisan split, most are closer to 60-40. And the division of partisans is becoming more lopsided in some states. In other words, political polarization is real in many states. The authors of one book on the subject of political polarization put it this way, "Geography matters politically. States are not merely organizational entities. . . . States have real, significant cultural and political differences. And despite the homogenizing tendencies of national media, drastically lower transportation costs, and a franchised economy, regional differences have not gone away."[18]

In other words, changes in technology, mobility, and mass consumerism have not eliminated state differences. Some argue, in fact, that the differences are growing as technology and mobility allow people to live where they want and among the people they wish to have as neighbors.[19]

In his book, *The Big Sort: Why the Clustering of Like-Minded America Is Tearing Us Apart*, Bill Bishop wrote, "[P]eople do not live in states. They live in communities."[20] This is not an entirely accurate statement, of course. People do live in states. What Bishop meant was that people choose to live in particular communities, or particular neighborhoods that just happened to be in a particular state. His point is that people are "sorting" themselves by their religious and civic attitudes into like-minded local "tribes."[21]

But the fact of the matter is that cities and counties are creations of state governments. The way that local governments operate—their taxing authority, their policy-making abilities, the way they are organized for governance—are, ultimately, matters determined by the state constitution and the state legislature. As citizens, our specific behaviors vis-à-vis the polity likely are constrained or encouraged by state legal codes far more than by the federal code. As Gimpel and Schukneckt note, "State boundaries have taken on great meaning partly because of the social and economic practices that are legally permitted or prohibited within them."[22] States are important in that they help structure civil society. So, not only do people live in states, but it matters in which state.

The Contemporary Context

It is interesting that in this time of globalization there remain substantial differences between the states on an entire range of economic, demographic, cultural, and other dimensions. We are reminded that states do indeed represent different mixes of people, characteristics, and cultures and that is, in Elazar's phrase, "what transforms each state into a civil society, possessing a political system that is in some measure autonomous."[23] A glimpse at the differences among the states on several dimensions is provided in table 1.2. The differences are striking. California has *seventy times* more people within its borders than does Wyoming. In fact, one county in California, Los Angeles County, has a larger population than about forty states. As you can imagine, this imposes very different policy and administrative demands on the states (and their local governments) as governing units.

States vary in many other meaningful ways. California's economy, measured as gross state product, would rank ninth in the world between those of Italy and Russia. In contrast, Vermont's would rank ninety-second, just ahead of Cameroon.[24] Per capita income varies widely across the states. Of course, the source of state wealth differs; some states have been blessed with valuable natural resources (think oil) while other states have deliberately pursued certain public policies designed to generate money (think gambling). The proportion

TABLE 1.2
Top Five, Bottom Five, and Median States, Selected Demographic and Socioeconomic Variables

Rank	Population (millions)	Gross State Product (in millions $)	Per Capita Income (thousands)	Percent Hispanic	Percent Black	Percent White Evangelical	Percent Catholic	Percent College Degree	Percent Mobile Homes	Violent Crimes (per 100,000)
1	CA 36.9	CA 1,958,904	CT $56.3	NM 44.9	MS 37.2	TN 47.0	RI 51.0	MA 38.1	SC 17.9	SC 788
2	TX 24.8	TX 1,308,132	NJ 51.4	CA 36.6	LA 32.0	OK 46.3	CT 45.6	CO 35.6	NM 16.4	TN 753
3	NY 19.5	NY 1,157,969	MA 51.3	TX 36.5	GA 30.0	AL 46.1	MA 44.0	CT 35.6	MS 15.2	NV 751
4	FL 18.5	FL 754,255	NY 48.8	AZ 30.1	MD 29.4	WV 44.2	NM 40.2	MD 35.2	AL 14.3	LA 730
5	IL 12.9	IL 670,727	WY 48.6	NV 25.7	SC 28.4	AR 44.0	VT,NY 38.0	NJ 34.4	NC 14.3	FL 723
Median	LA, KY 4.4	IN, WI 266,473	TX, SD 38.2	VA, DE 6.8	KY, MA 7.3	MI, OH 25.0	CO, MT 22.5	NC, PA 26.2	VT, MO 6.8	CO, OH 345
46	SD 0.8	ND 40,328	AR 32.4	MS 2.2	ND 1.1	NJ 9.7	AL 6.6	LA 20.3	RI 1.0	SD 169
47	AK 0.7	SD 40,117	KY 32.1	ND 2.1	ME 1.0	UT 8.2	AR 6.5	KY 19.7	NJ 1.0	ND 142
48	ND 0.6	MT 37,990	UT 31.9	VT 1.4	ID 0.9	NY 8.0	UT 6.1	MS 19.4	MA 0.9	NH 137
49	VT 0.6	WY 37,990	WV 31.6	ME 1.3	VT 0.9	CT 7.3	TN 6.0	AR 18.8	CT 0.8	VT 124
50	WY 0.5	VT 25,905	MS 30.4	WV 1.1	MT 0.7	RI 6.7	MS 4.7	WV 17.1	HI 0.2	ME 118

SOURCES: Gross State Data from US Department of Commerce, Bureau of Economic Analysis, www.bea.gov/newsreleases/regional/gdp_state/gsp_newsrelease.htm; religion data from John Green, Ray Bliss Institute of Applied Politics, University of Akron as posted on www.beliefnet.com. All other data from 2012 Statistical Abstract, found at www.census.gov/compendia/statab/rankings.html.

of college-educated individuals is much higher in some states than others. The crime rate is dramatically different. The racial and ethnic makeup is varied. Religious affiliations are not the same. Indeed, not only are religious affiliations different (compare, for example, Connecticut and Tennessee in columns 7 and 8), but the depth of feeling about religion is very different. A Gallup Poll in 2009 found that at least 80 percent of the respondents in Mississippi, Alabama, and South Carolina said that religion was an important part of their daily lives, while less than half of the people in the New England states made that claim.[25] The depth of religious meaning to one's daily life is known as "religiosity" and has been linked to very specific policy preferences, especially certain social policies such as same-sex marriage, abortion, and school vouchers (all of which are discussed in chapter 5).

Given all of this variation, can any state be thought to be representative of the nation? One attempt to answer this question produced surprising answers. Looking at fifty-one different indicators, the most representative state was Kansas, followed by Oregon and Delaware. Isolating just economic variables, Iowa was the most representative, followed by Oregon and Georgia.[26] Of course, many people might well reject these findings because they see these states as being very different from their own states and what they think is typical of the nation.

The key point here is that the states are not just fifty shades of vanilla. They are different geographically, demographically, economically. All of this adds up to the realization that the people in the different states have somewhat different political and social values—different civil and political societies. Students of comparative state political systems are familiar with the term "political culture" and the idea that different states have different orientations to government and politics. The old designations of individualistic, traditionalistic, and moralistic political cultures may no longer be an especially accurate or appropriate reflection of today's state-by-state differences in the United States.[27] But the idea that substantial differences exist, and that they affect policy preferences differently, is still very real. It may even be more accurate today than it was a generation ago. To some extent, sorting may be part of this. And to some extent, the political stalemate at the national level means states are left with more latitude to pursue their own policy agendas on some issues—and what is considered sound policy in one state might not be in another. For example, in a single year (2007) the state of New Hampshire approved of civil unions while the Texas legislature adopted a bill to protect religious speech in public schools.[28] As Bill Bishop notes, "Congress has balkanized. . . . Meanwhile, in states and cities where the Big Sort has resulted in increasingly larger majorities, there has been an explosion of innovation and legislation. Federal leadership has been replaced by a wild display of federalism, as like-minded communities put their beliefs into law."[29]

The 2012 election provides some clear illustrations of this point. On the one hand, same-sex marriage laws were approved in Maine, Maryland, and

Washington. Meanwhile, in Colorado and Washington, voters approved the legalization of marijuana for recreational use. By American standards, these are pretty liberal views. But on exactly the same day, Alabama, Missouri, Montana, and Wyoming voted to block implementation of the Affordable Care Act ("ObamaCare")—a strongly preferred outcome among conservatives.

We are likely to see more evidence of the divergence in state policies as some states are increasingly controlled by one political party and some other states by the other party. After the 2012 election there were more states with unified control of government (i.e., the governor, the state senate, and the state house all controlled by the same party) than at any time since 1952.[30] Currently, only twelve states do not have unified government (i.e., twelve states have divided government). To put it another way, currently in 75 percent of the states one party is in control of policy making. Figure 1.1 shows these trends since 1960. The figure actually shows two trends that bear on partisan control of state government. The solid line shows the percentage of states with unified government.

In 1960, 63 percent of the states operated under unified government; in 1962, the figure reached 65 percent (32 states). But over the next forty years, there was

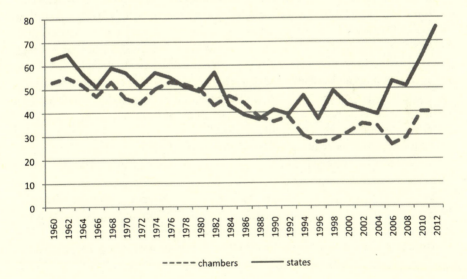

FIGURE 1.1
Percentage of states with unified government and percentage of legislative chambers with extraordinary majorities, 1960–2012. Source: Raw data are from Karl Kurtz, National Conference of State Legislatures. We converted to percentages. "Unified" is defined as both legislative chambers plus governor's office is controlled by the same political party. "Extraordinary Majority" is defined here as one party controlling at least two-thirds of the seats in the chamber. Because it is both unicameral and nonpartisan, Nebraska is excluded, so percentages are based on ninety-eight chambers and forty-nine states.

a relatively steady decline in the number of states with unified government, as southern states and some northeastern states began the slow process of partisan realignment. Fewer than half of the states experienced unified government in any given electoral cycle between 1984 and 2006. In other words, divided government became the norm. On several occasions between 1986 and 1996, over 60 percent of the states had divided government. By 2006 a new and dramatic trend occurs, however. There is a steep rise in the percentage of states experiencing unified government. As of 2013, there are more states with unified government than we have seen in several generations.

And it is not simply that states are now more apt to have unified governments, but in many states the majority party enjoys unchallenged dominance. After the 2012 elections, Democrats, for example, control 89 percent of the state legislative seats in Hawaii and Rhode Island, and 84 percent of the seats in Massachusetts. At the other extreme, Republicans hold 87 percent of the seats in Wyoming, and 82 percent of the seats in Idaho and Utah. As represented by the dotted line in figure 1.1, the proportion of legislative chambers in which one party has extraordinary control (defined here as holding at least two-thirds of the chamber seats) is higher today than at any time since 1986. Although party competition can still be found in some states, many clearly tilt heavily in one party's favor. Given that Republicans dominate in some states while the Democrats are in clear control in others, we can expect contrasting approaches to governance emerging across the states. As Larry Sabato pointed out after the 2012 election, "The red states are getting redder and the blue states are getting bluer. This is a highly polarized era."[31] Karl Kurtz, of the National Conference of State Legislatures, says that in terms of policy, the red and blue states "are like trains going in opposite directions on parallel tracks. On highly charged partisan issues like collective bargaining, immigration, gay marriage, abortion health care exchanges and voter ID, Republican governors and legislators are moving in one direction while Democrats head the opposite way."[32]

As *Governing* magazine recently reported, "This is more than just policy polarization. It is part of a tectonic shift away from federal authority and toward power in the states."[33] That is certainly an overstatement, but we share the basic sentiment that states matter, and they seem to matter more now than they have for some time.

The Federal Government and the Future

There is little doubt that significant changes are coming to the federal budget. Federal spending today so outstrips revenue that the national debt, relative to national economic output, is at the highest level since World War II. The debt to economic output (GDP) ratio has fluctuated considerably over the past seventy years, but it has grown rapidly since 2000. As the baby boom generation begins to retire, the federal budget obligations to social insurance programs like Medicare and Social Security mean that the debt will increase unless there are substantial changes to those programs, putting greater pressure on the federal budget. And with the outcome of the 2012 election and the US Supreme Court decision in *National Federation of Independent Businesses v. Sebelius* guaranteeing implementation of the Affordable Health Care Act, there is little doubt that federal entitlement obligations to health care will increase. One of the implications for the states is that they are likely to see a decline in federal aid to programs outside of health care.

In other words, in the future states are likely to have to deal with more problems using their own resources. This is not going to be an easy transition. To those who desire the return of more governing responsibility to the states, the adage, "Be careful what you wish for" is relevant. One option for state policy makers will be to increase taxes—almost never a popular option among the voting public. Another choice will be to cut back or completely eliminate some programs. In some cases, this means eliminating programs relied on heavily by the poor and most vulnerable segments of society, another option that the public usually resists. A third alternative will be for states to try innovative—some might say "radical"—solutions by drastically changing the way that services are provided and the manner in which costs are borne. Major changes to education, corrections, welfare, and transportation can be expected. For the American states, the next decade will be a time of significant changes. Those changes will probably not look the same from one state to another. But it should be pointed out that change is nothing new to the states.

In the remainder of this book we discuss some key areas in which states matter and ways in which changes have occurred. In chapter 2 we begin, basically, at the beginning: by discussing the adoption of the US Constitution, the establishment of the federal system, and the continual tug between national and state influences on policy making. We will also see how federalism has played out differently in other countries. While most of the discussion concerns the interplay between national and state levels, we will also look at the relationship between state and local governments.

Chapter 3 examines how the basic structures of state government developed and makes the case for why these governments are important in specific policy arenas. While states are clearly constrained by the US Constitution, US Supreme Court decisions, and actions by the president, the Congress, and the federal agencies, there are plenty of areas in which states have authority to chart their own courses.

As mentioned earlier, states are facing major challenges in the immediate future. Much of the burden to meet these challenges fall on the institutions of state government—the executive, legislative, and judicial branches. Chapter 4 demonstrates how these instruments of state government, which were so inadequate sixty years ago, are much better prepared to take on increased responsibilities today. The capacity of the states to govern effectively is much greater today than a generation or two ago.

In chapter 5 we make the case that states are significant policy makers in many functional areas. As one well-known American government text states, "The states play a key role in social welfare, public education, law enforcement, criminal justice, health and hospitals, roads and highways, and managing water supplies. On these and other matters, state constitutions are far more detailed and sometimes confer more rights than the federal one."[34] Thus, even while losing a modicum of policy-making discretion to the national government in areas like public education, state governments still make most of the relevant decisions about publicly funded schools, at both the K–12 level and higher education, as well as in a host of other policy areas. Often, some states are out in front of the national government in developing innovative, imaginative solutions to public problems. In some cases, they are way out in front of the national government. In many instances, the variation in public policy from one state to another is quite substantial.

One of the ways that states matter most is in the electoral arena. Unfortunately, this is not often recognized by the general public, except when incredibly close elections expose the reality. Chapter 6 provides an explanation of the critical role states play in national electoral politics. We also discuss the various instruments of direct democracy that play a very important role in state policy making but that are nonexistent at the national level. Some of the innovative policies discussed in chapter 5 are, in fact, driven by the referendum and especially the initiative processes which exist in many states.

Some of the most important and least understood aspects of state governments are their fiscal systems. It is a complicated topic, but one that is critical for students and citizens of the states to grasp. In chapter 7, we tackle this crucial and fascinating topic. It is especially important today, as the expanding federal deficit will have significant effects on state fiscal policies. Finally, in chapter 8 we conclude with an assessment of how the world of state government and politics is changing and why states will remain important for the foreseeable future—that is, why states matter.

2

States and the Federal System

States matter because:

- They are an essential part of the federal system.
- They still have primary responsibility for policy making in many issue areas.
- They employ more government workers than the national government.
- They have authority to define the nature of local government operations.
- Citizens look to the states when there is stalemate at the national level.
- Efforts to address the federal deficit will put a greater burden on the states.

IN FEBRUARY OF 2011, several hundred people packed the House State Affairs Committee hearing in the Idaho state legislature. Most had come to urge the committee to act favorably on House Bill 117, a bill to nullify the Patient Protection and Affordable Care Act (PPACA, also known as "ObamaCare"), which the US Congress had passed the previous year. House Bill 117 stated that,

> The Legislature of the state of Idaho, therefore, on behalf of the citizens of this state and to secure the blessings of liberty, hereby asserts its legitimate authority to interpose between said citizens and the federal government, when it has exceeded its constitutional authority and declares that the state shall not participate in and considers void and of no effect the PPACA.[1]

Essentially, supporters of the bill contended that states have the authority to nullify laws passed by the national government. This argument for "interposition and nullification" has been around since the adoption of the US Constitution. It is, in effect, an interpretation of federalism that gives primacy to states' rights. While the US Supreme Court has never accepted the "nullification" doctrine, the phrase is resurrected from time to time. In 2011 and 2012, it was in the news quite frequently, as "ObamaCare" nullification bills were introduced in more than a dozen state legislatures. Attorneys General of twenty-six states filed a lawsuit to challenge the law and the governors of at least three states vowed to block implementation of it in their states.[2]

To put it simply, one cannot talk about the role of the states without talking about federalism. Federalism is defined as "a political system in which power and authority are divided between two or more levels of government."[3] That is a pretty imprecise definition because federalism is a pretty imprecise arrangement. What does it mean to say that "authority is divided between levels of government?" Divided in what proportion to which level: 50-50, 80-20, 20-80? Is authority divided differently for different policy areas, so that the division is different on transportation policy compared to welfare policy? These and similar questions have been around since the debates over the drafting and adoption of the US Constitution. And here is the key point: the questions are never resolved. As John Donahue wrote in his book, *Disunited States*, "The Framers at Philadelphia launched not only a nation, but an appropriately endless argument over the proper balance between federal and state authority—an argument whose intensity ebbs and flows and whose content evolves, but which is never really settled."[4]

Federalism is always a complicated arrangement. It is further complicated in the United States because the division or sharing of power involves fifty subnational (regional) units. Whether they are called states, provinces, cantons, or länder (the German term for "lands"), no other federal system in the world has so many regional units as the United States. Australia has but six; Canada, ten. There are thirteen states in Malaysia, while Germany has sixteen; Brazil has twenty-six and India has twenty-eight.[5] The only country besides the United States with more than thirty regional governments is Nigeria, with thirty-six.

Given the complexity of federal systems, it is no surprise that relatively few countries adopt this arrangement. There are about two hundred sovereign nations in the world today, and only about twenty-five of them have a federal system. On the other hand, federal systems are relatively common among countries with a large geographic size (e.g., Argentina, Australia, Canada, Brazil, India, United States), or with a large population (e.g., Brazil, Germany, India, Mexico, Nigeria, Pakistan, United States). Geographically, six of the eight largest countries are federal, as are five of the eight most populous countries. The ways that these federal systems operate are different from one another, depending on a whole host of variables including size, ethnic and racial diversity, history, and economy. And some are very new and not necessarily stable federations at this point. One recent study maintains that if we impose some conditions such as stability and the presence of truly democratic elections, the number of functioning federal systems is only eleven.[6] Federal systems are difficult to maintain because of the constant tension between the central (national-level) government and the peripheral (state, regional, provincial) governments. As one scholar of federal systems notes, "Characteristic of federal systems is the simultaneous existence of powerful motives for constituent units to be united (for certain shared purposes) and their deep-rooted desires for self-government (for other purposes)."[7] To put this another way, there are both centrifugal (pull away from the center) and centripetal (pull toward the center) tendencies. Such tendencies may vary between federal systems, over time within a particular federal system, or by policy area within a particular federal system.

Almost all the federal systems in existence today were established after World War II. According to one authority, there were only four countries with true federal systems of government prior to the twentieth century.[8] The oldest continuous federal system in the world is the United States; inaugurated in 1789, it celebrates its 225th anniversary in 2014. But the federal system in the United States today hardly looks like the federal system of 1789. Of course, the United States itself hardly looks like the country of two centuries ago, as table 2.1 makes clear. We have evolved from a relatively small, rural and agrarian nation of 4 million people and thirteen states to a large, extremely complex, urban and technologically sophisticated country with fifty states. The population is almost one hundred times greater; the number of states has quadrupled; the shift from rural to urban and now to suburban locations is dramatic. The 1790 census indicates that almost 20 percent of the enumerated population was black (of which 8 percent were free and 92 percent were slaves). The

TABLE 2.1
The Evolution of a Federal System

Date	National Population (in millions)	Percent Rural Population	Population of Largest Cities	Number of States	Constitutional Amendments
1790	4	95	33,181 (New York 28,552 (Philadelphia)	13	1–10 (1791)
1860	31	80	813,559 (New York) 565,529 (Philadelphia)	33	13–15 (1865–1870)
1910	92	44	Three cities over 1 million*	46	16–19 (1913–1920)
1960	179	30	Five cities over 1 million**	50	23–26 (1960–1971)
2010	308	16	Nine cities over 1 million***	50	None since 1992

*New York, Chicago, Philadelphia (in descending order of population)
**New York, Chicago, Los Angeles, Philadelphia, Detroit
***New York, Los Angeles, Chicago, Houston, Philadelphia, Phoenix, San Antonio, San Diego, Dallas.

Source: US Census Bureau, various tables.

remainder of the enumerated population was almost entirely of European descent.[9] Native Americans were not included as a category in the first census, but probably numbered at least six hundred thousand, mostly in the territory beyond the recognized borders of the thirteen states.[10]

One quick measure of the magnitude of change is travel time. Consider, for example, a trip from one end of the country to the other; basically that would have been from Boston to Savannah (note that Atlanta did not yet exist; it wasn't founded until 1837). Today, by air travel, it is about a two hour direct flight between these two cities. In 1790, if a person owned a horse and chose to ride from Savannah to Boston, he could expect the journey to take a little over one month—about thirty-five days if the weather was decent and the roads were passable. The fastest mode of travel would have been by ship, and with luck the trip could be accomplished in about one week. It would also be quite expensive. Obviously, most people did not travel much at all. Each community, and certainly each state, was something of a world unto itself. This bears no resemblance at all to the world we know today.

Table 2.1 represents five eras in the United States. They were chosen because, except for the first (1790), they are half a century apart and because (except for the last one, 2010) they were characterized by significant constitutional changes. In fact, all but six of the amendments to the US Constitution occurred during the periods represented in table 2.1. The federal relationship has changed as well. In fact, it has changed substantially—a theme of much of the rest of this chapter.

The US Constitution and the Roots of Federalism

Conflict and controversy is endemic to a federal system. Recall that under the Articles of Confederation the states were widely understood to be sovereign and basically independent of one another. The confederation was little more than a treaty among thirteen sovereign entities. But to say the states were sovereign does not necessarily mean they were effective or powerful. It was their ineffectiveness that led some to call for a formal meeting in Philadelphia to discuss ways to improve the system. Nonetheless, giving up some portion of one's sovereignty is not something most do willingly. Even with the admittedly serious problems that the states experienced under the Articles, there were many citizens and political elites in the states who did not want to relinquish any sovereign power to another, "higher" government.

At the Constitutional Convention there was controversy, disagreement and different interpretations of the "proper" relationship between the national government and the states. There was general agreement that the national government needed to be stronger, but disputes over how strong it should be. And even today, many of those disagreements and differences of interpretation have never been resolved. This is a core characteristic of American federalism.

The emphasis, quite understandably, in contemporary high-school history and civics courses is on the debates, the various plans, and the compromises that resulted in the drafting of the Constitution. But let us not forget that not all who were at the Philadelphia convention agreed with those compromises. When it came time to affix their name to the document, three of the people in the room at Independence Hall refused to sign. All three were notables in their day and are well known even in our time: George Mason and Edmund Randolph of Virginia and Elbridge Gerry of Massachusetts. At least four others left the convention in protest of the proceedings. Another nine left early, claiming they were needed at home.

Another twenty-one individuals who were invited to attend declined to show up at all—including the entire Rhode Island delegation. Some of these men (and indeed they were all men—another difference between the political world of 1790 and today) were simply unable to attend. But others assuredly boycotted the convention because they were opposed to any effort to reduce the independence of the states. Patrick Henry was one of those who was invited but refused to attend, later claiming he declined because "I smelt a rat," meaning he suspected there was a move afoot to weaken the independent status of the states.[11]

Controversy certainly did not end with the adjournment of the convention in Philadelphia. While some states, like Delaware, adopted the new form of government almost immediately, others remained unconvinced. Recall that the mechanism for adoption of the new constitution was not the various state legislatures, but ratifying conventions to be held in each state. For our purpose, this is significant for two reasons. First, it was assumed that a number of state legislatures would be opposed to the new government since it clearly diminished the power of the states. And, as the key decision making units in the states under the Articles of Confederation, the state legislatures would especially be diminished by the new system. Second, under the Articles, the state legislature was in effect the government of the State. In other words, the legislature represented the *State as a sovereign entity*. The ratifying conventions, on the other hand, could be thought of as representing *the people* of the state. For many, this is a crucial distinction.

From the outset, then, there was disagreement as to whether the Constitution was adopted by the people or by the states.[12] To reiterate, at core the question comes down to the nature of the ratification assemblies called in the various states to consider and act upon the newly proposed constitution. The Federalist argument was that the delegates to the various ratification assemblies represented the people of the various states, and thus it was the people—the citizens themselves—who chose to discard the government under the Articles of Confederation and to adopt a new government with a more robust national presence.

The Antifederalist argument was that the ratification assemblies represented the sovereign states, not the people directly. Because the states themselves were the sovereign units under the Articles, only the states had the authority to accept, reject, or modify the conditions of the proposed arrangement under the Constitution. In this view, the Constitution was basically a compact among sovereign states. And since a compact is little more than a voluntary association, any state that agrees to the compact has the right to disassociate when it feels the policies of the compact government (i.e., the federal government) are not in the interests of the aggrieved state.

Thus, the conflicting views over whether "the people" or "the sovereign states" are the true adopters of the Constitution and therefore of the new federal arrangement is at the heart of the "states' rights" argument and a key rationale in the argument for "interposition and nullification." Typical of this reasoning is the statement adopted by one state legislature in 1809, "Whenever the national compact is violated, and the citizens of this state are oppressed by cruel and unauthorized laws, this legislature is bound to interpose its power, and wrest from the oppressor its victim."[13]

While we usually associate such a sentiment with the southern states, this quotation is from a report of the Massachusetts state legislature in reaction to an embargo placed on American ships by President Thomas Jefferson. Similar expressions of the right to interposition (and nullification) can be found among other New England states over the embargo, and later over the efforts to draft state militia during the War of 1812. It is worth pointing out the irony here; these northern states were using the principles of interposition and nullification against the actions of Presidents Thomas Jefferson and James Madison—the authors of the original drafts of the Kentucky and Virginia Resolutions. By late 1814 the dissatisfaction with the embargo and the War of 1812 (1812–1815) led representatives of several New England states to meet to discuss their grievances. This was the Hartford Convention, which met in secret for several weeks during the winter of 1814–1815. Most of the Hartford delegates were members of the Federalist Party, so it is surprising that both nullification and secession were apparently discussed.

Any discussion of nullification usually begins with the Kentucky and Virginia Resolutions (1798–1799), drafted by Thomas Jefferson and James Madison, respectively. Recall the state legislatures of Kentucky and Virginia, controlled by Antifederalists, adopted these statements in response to the Alien and Sedition Acts of 1798, which were passed into law by the Federalist Party–controlled US Congress. These laws were viewed by many as a severe restriction on the right to free speech. Alarmed by what they considered an unconstitutional usurpation of power by the national government, the state legislatures of Kentucky and Virginia argued that they had the authority—indeed, the duty—to resist the repressive tendencies of the national government on behalf of their state citizens. In other words, the state had the right to "intervene" between its citizens and the national government to protect the rights of its citizens. Kentucky further argued that they had the right to nullify the federal action, while the Virginia resolution did not go quite this far.[14] At any rate, these sentiments express a thread that runs through the fabric of American history.

"Interposition" and/or "nullification" appear in the public discourse in the Kentucky and Virginia Resolutions (1798–1799); the New England resistance (c. 1805–1815); the "nullification crisis" of 1832 involving John C. Calhoun, South Carolina, and the congressional tariff laws; the period immediately prior to the Civil War; the desegregation and civil rights period (c. 1954–1965); and the reaction in some quarters to the PPACA (2010–present).

· Since the terms have reappeared recently, in response to both the Real ID Act of 2005 (the congressionally imposed requirements on state driver's licenses, making them essentially national identification cards) and especially in response to the PPACA, perhaps it is worth explaining the terms as used in their historical context. The terms "interposition" and "nullification" are often used interchangeably but they do not actually have the same meaning. As used by Madison and others of the time, "interposition" meant a state should intervene on behalf of its citizens when the national government exceeded its constitutional authority. Basically, this was an oversight function, a calling of attention to an act or policy that deserved resistance or questioning. Moreover, "interposition" was viewed as a collective endeavor, something that several or many states would undertake, and together they might exert enough pressure to get the national government to reconsider or amend the policy in question. Within this context then, interposition is a perfectly legitimate action; whether it is successful in getting the egregious act repealed is another matter. Used in this manner, interposition is a procedure by which states can "converse" and perhaps bargain with the national government. Political scientist John Dinan speaks of the "various ways that states can 'talk back' to federal officials" which we think captures the spirit of interposition as conceived by Madison.[15] Thus, the Kentucky and Virginia Resolutions called upon other states to join them in resisting the congressional laws. But no other state joined them.

In contrast, "nullification" is the act of voiding or rejecting the application of a congressional or presidential act, or federal judicial decree within a specific state. It is an act of defiance meant to nullify a national policy within the confines of a particular state. Nullification has been consistently rejected by the federal courts as unconstitutional.[16] This does not preclude the term from finding its way into the public discourse these days. Just type in "nullification" to any Internet search engine and see what pops up—from news stories to definitions to all manner of blogger rants.

The Evolution of American Federalism

While "interposition and nullification" are instruments that have been argued about since the ratification of the Constitution, let us not lose sight of the fact that they are remedial instruments designed to correct a perceived transgression on the part of the national government vis-à-vis the state governments. The period surrounding the Constitutional Convention and the ratification process demonstrate considerable resistance by Antifederalists because they feared what they saw as the centralizing tendencies in the document.[17]

A half century ago, Cecelia Kenyon described the Antifederalists as "men of little faith." She was not referring to their religious attitudes but to the fact that they were, from the outset, distrustful of the constitutional arrangement and were unconvinced that under the new arrangement the states would be able to hold the national government in check. Their argument rested on "four great pillars of consolidation."[18] The four features of the Constitution that most concerned these defenders of the states were (1) the power of the national government to tax, (2) the power of the national government to raise and maintain a military force, (3) the necessary and proper clause at the end of Article I, Section 8, and (4) the national supremacy clause in Article 6. From the point of view of those who believed the states were the essential sovereigns and preferred it that way, their fears that the Constitution provided for national consolidation were both real and eventually realized.

For the most part, the centralization process has been slow and it is by no means complete. Some historical events were instrumental in redefining the relationship between the national and state governments: the Civil War and the Great Depression are the two most obvious. Many other events or trends contributed to the changing relationship over 225 years. A complete accounting and description of all these phenomena is not possible here, but the list would include, at a minimum, the following:

1. *The Supreme Court's adoption of the implied powers doctrine in 1819.* The Antifederalists' concern that the "necessary and proper" clause could be a vehicle for the expansion of the role of the national government seems prescient with the US Supreme Court's decision in the case of *McCulloch v. Maryland* in 1819.[19] As Cecelia Kenyon noted, "This was a clause so sweeping in its possible implications . . . that the Antifederalists could see no logical limit to the powers of the central government."[20]

Recall that the issue in the *McCulloch* case involved the authority of the national government to establish a national bank.[21] Creation of such a bank is not one of the specific, enumerated powers of the national government stipulated in Article I, Section 8 of the Constitution; some states therefore argued that the creation of banks was a state power and not a power held by the national government. Chief

Justice John Marshall noted that the "general government" (by which he means the national government) is a government of enumerated powers,

> But the question respecting the extent of the powers actually granted is perpetually arising, and will probably continue to arise so long as our system shall exist. In discussing these questions, the conflicting powers of the General and State Governments must be brought into view, and the supremacy of their respective laws, when they are in opposition, must be settled.[22]

Marshall goes on to note that the enumerated powers are supported by a variety of actions and means which are not necessarily enumerated and, he notes, this is one of the ways in which the system established under the Constitution is clearly different than that under the Articles of Confederation.

> Among the enumerated powers, we do not find that of establishing a bank or creating a corporation. But there is no phrase in the instrument which, like the Articles of Confederation, excludes incidental or implied powers and which requires that everything granted shall be expressly and minutely described.[23]
>
> Let the end be legitimate, let it be within the scope of the Constitution, and all means which are appropriate, which are plainly adapted to that end, which are not prohibited, but consist with the letter and spirit of the Constitution, are Constitutional.[24]

The expansion of national powers through the implied powers doctrine did not occur on a grand scale immediately. But the precedent was set with McCulloch and this becomes especially important almost a century later when one of the enumerated powers—the power to regulate interstate commerce—is broadly interpreted.

2. *The Union victory in the Civil War (1865) and the passage of the Civil Rights Amendments.* Obviously, the victory of the Union over the Confederacy was essential to the maintenance of the federal system. Virtually by definition, the right to secede reduces the federal system to a confederation. The immediate result of the Union victory is the nationalization of the rights of the former slaves through the adoption of the Thirteenth, Fourteenth, and Fifteenth Amendments between 1865 and 1870. While these amendments were vigorously enforced during the Reconstruction of the Southern states, the application of the Fourteenth and Fifteenth soon waned. By the end of the nineteenth century, a return to the "dual federalism" of the first half of the century is evident in such cases as *Plessy v. Ferguson* (1896) and *Williams v. Mississippi* (1898). Nonetheless they return to prominence and become instrumental in redefining the federal relationship in the civil rights era of the mid-twentieth century. As one observer notes, "These amendments would become the instruments for a recasting of federal-state relations."[25]

3. *The adoption of a broad interpretation of congressional authority to regulate interstate commerce.* Since the close of the nineteenth century, one of the most important channels for the expansion of national power is the interstate commerce clause. Article 1, Section 8 of the Constitution says, in part, that Congress has the power to regulate commerce "among the several states." Unlike many aspects of the Constitution, this particular power apparently was not seriously contested by Antifederalists.[26] Perhaps this was because they recognized the need for some regulation, given the disastrous economic situation under the Articles of Confederation.

The pivotal case for our purposes is *Wickard v. Filburn* (1942), a case in which the US Supreme Court determines that economic activity that is not ostensibly interstate may nonetheless be regulated by Congress.[27] It marks the beginning of a period in which the court gives a very free rein to congressional action in the name of regulating interstate commerce. Indeed, the court finds no limit to congressional authority to regulate via the interstate commerce clause for the next half century, until 1995.[28]

4. *The adoption of the Sixteenth Amendment (1913) and the development of fiscal federalism.* Earlier, we noted that Antifederalists were concerned about the centralizing effect of granting the national government the right to tax, under Article 1, Section 8 of the Constitution. Previously, under the Articles of Confederation, the central government had no authority to tax. Many of the framers, especially Alexander Hamilton, recognized the need for the new national government to be able to raise revenue on its own.

Although some opponents of the Constitution feared granting this authority to the national government, the fact is that the states (and their local governments) exercised most of the taxing authority until well into the twentieth century. With the passage of the Sixteenth Amendment, creating an annual federal income tax, the fiscal dynamics begin to change. Some observers contend that this amendment is the single most important factor in altering the relationship of the national and state governments.[29] In particular, the development of fiscal federalism on a significant scale is not possible until the national government has a substantial and steady source of revenue through the income tax. Today, about half of all federal revenue is derived from the income tax.[30] Later, we will discuss fiscal federalism in more detail, but for now it is enough to note that federal grants-in-aid give the national government great leverage in the policy-making arena. Federal aid typically represents about 30 percent of the revenue for all states combined. The dependence on such fiscal aid varies quite a bit by state, however, with some states relying for less than one-quarter of their general funds on fiscal federalism, while in a few states about half of their funds are in the form of federal aid.[31]

5. *The adoption of the Seventeenth Amendment (1913) and direct primaries.* It is fashionable today, especially among Tea Partiers, to call for the repeal of

the Seventeenth Amendment. This amendment, ratified at the height of the Progressive Reform Era, mandates the direct popular election of US senators. Article I, Section 3 of the Constitution originally stated that "The Senate of the United States shall be composed of two Senators from each State, chosen by the Legislature thereof for six Years; and each Senator shall have one Vote." In the context of the role of the states in the new federal system, there are two important components to this Article. The first is that the states have an equal representation in the Senate. As Madison notes in *Federalist* 62, "The equal vote allowed to each State is at once a constitutional recognition of the portion of sovereignty remaining in the individual States, and an instrument for preserving that residuary sovereignty."[32] Thus the House of Representatives would be the "people's chamber" and the Senate would be the "states' chamber."[33]

The second important point is the legislature of each state would select its US senators. The Framers assumed this would ensure that the states had some influence over Congress because the senators would be held accountable to the state legislature. Once the Seventeenth Amendment was ratified and direct elections of US senators was in effect, the power of state legislatures to control US senators was gone.[34] Some see this as being of "transcendent importance to federalism" because it marked the abandonment of one of key constitutional protections for the states.[35]

But, as William Riker notes, this power of the states over their senators was never as strong as some would believe. Central to this effort on the part of these legislatures to control their US senators was the doctrine of instructions.[36] This doctrine held that the state legislatures could instruct their US senators how to vote on important issues. As Riker demonstrates, the doctrine of instructions was applied, off and on, for about 120 years but was never entirely successful because there was no firm way to enforce sanctions against senators who ignored instructions. The ratification of the Seventeenth Amendment diminished what leverage states, through their state legislatures, held in the US Senate, although such leverage was never as strong as the Founders had anticipated it would be.

The Seventeenth Amendment was part of the agenda of the Progressive Reform movement to weaken the state and city-based political party organizations, which were seen as corrupt, undemocratic, and controlled by party bosses and machines. In some cases, this included state legislatures. As Alexander Heard wrote, "United States Senators were once elected by state legislatures. This and other functions made these bodies at times more a focus of attention for special interests than any other organ of government—federal, state or local."[37]

Another such reform was the direct primary, instituted in most states by 1915. Primary elections "stripped the parties of a critical source of power: control over nominations."[38] Control over who gets the party's nomination for the general election is an important power; if a small group or a single "boss" controls the nomination phase, they have the opportunity to influence the nominee's behavior once elected. The combined effect of direct primaries and the Seventeenth Amendment is to weaken the linkage between the state party organizations and the members of Congress.

6. *The Great Depression and the development of national social welfare policy.* Prior to the 1930s, the domestic reach of the national government was quite limited. Until then, the activities of the national government and the state governments did not often intersect. The history of US federalism up until the 1930s is often described as "dual federalism" in which the national government had primary authority over foreign affairs and some regulation of economic activity and state governments had primary authority in the other arenas. This is a generalization and not entirely accurate, but it is not far from the reality of the way things operated. This changes markedly, however, with the crushing effects of the Great Depression.

For those of us who did not live through the Great Depression of the 1930s, it is difficult to imagine its harshness, and the hardships it imposed. True, the recent "Great Recession" of 2008–2010 and its lingering effects for several years later was an extremely difficult time for citizens and governments. But the Great Depression was much worse. Unemployment rates reached 25 percent (compared to less than 10 percent in the recent recession) and the decline in the domestic economy (GDP) was -25 percent (compared to -3.3 percent in the recent recession). While fewer than a hundred banks failed in the recent recession, over nine thousand banks went under during the Great Depression. The point is that the Great Depression resulted in economic devastation and social disruption of an entirely different magnitude than what we recently experienced. It is on this basis that we must understand the actions of the national government under Franklin Roosevelt. As Martha Derthick states, "In response to a catastrophic economic collapse . . . [a] new constitutional law emerged after 1937 that swept away previous limits on Congress's power to regulate commerce and solidified its power to tax and spend for any purpose associated with the general welfare."[39]

7. *The Civil Rights/Great Society era (c. 1954–1968).* It is important to remember that it was a mere fifty years ago, in 1963, that George Wallace, in his inaugural address as the newly elected governor of Alabama said, "I draw the line in the dust and toss the gauntlet before the feet of tyranny and I say segregation now, segregation tomorrow, segregation forever."[40]

This period is about more than civil rights. But it was the drive to desegregate and expand the civil and voting rights of African Americans that led the national government into a more activist role in the domestic affairs of the states, unprecedented since Reconstruction. It is a period in which the Fourteenth and Fifteenth Amendments are rediscovered. The school desegregation case of *Brown v. Topeka Board of Education* (1954); the use of federal troops by Presidents Eisenhower and Kennedy to enforce this court decision in southern cities such as Little Rock, Tuscaloosa, and Oxford; and the passage of landmark legislation such as the Civil Rights Act (1964) and the Voting Rights Act (1965) demonstrate a strong commitment by all branches of the national government during this period to end the pernicious activities of both private citizens and public entities in the South.

During this battle, echoes of earlier conflicts over federalism were heard. Notably, the words "interposition and nullification" reappeared, as politicians in several southern states invoked the right of the state to disregard the actions of the US Supreme Court and Congress.[41] It is largely the use of these terms in this context that colors most current Americans' understanding of them.

Beyond the civil rights question, this period finds the national government, driven by an activist Congress, developing preemptive policies. As Joseph Zimmerman notes, "A revolution in national-subnational relations commenced in 1965 when the Congress enacted the first minimum standards preemption statute—the Water Quality Act of 1965. . . . Minimum standards statutes regulate private and subnational governmental activities."[42] Ultimately, what this means is that the national government sets standards that all states must meet or exceed; otherwise, the national government will take over the administrative or regulatory control of that policy area from the state. This allows Congress—and the federal bureaucracy to which Congress often delegates authority—major policy influence in areas previously left to the states.

This is also a period in which fiscal federalism increased at warp speed. During the decade of the 1960s, federal aid tripled and continued to grow at a rapid rate for another decade after that. It was not just the amount of money distributed to subnational governments, but the expansion in functional areas for which the money was intended. The development of fiscal federalism as both a carrot and stick to facilitate state compliance with expanding national goals was a defining feature of this period.

At the center of this active period was the US Supreme Court. Writing about the role of the Supreme Court during this time, Derthick states, "It emerged as a reformer, and the institutions it chose to change were those of state governments."[43] This is an intriguing statement, because it points to the fact that many states were slow to adapt to a quickly changing political and social environment. Many states were poorly funded and ineffectively administered. As we show in chapters 3 and 4, the capacities of states today are substantially greater than in 1960.

The court, focusing on issues of equality of rights for American citizens, rendered transformative decisions involving school segregation, criminal justice and rights of the accused, public school prayer and "one person, one vote" definition of voting equality. When one looks at the totality of the national effort during this period—the activist role of the US Supreme Court and the efforts on the part of Congress and the president to end segregation, guarantee individual rights, and expand the reach of minimal national standards through statute and fiscal federalism—this period stands out as one in which the character of federalism changed more than any other period—perhaps even more than the New Deal period.

8. The new century. Toward the end of the twentieth century, much was being written about a rolling back of the national government's influence—a devolution in the federal relationship. There were certainly some signs pointing in that direction. The landmark agreement between the Republican Congress and President Clinton that restructured a key component of social welfare policy and shifted more control to states was one such sign. Numerous decisions by the Rehnquist Court that signaled a rethinking of the unfettered use of the interstate commerce clause as a rationale for congressional policy making in traditionally state arenas is another. The election of a Republican president, George W. Bush—a former governor—coupled with a Republican-controlled Congress, led many to expect an administration sympathetic to a state-oriented version of federalism.

Whatever devolutionary momentum existed was stopped by the events of September 11, 2001. In response to 9/11, President Bush and the Congress pushed for a very strong antiterrorism role for the national government in domestic policy. The Patriot Act (2001) and the Real ID Act (2005) were two centerpieces to this centralization effort. Moreover, President Bush successfully pushed a major educational reform effort, the No Child Left Behind Act (2001), which broadened national control over what has always been viewed as a state function—public education.[44]

The Great Recession further weakened the states and, as we discuss in chapter 7, led to a substantial increase in the reliance on federal financial assistance for several years. In addition, the policy centerpiece of the first Obama administration, the PPACA, extends national policy making over health-insurance policy in dramatic ways. About half the states challenged the president and Congress' authority to pass this legislation, which imposes an individual mandate to purchase health insurance. The Supreme Court's decision in this regard was much anticipated. The result, in a complex decision with multiple opinions, was a blow to state sovereign power in that the court upheld the national government's authority to require such a mandate. The victory was not complete, however, and it remains to be seen how far the decision moves the national–state pendulum. States will make important decisions about the implementation of the program.

Federalism and the Inherent Tension among Values

The federal system created under the US Constitution is a remarkably complex one. It creates a complicated structure with separate executive, legislative, and judicial powers and two levels of government, each with its own claim to sovereignty, or at least partial sovereignty. The structure, as created in Philadelphia, was new to the world. And because it was new and unfamiliar, there was room for different interpretations. This was true in 1789. It is still true today. Martha Derthick, an astute analyst of the American form of federalism, notes that "It is, however, a very confusing form of government, with authority widely diffused and obscurely allocated. And it requires much tending. Issues of intergovernmental relations consume a great deal of official attention, including that of the Supreme Court."[45]

Under the Constitution, the federation seeks to balance a number of values such as national interests and state interests, majority power and minority rights. Larry Gerston points out that two values our federal system constantly struggles to balance are liberty and equality.[46] *Liberty* is an expression of the freedom to pursue individual self-interest. It was a value emphasized by the Antifederalists who feared the loss of liberty under a strong national government. *Equality,* or fairness, is a value best fostered by the central government that could guarantee uniformity of policy throughout the states. Finding the balance between these values is almost impossible: "To the extent that government institutions promote liberty, the public policy rules are bound to differ from state to state. And to the extent that government institutions endorse equality, states are disallowed from behaving in ways unique to their individual existences. Therein lies a conundrum of American federalism."[47]

Derthick makes a similar point, arguing that the primary tension is between "place-based groups" such as states and communities and the rights of individuals as guaranteed by the national constitution. She concludes that "one type of group—the place-based group that federalism had honored—yielded to groups otherwise defined, as by race, age, disability or orientation to an issue or cause."[48]

It is, as David Walker noted, a "conflicted" system—one in which both centripetal and centrifugal forces may occur concurrently: "The system is conflicted insofar as it reflects simultaneously centralizing and decentralizing, cooperative and competitive, co-optive and more discretionary, and activist as well as retrenching tendencies."[49]

This is the case because the operation of federalism may be different in different policy areas at different times. Furthermore, it can be the case because different institutions may pull in different directions or be constrained in different ways during the same time period; for example, Congress and the bureaucracy may seek to expand control through fiscal federalism at a time when the Supreme Court may seek to limit the reach of the national government in certain domestic arenas. It can be the case because, while the general public professes to distrust and dislike the growth of the national government, that same public advocates for the expansion of specific programs funded and administered by the national government. It can also be the case because we focus so much on the formal measures of who is "winning" (the Supreme Court's rulings on federalism; the broadening of congressional statutory authority; the expansion of fiscal federalism) when there are more informal, less obvious trends at work. Relevant in this regard is the argument recently made by John Nugent that states have learned how to influence national policy makers through alternative mechanisms.[50] Notably, state officials are involved in what Nugent calls "constructive engagement" with members of Congress and federal agencies over (1) the shape of future policy, (2) the conditions associated with federal grants, and (3) the amount and shape of administrative discretion given to the state agencies that often are the primary implementers of federal policies.

While some of this negotiation occurs in a series of single-state to national official interactions, a good deal of it occurs through associations of state officials. These associations essentially serve as interest groups on behalf of the states and their local governments. One group of such organizations is known as "The Big Seven" and is especially active and influential on behalf of state and local governments, with a substantial lobbying presence in Washington, D.C. The Big Seven include the National Governors' Association (NGA), the National Conference of State Legislatures (NCSL), the Council of State Governments (CSG), the US Conference of Mayors (USCM), the National Association of Counties (NACo), the National League of Cities, and the International City/County Management Association (ICMA). Other groups representing various state officials and interests include the National Association of State Budget Officers (NASBO), the National Association of Attorneys General (NAAG) and the National Association of Secretaries of State (NASS), among others. The activities of these organizations are often overlooked in discussions of federalism. Perhaps this is because they involve organized interest group activity and the policy discretion of administrative agencies, two developments not generally anticipated by the Founders (*Federalist* 10 notwithstanding).

Nugent further argues, and as we show in chapters 3 and 4, state governments today are far more competent and sophisticated, and have dramatically increased their capacity for effective governance. They have, in Nugent's terms, "developed a robust set of institutions to facilitate interstate cooperation and to strengthen their individual and collective hands in dealing with federal officials."[51] This is an important point that is often overlooked; the states today are not the states as they existed in the middle of the twentieth century.

Even when the national government is perceived to have won a struggle with the states over policy making, the victory is not necessarily total. A good example is the decision in *NFIB v. Sebelius*, the 2012 Supreme Court decision on the constitutionality of the PPACA. The court upheld the national government's right to mandate that states enforce the congressional requirement that health insurance be required of all citizens, and this significant decision became the focus of virtually all media reports on the Supreme Court decision. But another provision of the PPACA required states to expand Medicaid coverage by stipulating that states must accept people into the program who might not otherwise be eligible. These are the "working poor," those who make too much money to qualify for certain programs because their income is above the federal poverty line, but who do not make enough money to easily afford health insurance. This group is defined as those making up to 138 percent of the federal poverty line (around $32,000 for a family of four in 2012). To ensure that states would comply, the national government threatened the loss of federal aid if a state balked. But the *NFIB* decision struck down this provision. States cannot be penalized if they choose not to expand Medicaid coverage to the working poor in their state. As *Governing* magazine recently observed, "That means states have a real choice about whether to participate."[52]

As we trace the historical events and eras that, over 225 years, have led to a more nation-centered federalism, we might despair of the states and their roles. But that would be a mistake. Without a doubt, the role of the national government has grown substantially. But, in many respects, so has the role of the states. It is tempting to think of the federal relationship as a zero-sum game; if the national government expands its power, the states must be losing power. But this assumes that the size of the game itself remains constant—that the sum of all national and state power is a constant. But it is not. Governments at all levels—national, state, and local—are a bigger part of the citizens' lives now than previously. They are certainly a much bigger part of life than any or all government was in 1789. How could it be otherwise in a society as large, complex, and technological as today's? Furthermore, while it is clear that the authority of the national government to make policy in the domestic arena has expanded dramatically, such authority is often enacted in such a way as to increase the implementation and regulatory authority of state governments.[53]

It is also the case that states can resist some initiatives of the national government by refusing to accept federal funds for such policies. For example, some states declined funds for "abstinence only" sex education pressed by the administration of George W. Bush, while others refused to accept hundreds of millions of dollars in federal grants for planning and construction of high-speed rail systems.[54]

Let us be clear on the message here: we are not saying that government *ought* to be as big of a presence in citizen's lives as it is. We are certainly not saying that the federal system in the United States today *ought* to be as centralized as it has become. But we are saying that limited government in the way the Founders understood it—in a rural, agrarian society with a relatively small population and few technological advances beyond the printing press and rudimentary steam engines—is very different than what is feasible today.

It is also worth keeping in mind that, while the role of the national government in today's American federation is clearly central, it has not eliminated the need for the states. States retain significant policy-making power in most areas of domestic policy. States are often ahead of the national government when it comes to innovation. As one analyst has pointed out, "State governments are usually first to act in response to new problems or issues, of which many arise in a time of rapid technological and cultural change."[55] Examples include immigration policies in a number of states, California's tougher auto-emission standards enacted in the 1990s, and policies enacted in several states to address stem-cell research and global-warming concerns.

Federalism Elsewhere

The United States is not the only federal system. As mentioned earlier, of the approximately two hundred sovereign nations in the world, about twenty-five adopted a federal system. By now it should be evident that there are many gradations of federalism, with some leaning toward a regional- or state-centered system and some more toward a nation-centered federalism. Because each is a product of the culture, history, and specific geographical, political, and economic conditions within a particular country, each federal system is unique. And even within a single country, the federal relationship shifts over time, as we have demonstrated in this chapter.

Any comparison of federal systems leads to the conclusion that there are numerous ways in which the power is distributed between the center and the periphery. Some federal systems (e.g., Argentina, Spain, South Africa) are clearly more centralized than the American federation. On the other hand, a few federations are definitely less centralized and more oriented toward the peripheral, regional-level governments. One is Germany.

In Germany, the basis for a federal system was established after World War II and extended with the 1990 reunification of East and West Germany. As one text notes, "Its 16 states, or Länder, exercise a great deal of power, far more than states do in the United States . . . The central government has exclusive authority over foreign affairs, money, immigration and telecommunications. But the Länder retain residual powers over all other matters."[56] This includes education, health and welfare, and civil and criminal law.

Canada is another federal system in which the balance between center and the periphery is tipped toward the latter. In Canada, it is the regions—the provinces—that enjoy substantial autonomy. Canada is probably the most periphery-oriented federal system in the world. In part this is because of the dual cultures that characterize Canada. The bargain for keeping francophone Quebec in the system is substantial autonomy for provinces on many matters. This includes the fact that the provinces tax and spend at a higher rate than the federal government.[57] Moreover, there is a significant distribution of federal revenues to the provinces but without a heavy burden of national mandates attached to the funds.

State and Local Government Relations

The focus of this chapter is on the relationship between the national government and the states. By now it should be clear that it is a complex relationship, ever changing, inconsistent, and often times variable by policy area. It is clear that today's federalism is very different from that of 1788 or 1789. Federalism—here meaning the political and constitutional arrangement between the national and state governments—is just one type of intergovernmental relationship involving the states. States must also interact with local governments. The difference is that, while states may assert some measure of sovereign authority vis-à-vis the national government, local governments can make no such claim. They are creatures of the state government—meaning they were created by the state. From a legal perspective, local governments in their various incarnations—counties, cities, special districts, school districts and townships—are entirely dependent on state governments for their regulatory and taxing authority.

While the local governments are "creatures of the state," they are also "agents of the state" in that they carry out state powers at the local level.[58] They provide services authorized by the state and they regulate behavior as mandated by the state. Precisely how these activities are divided between the state and the local governments is highly variable. For example, in some states most of the welfare function is carried out at the local—usually county—level, while elsewhere it is centralized at the state level. One study found that the proportion of public services delivered by the state (rather than by the local governments) ranged from almost 80 percent (Vermont) to less than 40 percent (Nevada).[59]

Technically, then, the relationship between the state and its local governments is a unitary system, not a federal one. Local governments are not sovereign; they owe their claim to govern to a grant of authority, called a charter, from the state government. The charter stipulates what local governments can or cannot do, and what they are required to do. Some states, either through the state constitution or legislative statute, determine the precise organizational structure that a county or municipality (city) must have. The degree of latitude offered to local governments by the state authority is different from one state to another. In some, local governments are permitted substantial authority and freedom to operate as they see fit, usually referred to as "home rule." In others, the state—especially through the state legislature—places strict limits or constraints on the powers and the taxing authority of local governments. In some cases this brings local governments—especially school districts and cities—into conflict with the state legislature. One particularly salient example is public-school funding.

Although states have the legal authority over local governments, it is the case that for at least the first half of this country's existence, local governments were where most of the "governing" occurred. Political scientist (and future US President) Woodrow Wilson observed this fact in 1898.[60] It remained true into the early part of the next century: "At the turn of the twentieth century, local governments were raising more revenue, doing more spending, and had more debt than the federal and state governments *combined*."[61] The relevant point is that states are much more engaged in the activities of local governments today than they were a hundred years ago. In some ways, this is where the role of states has increased most dramatically. Because the focus so often is on the relationship between the states and the national government, the stronger role today of the states vis-à-vis their local governments is often overlooked. This is a powerful point once we recognize the pervasiveness of local governments; today there are about ninety thousand such units in the various states. There are almost seven thousand local governments in Illinois, and more than four thousand in Pennsylvania, Texas, and California each.

This engagement of states in local government administration extends, increasingly over time, to funding. For decades the primary source of revenue for local governments was the property tax, a cumbersome revenue source that is inefficient and unpopular. Consequently, states have shifted some of the local reliance on the property tax to other revenue instruments. These include local option taxes and user fees. It also includes state aid to local governments. This is especially true of local school districts, which receive over half their revenue from the state in many instances. Cities and counties also receive revenue transfers from the state. Just how much of the financial burden for local government is undertaken at the state level is highly variable by state. Nonetheless, it is clearly the case that states are now far more actively involved in assisting local governments, as well as regulating local governments, than they were in the past.

Conclusion

We began this chapter with the story of the resistance by some states to the controversial health-care reform legislation passed by a Democratically controlled Congress, at the Democratic president's urging, in 2010. Almost all the resistance was from Republican governors and Republican-controlled state legislatures. Partisanship and ideology are often part of the "endless argument" over federalism. Regardless of the source, it is indeed an endless argument, a contest that is never entirely resolved.

There is, however, no doubt at all that the balance has tipped in favor of the national perspective. We have outlined a number of trends and events that led to the current state. While states have less power today, relative to the national government, this does not mean that states are powerless—far from it. In many functional areas, states are energetic, imaginative, and primary policy makers, as we will demonstrate in chapter 5. The institutions of state government today are clearly more capable and competent than fifty years ago, as we will demonstrate in chapters 3 and 4.

Furthermore, while states may have less relative power compared to the national government, one can make a case that they have more absolute power than previously—certainly more so than in 1789. Everyday life was fundamentally different then, and the need for regulation and public services was minimal. In today's society of 300 million people, living in urban environments experiencing rapid technological and social change, government at all levels—including state governments—have a much larger role to play. Moreover, because of the emphasis on the most visible institutions and most salient issues, we often underappreciate the ability of states to influence federal policies in a meaningful way. Much of this is done through bureaucratic channels.

Finally, we should note that increased concern over the national government's fiscal policies and the growth in the federal debt almost certainly will require a recalibration of the relationship between the national and state governments. As economist Alice Rivlin recently noted, "A thorough rethinking of fiscal federalism is in order. A clearer demarcation of responsibilities between the federal and state levels could improve efficiency, accountability, and performance at both levels."[62] Others have made similar calls for a rethinking of the roles of the national and state governments.[63]

The extent to which these prescriptions are honored or ignored remains to be seen. The next few years will be especially important ones in terms of the relative role of the states in the federal system. As we show in the next few chapters, states are better prepared than ever, despite the growing challenges of governing in our federal system.

3

The Policy-making Environment
of the States

States matter because:

- State government structures are distinctive from those of the federal government.
- State legislatures operate with a variety of structures and resource levels.
- Governors have become powerful, with great influence over the policy-making process.
- Bureaucracies have evolved to handle the policy burdens shouldered by the states.
- State courts operate with different structures and different means to gain the bench.

IT IS EASY TO THINK of the fifty state governments as being smaller versions of the federal government. In this view, the governors are simply minor league versions of the president, state legislatures pale imitations of Congress, and state courts the judicial officials left to handle traffic violations and property disputes while their federal colleagues tackle the heavy legal issues. But such a perspective is fundamentally misguided; state governments have their own evolutionary histories and have developed their own governing structures, none of which exactly mirror the federal experience. Moreover, as discussed in chapter 2, the lines of policy authority between the federal and state governments have never been clear and have been continually shifting. Thus, it is critical to understand how the state governments we have today have come to be as they are, and how their decision-making power over the large number of policy decisions that shape our daily lives has developed, because it is not self-evident from understanding government at the federal level.

In this chapter we trace the development of the policy-making environment in the states. We discuss why over time legislatures came to lose power while the executive and courts increased their influence over policy making. We then discuss why these changes matter and what difference they make to the policy-making process. Finally, we turn to an examination of which policies the states dominate and how the mix of policies over which the states govern has changed over time.

Designing Governments

It is essential to appreciate that the original thirteen states were governing entities before any national government was established. When the first states emerged during the early movement toward independence, they had to create ruling structures to replace the colonial structures against which they were rebelling, without having any national model to emulate. The initial governing device employed in most of the emerging states was called the provincial congress. These bodies were representative assemblies that assumed legislative, executive, and, to a much lesser extent, judicial functions. They governed from roughly 1774 until 1776, when the newly written state constitutions took effect.[1]

In designing new governing structures, those who wrote these constitutions wanted systems that functioned more effectively than the provincial congresses had. Indeed, in the preamble to New York's 1777 constitution, the authors admitted, "And whereas many and great inconveniences attend the said mode of government by congress and committees, as of necessity, in many instances, legislative, judicial, and executive powers have been vested therein." Thus, the new governments were created with the now familiar idea of separate legislative, executive, and judicial branches. But in reality, this initial separation of powers was really very fuzzy and uneven. What was actually created in the first states was a system where the legislative branch clearly dominated the other two branches. Thus, policy making effectively rested entirely in the hands of each state's lawmakers.

The Rise and Fall and Resurrection of the State Legislatures

Explicit references to a separation of powers were present in about half of the original state constitutions. But only in New York and Massachusetts was the notion given much attention, and even in these constitutions clear lines dividing the branches were not to be found. The muddled nature of separation of power greatly bothered James Madison, who later complained in the *Federalist 47*, "If we look into the constitutions of the several States we find that, not withstanding the emphatical and, in some instances, the unqualified terms in which this axiom has been laid down, there is not a single instance in which the several departments of power have been kept absolutely separate and distinct."[2] In designing the new federal government, Madison and his colleagues made a conscious effort to establish a more clearly defined and balanced distribution of power among the three branches.

In particular, those who wrote the federal Constitution were concerned that in the state constitutions too much power had been concentrated in the hands of the state legislatures. There was considerable evidence to support their apprehensions. In eight of the new states, the legislature elected the governor. And in a slightly different set of eight states, the legislature selected judges. This meant that in a majority of the new states, the governor and the judges were directly beholden to the legislature for their positions. Not surprisingly, the legislature could use their dominant position to bully the other branches to do their bidding. In a celebrated 1786 legal decision, Rhode Island's supreme court issued a decision declaring a measure passed by the legislature to be unconstitutional, the first time any state court had done so. Lawmakers responded by demanding that the justices appear before them to justify their decision. The justices' arguments were not persuasive and when their terms expired the following year, legislators voted to replace all of those who had supported the decision.

But the era of legislative supremacy did not last long in most states. As early as the 1780s, efforts were made to rein in the legislatures, in part by taking away control over appointment of the executive and also by giving greater independence to the judiciary.[3] When the original states replaced their initial constitutions, the newer documents included provisions that constrained lawmakers; when new states were admitted to the union, their constitutions limited legislative power from the start. As will be discussed below, these changes unyoked both governors and judges from legislative dominance. And constitutions also came to place explicit limits on the kinds of laws the legislature could pass. Article IV, Section 27 of the 1865 Missouri constitution, for example, contained specific prohibitions against the legislature "establishing, locating, altering the course, or affecting the construction of roads, or the building or repairing of bridges; or establishing, altering, or vacating any street, avenue, or alley in any city or town" and "extending the time for the assessment or collection of taxes, or otherwise relieving any assessor or collector of taxes from the due performance of his official duties." Limitations of these sorts appeared in most nineteenth-century state constitutions.[4]

Perhaps the most prominent among the constitutional restraints imposed were provisions allowing legislatures to meet only once every other year. In the original states, legislatures were required to meet every year because it was thought frequent meetings promoted closer ties between representatives and the represented, and also gave the legislature greater control over the

Chapter 3

TABLE 3.1
The Rise and Fall and Resurrection of Legislative Power

Year	Number of States	Number of States with: Annual Sessions	Biennial Sessions	Quadrennial Sessions
1777	13	13	—	—
1832	24	21	3	—
1861	33	15	18	—
1889	38	6	32	—
1906	45	6	38	1
1931	48	6	41	1
1960	50	19	31	—
1999	50	43	7	—
2013	50	46	4	—

Source: Adapted from Peverill Squire, *The Evolution of American Legislatures: Colonies, Territories, and States, 1619–2009* (Ann Arbor: University of Michigan Press, 2012), 243–49, 270–73.

executive.[5] When legislative supremacy began to fall out of favor, the rationale behind legislative sessions shifted. Because it was thought that legislatures abused their powers, holding sessions only every other year came to be preferred because it was calculated that lawmakers would be able to cause less trouble, the system of laws would become more stable, and the cost of running the legislature would be reduced.[6] As documented in table 3.1, the trend over the course of the nineteenth century was unmistakable. At the beginning of the century, almost every state had annual sessions. By the end of the century almost every state had biennial sessions. In 1901, Alabama even went so far as to institute quadrennial sessions, having regularly scheduled meetings only once every four years. As we will discuss later, governors were the main beneficiaries of the trend toward having legislatures meet less often. In essence, a power vacuum was created and the executive filled it.

The trend toward less frequent legislative sessions reversed course in the twentieth century, as public pressure on the states to perform better began to build. As more demands were made of the legislature, it seemed prudent to have it meet annually. It was also thought that, echoing ideas in the original constitutions, annual sessions would help rein in gubernatorial power.[7] As table 3.1 documents, by 2013 only four states still meet every other year; the rest have annual sessions.

State legislatures, of course, underwent other important changes during the twentieth century, as will be detailed in chapter 4. Most important, as they came to meet annually, their sessions also became longer and they met for more days. Because legislative service became more demanding, legislative compensation and benefits improved. Staff also increased, giving lawmakers a greater ability to generate and evaluate information needed to make decisions. Facilities generally improved as well; members came to have offices and access to computers and other technological innovations that improved their capacity to do their job. All of these changes are subsumed under the concept of legislative professionalization. The idea driving these changes was to make the legislatures more competitive with the governor and the executive branch in the policy making process. Thus, during the American federal experience, state legislatures have traveled from being the dominant governing institution to being weakened to the point of near irrelevancy to being rehabilitated to once again be important actors in policy making.

The Increasing Importance of the Governor and the Executive Branch

The American colonies had governors who were, in most cases, imbued with impressive formal powers. But in reality, their ability to exercise those powers was greatly constrained by the fact that control over taxing and spending came to be asserted by the colonial assemblies. As noted above, when the new states wrote their constitutions they opted to make the legislatures powerful and the governors (called presidents in several states) weak. Indeed, New Hampshire chose to go without any chief executive at all until its 1784 constitution! Many distinguished Americans served as governor early in their states' histories: John Hancock and Samuel Adams in Massachusetts, George Clinton and John Jay in New York, John Rutledge in South Carolina, and Patrick Henry and Thomas Jefferson in Virginia. But the office they held was not imbued with much power. As James Madison noted during the federal Constitutional Convention, "The executives of the states are in general little more than ciphers; the legislatures omnipotent."[8] The original governors' lack of power can be documented in two ways, as shown in table 3.2. First, in eight of the states the governor was elected by the legislature. This method of election put the executive under the legislature's thumb. If these governors wanted to retain office they had to appease lawmakers. Second, in nine of the states the governor was given only a one-year term, leaving them remarkably little time to accomplish any significant goals. Election by the legislature and short terms of office were adopted to ensure that all important decisions were made by the legislature.

The problems with this institutional design became apparent relatively quickly. Those who wrote the federal constitution, for example, decided against having Congress elect the president and gave the office a four-year term. In the states, as legislatures came to be seen as abusing their exalted position, power was taken from them and given largely to the executive.[9] By 1833, only four of the twenty-four governors were still elected by the legislature, meaning that most of them were put into office by the voters. Indeed, every state that entered

TABLE 3.2
Gubernatorial Terms of Office over Time

Year	Number of States	Length of Gubernatorial Term by States			
		One-Year	Two-Year	Three-Year	Four-Year
1776–1777	13[a]	9 — CT, **GA, MD**, MA, **NJ, NC, PA**, RI, **VA**	1 — **SC**	2 — **DE, NY**	0 — —
1789	13	8 — CT, **MD**, MA, NH, NJ, **NC**, RI	1 — **SC**	4 — **DE, GA, NY, VA**	0 — —
1833	24	9 — CT, ME, **MD**, MA, NH, **NJ, NC**, RI, VT	6 — AL, GA, MS, NY, OH, **SC**	3 — IN, PA, **VA**	6 — DE, IL, KY, LA, MO, TN
1889	42	2 — MA, RI	20 — AL, AR, CO, CT, GA, IA, KS, ME, MI, MN, NE, NH, ND, OH, SC, SD, TN, TX, VT, WI	2 — NJ, NY	18 — CA, DE, FL, IL, IN, KY, LA, MD, MS, MO, MT, NV, NC, OR, PA, VA, WA, WV
1933	48	0	24 — AZ, AR, CO, CT, GA, ID, IA, KS, ME, MA, MI, MN, NE, NH, NY, NM, ND, OH, RI, SD, TN, TX, VT, WI	1 — NJ	23 — AL, CA, DE, FL, IL, IN, KY, LA, MD, MS, MO, MT, NV, NC, OK, OR, PA, SC, UT, VA, WA, WV, WY
1989	50	0	3 — NH, RI, VT	0	47 — AL, AK, AZ, AR, CA, CO, CT, DE, FL, GA, HI, ID, IL, IN, IA, KS, KY, LA, ME, MD, MA, MI, MN, MS, MO, MT, NE, NV, NJ, NM, NY, NC, ND, OH, OK, OR, PA, SC, SD, TN, TX, UT, VA, WA, WV, WI, WY
2013	50	0	2 — NH, VT	0	48 — AL, AK, AZ, AR, CA, CO, CT, DE, FL, GA, HI, ID, IL, IN, IA, KS, KY, LA, ME, MD, MA, MI, MN, MS, MO, MT, NE, NV, NJ, NM, NY, NC, ND, OH, OK, OR, PA, RI, SC, SD, TN, TX, UT, VA, WA, WV, WI, WY

States in bold indicate executive was elected by the legislature.

a. New Hampshire did not have a formal executive until 1784. Pennsylvania operated with a Supreme Executive Council headed by a president until 1790. Massachusetts did not adopt its constitution until 1780.

Sources: Gathered by the authors from state constitutions.

the union following the first thirteen states required its governor to be elected by the people. By 1889, the governors of all of the states were directly elected, with South Carolina being the last state to give way on this score in 1866. Being directly elected gave governors an independent political base, which in turn could be leveraged to increase their ability to influence policy decisions.

Governors also came to enjoy longer terms, affording them more time to accomplish their objectives. In 1833, less than half the states still retained one-year terms, while a quarter of them allowed their governor four years in office. A century later, no state had one-year terms; half had two-year terms, and the other half either three- or four-year terms. The trend toward longer terms has continued. Currently, only two states (New Hampshire and Vermont) have two-year terms, the rest have four-year terms. Governors now have considerable time to pursue their agendas and lawmakers and others in the political process have to take that fact into account.

The second way it can be shown that governors have increased their powers is given in table 3.3. Today, every governor enjoys some variant of the veto power—the ability to prevent legislation that has passed the legislature from becoming law.[10] The veto gives the executive the ability to greatly influence the legislative process. Most colonial governors had exercised an absolute veto, one that the legislature had no ability to override. In reaction, in the majority of the new states the writers of their constitutions shied away from endowing the governor with any veto power. South Carolina's governor briefly enjoyed a veto of the sort his colonial predecessors had, but that was taken away completely within two years. In New York, the veto power was exercised collectively by the governor jointly with the council and the court. The only state with a veto that would be familiar today was Massachusetts, whose veto power was the model for the veto given the president in the US Constitution.

Relatively quickly, however, most governors acquired a veto power, as voters came to fear legislative overreach more than arbitrary decisions by a monarchial chief executive. Among the original thirteen states, most gave their governor a veto as soon as they replaced their first constitutions. A few of them, however, did lag, most notably North Carolina, which did not grant its governor a veto until 1996. Among the states admitted after the original thirteen, almost all of them gave their governor a veto in their initial constitutions. Thus, all governors today have some ability to veto measures passed by their legislatures, giving them significant leverage in the legislative process.

But, of course, not all vetoes are created equal. A line-item veto gives an executive the ability to pick and choose which provisions of a bill to accept and which to block. The original veto power in the Massachusetts constitution (and the one still in the US Constitution) is an all-or-nothing proposition; the chief executive either accepts an entire measure or loses it all. A line-item veto gives a governor even greater leverage over the legislature by allowing him or her

TABLE 3.3
THE DEVELOPMENT OF THE GUBERNATORIAL VETO POWER

State	Veto in First State Constitution	Veto if Adopted Subsequent to First State Constitution	Adoption of Line-Item Veto
South Carolina	1776 (absolute)	No veto power in 1778 constitution, veto reappeared in 1868 constitution.	1895 constitution
New York	*1777 (shared with Council and Court)*	1821 constitution, governor given sole veto power.	1874 constitutional amendment
Massachusetts	1780 constitution	—	1918 constitutional amendment
Georgia	—	1789 constitution	1861 (Confederate) constitution; 1865 constitution
Pennsylvania	—	1790 constitution	1873 constitution
Kentucky	1792 constitution	—	1891 constitution
New Hampshire	—	1792 constitutional amendment	—
Vermont	*1793 constitution (shared with council, amendatory with one year suspension)*	1836 constitutional amendment	—
Louisiana	1812 constitution	—	1879 constitution
Indiana	1816 constitution	—	—
Mississippi	1817 constitution	—	1890 constitution
Connecticut	—	1818 constitution	1924 constitutional amendment
Illinois	*1818 constitution (shared with Council)*	1848 constitution, governor given sole veto power.	1884 constitutional amendment
Alabama	1819 constitution	—	1875 constitution
Maine	1820 constitution	—	1995 constitutional amendment
Missouri	1820 constitution	—	1875 constitution
Michigan	1835 constitution	—	1905 constitution
Arkansas	1836 constitution	—	1874 constitution
Florida	1839 constitution	—	1875 constitutional amendment
New Jersey	—	1844 constitution	1875 constitutional amendment
Texas	1845 constitution	—	1866 constitution
Iowa	1846 constitution	—	1968 constitutional amendment
Wisconsin	1848 constitution	—	1930 constitutional amendment
California	1849 constitution	—	1879 constitution

State	Veto in First State Constitution	Veto if Adopted Subsequent to First State Constitution	Adoption of Line-Item Veto
Minnesota	1858 (1857) constitution	—	1876 constitutional amendment
Oregon	1859 (1857) constitution	—	1916 constitutional amendment
Kansas	1861 (1859) constitution	—	1904 constitutional amendment
Nevada	1864 constitution	—	—
Nebraska	1866 constitution	—	1875 constitution
Maryland	—	1867 constitution	1891 constitutional amendment
Tennessee	—	1870 constitution	1953 constitutional amendment
Virginia	—	1870 constitution	1902 constitution
West Virginia	—	1872 constitution	1872 constitution
Colorado	1876 constitution	—	1876 constitution
Montana	1889 constitution	—	1889 constitution
North Dakota	1889 constitution	—	1889 constitution
South Dakota	1889 constitution	—	1889 constitution
Washington	1889 constitution	—	1889 constitution
Idaho	1890 (1889) constitution	—	1890 (1889) constitution
Wyoming	1890 (1889) constitution	—	1890 (1889) constitution
Utah	1896 (1895) constitution	—	1896 (1895) constitution
Delaware	—	1897 constitution	1897 constitution
Ohio	—	1903 constitutional amendment	1903 constitutional amendment
Oklahoma	1907 constitution	—	1907 constitution
Rhode Island	—	1909 constitutional amendment	—
New Mexico	1912 (1911) constitution	—	1912 (1911) constitution
Arizona	1912 (1911) constitution	—	1912 (1911) constitution
Alaska	1959 (1956) constitution	—	1959 (1956) constitution
Hawaii	1959 (1950) constitution	—	1959 (1950) constitution
North Carolina	—	1996 constitutional amendment	—

Note: The original thirteen states are in bold. Italics are used to indicate that a governor shared veto power. Dates in parentheses are when a constitution was adopted if different from when it went into effect.

Sources: Rui J. P. de Figueredo Jr., "Budget Institutions and Political Insulation: Why States Adopt the Item Veto," *Journal of Public Economics* 87 (2003): 2677–701; John A. Fairlie, "The Veto Power of the Governor," *American Political Science Review* 11 (1917): 473–93; National Conference of State Legislatures, *Inside the Legislative Process*, Table 98-6.10, www.ncsl.org/documents/legismgt/ILP/98Tab6Pt3.pdf, various state constitutions.

to threaten provisions that matter greatly to lawmakers without risking losing things that he or she wants.

The line-item veto first appeared in American politics in, of all places, the Confederate constitution. Georgia put one into its 1861 Confederate constitution a few days later. The line-item veto proved to be of sufficient interest that, by the end of the nineteenth century, most states had given their governor a version of it. Of course, within line-item vetoes some are more powerful than others—Wisconsin's "partial" veto is usually thought to be the most powerful.[11] But governors in forty-three states (Maryland's governor is effectively unable to use the line-item veto) now enjoy some ability to pick and choose provisions of legislation they wish to sign into law.

Being directly elected to longer terms and armed with extensive veto powers makes governors today much more powerful than their predecessors. But, as is always the case with the states, some governors are granted greater formal powers than are others. Along with their veto powers, governors also vary in the degree to which they can influence the budget process and in their appointment powers. In addition, while some governors can serve for an unlimited number of terms, most can only hold the post for two terms, and Virginia's governor is limited to a single four-year term.[12] Thus, the role a governor can play in his or her state's policy-making process varies across the states.

Another reason governors today exercise considerable power is because they each sit atop a large bureaucracy. As noted in earlier chapters, government at all levels did relatively little when the country was young. Thus, state bureaucracies were almost nonexistent. But as state populations increased and as their economies grew and diversified, more demands were made on government. The bureaucracy grew in response as, over time, more agencies were created to administer the programs demanded by voters.

The early growth of the bureaucracy can be demonstrated by the changes in New York between 1800 and 1925. At the beginning of the nineteenth century, New York had just ten state agencies. By 1850, another ten agencies had been added. At that point, state government growth accelerated: by 1900 there were eighty-one agencies, and another eighty agencies were established by 1925. This dramatic increase was driven by changes in society. Thus, as education came to be seen as an important governmental function, New York responded by creating a superintendent of public instruction in 1854. The state started agencies to regulate banking in 1829, insurance in 1859, and public utilities in 1882. As the industrial revolution swept the state, a commissioner of statistics of labor was established in 1883. Urbanization raised sanitation issues and a public health department was fashioned in 1880. Environmental issues also surfaced and in response game and fish protectors were created in 1880, followed by a forest commission in 1885, a fisheries commission in 1892, and a state water commission in 1905. All were eventually swept into a single conservation department in 1926. Similar growth trajectories driven by similar social trends were found in other states.[13]

Indeed, the growth of state government continued unabated over the rest of the twentieth century, as documented in table 3.4. Again, state agencies were added as new problems surfaced on the public agenda. In 1959, there were fifty-one agencies that existed in at least thirty-eight (or three-quarters) of the states. These were units devoted to what most would agree were deemed core governmental activities, such as corrections, education, and highways. As fresh issues emerged, states responded by creating bureaucracies to deal with them. Thus, among the twelve agencies initiated in most of the states in the 1960s were ones devoted to air quality, economic development, and highway safety. The 1970s saw a significant increase in the size of government, in addition to agencies overseeing civil rights, consumer affairs, and mass transit, arts councils, energy departments, and women's commissions were also added. Growth rates subsided in the 1980s and 1990s, but state governments still created agencies to oversee groundwater management, hazardous waste, lotteries, mining reclamation, public broadcasting systems, and underground storage tanks.

By 2013, state government bureaucracies touched on an impressive array of policy areas. Consider the list compiled by the Council of State Governments of *selected* state agencies found in almost every state: administration, agriculture, auditor, banking, budget, civil rights, commerce, community affairs, comptroller, consumer affairs, corrections, economic development, education, election

TABLE 3.4
Growth in State Agencies, 1959–1999

Year	Number of State Administrative Agencies Present in Thirty-eight or More States	Notable Examples
1959	51	Corrections Education Highways

Year	Number of New State Administrative Agencies Created in Thirty-eight or More States during Previous Decade	
1969	12	Air Quality Economic Development Highway Safety
1979	29	Civil Rights Consumer Affairs Mass Transit
1989	8	Groundwater Management Hazardous Waste Underground Storage Tanks
1999	8	Lotteries Mining Reclamation Public Broadcasting Systems

Source: Cynthia J. Bowling and Deil S. Wright, "Public Administration in the Fifty States: A Half-Century Administrative Revolution," *State & Local Government Review* 30 (1998): 52–64.

administration, emergency management, employment services, energy, environmental protection, finance, fish and wildlife, general services, health, higher education, highways, information systems, insurance, labor, licensing, mental health, natural resources, parks and recreation, personnel, planning, postaudit, preaudit, public library development, public utility regulation, purchasing, revenue, social services, solid-waste management, state police, tourism, transportation, and welfare.[14] In one way or another, state governments are now involved with almost every aspect of daily life. As the state's chief executive, this reality makes the governor more important today than in the past.

But it is again important to appreciate that although states have departments, agencies, and bureaus devoted to most of the same policy issues, the way the bureaucracies are configured across the states varies. In New Jersey, for example, the governor appoints the heads of most agencies, in some cases with the approval of the state senate. Occasionally, an agency head is allowed to make the appointment of a subsidiary bureau, but, of course, the agency head is a gubernatorial appointee. Thus, in New Jersey the state bureaucracy is under the governor's control. In contrast, in North Dakota a large number of agency heads are elected by the voters, giving each of them independent political standing. Thus, where the New Jersey Commissioner of Education is nominated by the governor, subject to state senate confirmation, and serves at the governor's discretion, the North Dakota Superintendent of Public Instruction is elected by the voters, leaving the current officeholder able to boast on his website that as "An extremely popular public official, Dr. Sanstead received more votes in his 1988 re-election than any other candidate for any office in the history of North Dakota."[15] Clearly, New Jersey's education leader has to be responsive to the governor's wishes in a way that North Dakota's educational leader does not have to fear.

The Courts as a Parallel Dimension of Federalism

Perhaps nowhere is the American federal system of government on better display than in the judicial system. American courts operate on parallel tracks, one federal, and the other state. Their similarities are largely superficial. Although the US Constitution's supremacy clause means that any conflict between federal and state law will be resolved in the former's favor, the design and scope of the two systems differs, and the laws and the interpretation of those laws also vary.

Courts existed during the colonial era, but what we take today to be exclusively judicial powers were actually shared among different governing institutions. Legislatures, for example, often heard legal cases and rendered decisions. Indeed, the archaic name still used by the state legislatures in Massachusetts and New Hampshire, "the General Court," harkens back to this reality. The first state constitutions did little to give the newly created state courts clearly defined jurisdictions. Indeed, as with the drafting of the US Constitution a decade later, the design of the court system was treated as something of an afterthought. Thus, under New Jersey's original constitution, the governor and his council functioned as the state's court of last resort. Final judicial authority was not granted to the state's court of last resort (or supreme court) until the constitution of 1844. Similar final authority power was only granted to every state's court of last resort in the middle of the nineteenth century.[16]

The separation of trial courts from appellate courts was also slow in developing in the states. Initially, appellate court judges also served as trial court judges, devoting part of their time each year to riding their circuit, moving from town to town in their district along with lawyers and court clerks, in something of a legal road show. The burden this system placed on judges proved great. But the system really changed only in response to the increased demands made on a state's legal system as populations and economies grew. Thus, during the nineteenth century, trial courts and appellate courts eventually became distinct operations, and later appellate courts usually split into a court of last resort with some subsidiary court of appeals, all to accommodate the increased demands being made on the legal system.[17]

As state judicial systems have continued to evolve, they have come to look different from the federal system, and often from each other. In simplified form, the federal court system consists of three levels, with trial courts, courts of appeal, and the Supreme Court. Similar unified courts systems, where trial courts handle all matter of civil and criminal cases, are only found in five states: California, Illinois, Iowa, Minnesota, and South Dakota. The other states have constructed more complicated systems.[18] New York, for example, has eight limited jurisdiction courts, with different systems for New York City (separate civil and criminal courts), Nassau and Suffolk counties on Long Island, and the rest of the state (Surrogates' Courts in sixty-two counties, and 1,487 Town and Village Justice Courts), along with a specialized Family Court, and a Court of Claims. Such complexity is not unusual. There are separate civil and criminal courts of last resort in Oklahoma and Texas. Water Courts were established in Colorado and Montana in the late 1960s and early 1970s to handle special issues involving water rights in those states. Vermont created an Environmental Court. Some states have separate courts that try cases involving taxes, workers compensation, and probate matters. Maryland has an Orphan's Court. In terms of structures, then, each state has largely devised its own system to handle legal cases.

States have also developed a range of approaches to judicial selection. The original thirteen states split in the way they put judges on the bench, as shown in table 3.5. In five states, governors appointed judges with the consent of the council; in the other eight states they were elected by the legislature. As noted earlier, legislative election made judges beholden to lawmakers. In contrast,

TABLE 3.5
State Judicial Selection Procedures over Time

Year	Number of States	Selection Procedure for Court of Last Resort		
		Gubernatorial Appointment	Legislative Election	Popular Election
1789	13	5 MD, MA, NY, PA[a], NH	8 CT, DE, GA, NJ, NC, RI, SC, VA	0 —
1833	24	11 DE, IN, KY, LA, ME, MD, MA, MO, NH, NY, PA	12 AL, CT, GA, IL, NJ, NC, OH, RI, SC, TN, VT, VA	1 MS
1889	42	7 CT, DE, ME, MA, MS, NH, NJ	6 GA, LA, RI, SC, VT, VA	29 AL, AZ, AR, CA, CO, FL, IN, IA, KS, KY, MD, MI, MN, MO, MT, NE, NY, NC, ND, OH, OR, PA, SD, TN, TX, WA, WV, WI
1933	48	6 CT, DE, ME, MA, NH, NJ	4 RI, SC, VT, VA	38 AL, AZ, AR, CA, CO, FL, GA, ID, IL, IN, IA, KS, KY, LA, MD, MI, MN, MS, MO, MT, NE, NV, NM, NY, NC, ND, OH, OK, OR, PA, SD, TN, TX, UT, WA, WV, WI, WY
1989	50	23 AK, CA, CO, CT, DE, FL, HI, IN, IA, KS, ME, MD, MA, MO, NE, NH, NJ, NY, OK, SD, UT, VT, WY	3 RI, SC, VA	24 AL, AZ, AR, GA, ID, IL, KY, LA, MI, MN, MS, MT, NV, NM, NC, ND, OH, OR, PA, TN, TX, WA, WV, WI
2013	50	25 AK, CA, CO, CT, DE, FL, HI, IN, IA, KS, ME, MD, MA, MO, NE, NH, NJ, NY, OK, RI, SD, TN, UT, VT, WY	2 SC, VA	23 AL, AZ, AR, GA, ID, IL, KY, LA, MI, MN, MS, MT, NV, NM, NC, ND, OH, OR, PA, TX, WA, WV, WI

a. In Pennsylvania, judges were appointed by executive council. In the other states the council consented to gubernatorial selections.

Source: data gathered by authors from www.judicialselection.us/.

gubernatorial appointment hinted at greater judicial independence. The framers of the US Constitution opted for this latter approach, allowing the president to nominate and the Senate to confirm federal judges to life terms. The idea that judges should enjoy independence from the political branches of government never gained complete favor in the states. By 1833, roughly half the states used gubernatorial appointment but, with one exception, the rest employed legislative election.

And that one exception proved enormously important. In its 1832 constitution, Mississippi became the first state to have all of its judges elected by the voters. New York followed suit in 1846, and by 1889 the vast majority of states elected their judges. The move to judicial elections was triggered in large part by dissatisfaction with the performance of the judicial branch, which many voters thought catered too much to elite and moneyed interests. They preferred to make the courts more responsive to the interests of the voters. Thus, instead of promoting judicial independence, the states opted for elections, which accentuated accountability. Judges would have to be able to defend their decisions to retain their place on the bench.

Judicial elections proved popular and every state that entered the union between 1846 and 1912 required them in its constitutions. However, a backlash against the use of elections to name judges developed during the second half of the nineteenth century. The concern was that elected judges were nothing more than another partisan cog in the political machines that dominated state politics. Judges were now thought to be beholden to party bosses and therefore susceptible to corruption.

An altogether new alternative approach to naming judges was proposed in 1914 by Albert Kales, a Northwestern University law professor. Kales devised a system that placed great value on merit. Under his plan, a governor would fill a judgeship by naming one of the people suggested by a panel consisting of lawyers and lay persons who would evaluate the qualifications of the candidates who applied. The people selected to be a judge would serve for a year or two and then face the voters in a retention election, a contest where the voters would only decide whether or not they wanted that judge to serve a full term. The idea was that this system would improve the legal qualifications of the people named as judges while still giving the voters, but not the parties, a say in whether they would stay on the bench. It was also reasoned that judges would be able to focus on the cases before them and not have to devote time and effort to campaigning.

It took a quarter century before any state opted to implement any variant of what came to be called the "merit plan." In 1940 Missouri finally became the first state to adopt a version of it. After another long period, starting in 1958, over the next two decades nineteen states adopted what was now becoming referred to as the "Missouri Plan." By 1989, roughly half the states selected their judges through some merit system.

Today, the variation in state judicial selection procedures is substantial. The governor nominates judges for the court of last resort, usually through a merit system, in half the states. Election by the legislature is still used in South Carolina and Virginia. The voters select judges in the rest of the states; partisan contests are held in six states, nonpartisan elections are employed in thirteen states, and in a strange hybrid approach judicial candidates in Michigan and Ohio are nominated through partisan mechanisms but elected in nonpartisan elections. To further complicate matters, some states use one system to select judges for the court of last resort, and another system to select lower court judges. And even in Missouri, the "Missouri Plan" is only used to select lower court judges in a handful of the largest counties; in the rest partisan elections are held.

There are two points to take away from this discussion. First, very few of the states follow the federal model of judicial elections in any significant way. Judges in Massachusetts, for example, used to be nominated by the governor for life terms, but in 1972 the voters passed a constitutional amendment requiring judges to step down at age seventy. In addition, states vary selection procedures between court levels, and often by county. Second, state selection procedures place greater weight on judicial accountability, whereas the federal system places greater weight on judicial independence.

What then, about the decisions judges make? As noted in this book's opening vignette, laws vary across the states. The way judges treat those laws also varies to some extent. In significant ways, states have developed their own legal histories. Perhaps the most significant development over the last generation has been the appearance of the "New Judicial Federalism." Starting in the 1970s, state courts began looking to state constitutions rather than the federal Constitution to drive their decisions on a number of important questions about civil liberties.[19] From this perspective, the federal constitution and the way the US Supreme Court interprets its provisions establishes the floor, or minimum standard, for civil liberties, while state courts interpreting state constitutional provisions have the opportunity to expand and strengthen those liberties.[20]

The new judicial federalism has been the source of some significant policy changes in recent American history. In granting same sex couples the right to marry in 2004, the Supreme Judicial Court of Massachusetts did so by finding the ban against it to violate provisions of the state constitution. There have, of course, been backlashes against such decisions and it is critical to understand that state courts operate in a context where their decisions can be resisted in ways that decisions by federal courts largely cannot. First, voters in some states can put measures on the ballot to overturn state court decisions. When the Supreme Court of California held same-sex marriage to be constitutional under that state's constitution in early 2008, opponents of the decision quickly launched a successful effort to overturn it at the ballot box. (An effort to allow the voters to overturn the Massachusetts Court's decision failed because under that state's rules only the legislature could place such a measure on the ballot and lawmakers resisted calls to do so. In California, voters could gather signatures to get the measure put on the ballot.) Second, in many states voters get to pass judgment on judges. Thus, after the Iowa Supreme Court found a ban against same-sex marriage to be unconstitutional under the state constitution in 2009, voters vented their displeasure by voting against retaining three of the judges when their names appeared on the ballot in 2010. Iowa voters could not, as California voters could, place the decision itself on the ballot, but they could replace the judges who made the controversial ruling. (As in Massachusetts, only legislators could put the measure on the ballot, and so far, Iowa legislators have declined to do so. And, in Massachusetts, judges do not go before the voters, leaving them insulated from any voter unhappiness.)

The Design of State Governments

As they have evolved, the structures of state governments have come to look much like the federal government, with three separate branches. But, as noted, upon closer inspection, there are notable differences, both between the federal government and the state governments, and across the state governments themselves. Indeed, the notion of separation of powers means something slightly different in each system. In Rhode Island, for example, only since voters passed a constitutional amendment in 2004 has the era of legislative supremacy ended. Prior to the amendment's passage, the legislature dominated the executive branch through lawmakers' control over appointments to regulatory agencies.[21]

This leads to one final point that needs to be emphasized. Each state government is, in some fashion, unique. They operate under somewhat different sets of rules, with somewhat different structures. Thus, the policy decisions they make are the products of different governmental structures and procedures.

State Governments and Policy Domains over Time

When they were first established, state governments did relatively little. But by their fifth decade, their involvement in various aspects of the economy and society was beginning to expand. Take, for example, the sorts of state laws passed in Georgia between 1819 and 1829.[22] Much legislative time was devoted to public education, both at the primary and higher levels. Transportation issues, mostly dealing with ferries and highways, were important. Writing and refining criminal law consumed time, as did the creation and maintenance of a judicial system to administer it. Oversight of the conduct of elections was prominent on the legislative agenda. Regulation of the economy commanded attention. The legislature determined "The mode of granting a license to" physicians, while individual lawyers were "authorized to plead and practice." Banks and corporations were chartered. The state was also involved with gaming issues, authorizing a large number of lotteries while determining the "Punishment for keeping gambling-houses, tables, or rooms." A public health officer was authorized for Savannah.

What is of particular interest about these policy areas is that almost two centuries later, they are still central to the policy jurisdictions of the states. As noted in chapters 2's discussion of federalism, although the US Constitution established a federal system and in some instances allocated specific powers to each governmental level, there is sufficient ambiguity in the overall design that there has been an ongoing resorting of policy powers. The federal government has, over time, become more intimately involved in most of these areas. But, as we assess the roster of policies that we still look to the states to deliver—education, transportation, the administration of justice, public health, and economic development—we find the same basic set that they took responsibility for when they were first established.

4

The Policy-making Capacity
of State Governments

States matter because:

- The policy-making capacity of state governments has increased markedly in the past two generations.
- The training and preparation of elected officials today is far advanced over past generations.
- The ability of governors to affect policy making is substantial; many people believe being governor is "the best job in politics."
- Despite the deleterious effect of strict legislative term limits in some states, today's legislatures are more capable partners in the policy-making arena.

OVER THE PAST SEVERAL DECADES, an increasing number of policy decisions have been deferred to state governments. As we have argued, this trend is positive for a number of reasons. But one important question has been left unanswered. As more and more policy decisions are pushed onto state governments, do they have sufficient organizational capacity to make competent decisions? By capacity, we mean the organizational resources to generate and analyze the information needed to make knowledgeable policy choices.

In this chapter we assess the policy-making capacities of the four governmental institutions intimately involved in the policy-making process: the governor's office, the executive branch, the state legislature, and the state court of last resort. Each institution is charged with making important policy decisions. The question to address is whether each has sufficient capacity to handle all that is now asked of them.

Before directly addressing these questions, we note a related trend. As mentioned in chapter 2, today there are numerous professional organizations that assist state officials. Examples include the Council of State Governments and the National Association of State Budget Officers. Some of these organizations, like the National Governors' Association, have been around for more than a century. Others, notably the National Conference of State Legislatures and the National Legislative Leaders' Foundation, have existed for only a few decades. Regardless of when they were founded, all have become more active in providing services, information, and training to state officials. Most are nonprofit organizations that the general public has never heard of and knows nothing about. But they are important support organizations that have helped state governments increase their capacity to govern. In addition, there are university-affiliated research and training operations, such as the Carl Vinson Institute of Government (University of Georgia) and the Hubert Humphrey School of Public Affairs (University of Minnesota) that devote many hours to the training and education of state (and local) officials. There are many such university-housed institutes or organizations, and they too have been an important part of the capacity-building efforts for state governments.

Gubernatorial Capacity

In the no-so-distant past, state governors were denigrated as being, "good-time Charlies."[1] In 1962, for example, James Reston, an influential political columnist for the *New York Times*, lamented that, "It is difficult to make a political swing around America these days without coming to the conclusion that the governors of the states, taken as a whole, are a poor lot."[2] Indeed, they often appeared to be less than engaged in the policy-making process. A reporter covering a National Governors Conference in 1970 noted, with some hyperbole, that "most of the governors snored through dozens of 'policy statements.'"[3] Such characterizations suggested that many governors were, at best, political hacks, interested more in doling out political patronage than in the nitty-gritty of policy making.

Over the following decade, however, that image began to improve. By the late 1970s, governors were seen as serious policy makers, focused on improving their state's lot. It is this latter image that appears to dominate today. In a recent treatise on governors, Alan Rosenthal chronicles the growth in policy-making influence of the governors over the past generation.[4] Interviews with numerous former governors led him to conclude that the governorship "according to nearly all of those who have held it, is now the best office in American politics."[5] For the most part, this is because state problems are more manageable than those at the national level, and governors tend to have the resources necessary to address at least some of those problems. A particularly telling comparison comes from those who have served as both state governor and US senator. Rosenthal claims that of the dozen members of the US Senate in 2010 who were former governors, all but one "preferred their job as governor to their job as senator."[6]

Indeed, as former governors Jimmy Carter, Ronald Reagan, Bill Clinton, and George W. Bush have intimated, in many regards governors today may be better able to influence state policies than the president is able to influence national policies. There are three plausible reasons why this might be the case. First, governors dominate state media. In the first eight months of 2012, for example, a search of Google News reveals 3,650 news stories mentioning Illinois governor Pat Quinn compared to only 272 stories mentioning the state house speaker, Michael Madigan, even though Madigan is a powerful official who has held his important post for all but two years since 1983. Governors can exploit their media advantage to set their state's policy agenda, leaving the legislature and others to only be in a position to react. Recent research by Kousser and Phillips shows that governors are especially influential in bargaining with the legislature over the state budget.[7]

Second, governors enjoy a significant information advantage over their state legislatures. The governor's job is, of course, a full-time position. And, as will be noted below, governors now have large staffs to assist them, and they can draw on the state bureaucracy's expertise as well. In contrast, legislatures in most states are part-time and many have relatively meager staff resources. This disparity gives a governor the upper hand in policy debates that turn on facts and analyses.

Third, as noted in chapter 3, most governors enjoy a powerful veto, one that gives them great leverage over the legislature. Unlike the president, who must take or leave an entire bill, governors in most states can pick and choose provisions that they wish to keep. Knowing that governors can selectively veto legislative provisions in a bill forces legislators to be more accommodating to them earlier in the legislative process. A veto threat can be a valuable bargaining chip.[8]

Thus, the evidence suggests that governors today are powerful. The question then becomes whether they are serious and capable policy makers. In table 4.1, we examine two personal characteristics of governors serving in 2013 that arguably act as indicators of their intellectual capacity as policy makers. The first indicator is a governor's level of educational attainment. The idea behind this measure is simple: higher levels of educational attainment suggest that a governor has the academic training to analyze the vast amounts of information available on policy issues. Not surprisingly, as table 4.1 reveals, governors today are well educated. Almost all of the governors had at least an undergraduate degree. All three who did not—Brewer (R-AZ), Herbert (R-UT), and Walker (R-WI)— attended college but without graduating. Overall, a much higher percentage of governors graduated from college than in the general public.

TABLE 4.1
Capacity Indicators for Governors, 2013

Capacity Indicator	Number of Governors with Indicator
Educational Attainment	
BA, BS, or other undergraduate degree	47
JD	26
MBA	4
MD	2
Other graduate degree or degrees	5
Elective Office Experience	
Local government	13
State legislature	25
State attorney general	9
Other statewide office	7
Lt. Governor	13
US House of Representatives	9
US Senate	3

Perhaps even more impressively, most governors had a graduate degree of some sort. As might be anticipated, just over half of them have a law degree. Another four have MBAs. Others held assorted degrees; both Robert Bentley (R-AL) and John Kitzhaber (D-OR) have MDs and Neil Abercrombie (D-HI), a PhD in American studies. These varied educational backgrounds suggest that governors possess the intellectual training to handle the complex policy problems confronting state governments.

The second indicator of policy-making capacity is political experience as measured by other elective offices held previously. The notion that governors who have held other offices may be better positioned to navigate the complexities of policy making in a governmental system characterized by the separation of powers is reasonably well accepted. Previous office holding, for example, is embedded in Beyle's widely used measure of gubernatorial power.[9] Governmental experience provides a governor with exposure to the myriad of policy questions and a measure of expertise on some aspects of them, as well as a network of connections both within and outside of government that can be drawn upon to assist in policy development.

Not surprisingly, the vast majority of governors—88 percent in 2013—had previous elective office experience. Some had served in local government; for example, Martin O'Malley (D-MD) was mayor of Baltimore and John Hickenlooper (D-CO) was mayor of Denver. A large number of others had served in the state legislature or in a statewide office. California governor Jerry Brown (D-CA) has a particularly impressive political resume, having previously served as secretary of state (1971–1975), governor (1975–1983), mayor of Oakland

(1999–2007), and state attorney general (2007–2011). Such experiences provide governors with extensive knowledge of the policy problems, policy-making processes, and policy makers in their states.

Even those governors without electoral experience often had some background in politics. Governor Mitch Daniels (R-IN, 2005–2013), for example, never held elective office prior to winning the governorship, but he had been chief of staff to US Senator Richard Lugar, a senior advisor to President Ronald Reagan, and director of the Office of Management and Budget (OMB) under President George W. Bush. In addition, he had also been an executive at Eli Lilly, a major pharmaceutical corporation. He too was well positioned to lead state policy making.

It must be pointed out, of course, that previous electoral experience does not perfectly predict success in office. In North Dakota, Republican John Hoeven had spent his career in banking prior to winning the governorship. During his tenure (2000–2010) he was enormously popular, in large part because of the state's strong economic performance. In contrast, Illinois governor Rod Blagojevich (2003–2009), a Democrat, had impressive political credentials before taking office, having served in the Illinois House of Representatives and the US House of Representatives. Now he serves in the Federal Correctional Institution in Englewood, Colorado. He was impeached and removed from office by a legislature controlled by his fellow Democrats and later convicted in federal court on corruption charges. But, despite these aberrations, political experience, on average, is beneficial.[10]

Similar insights are provided by looking at the experience immediately prior to ascending to the governorship. Here we find an interesting temporal trend. As Margaret Ferguson shows, the proportion of governors who held some other statewide office prior to becoming governor has grown from about 20 percent in the period from 1900 to 1980 to 30 percent in the period 1981 to 2011.[11] Thus, not only do governors have more experience, but the quality of that experience is impressive. Even more telling is the fact that in the earlier period, 1900 to 1980, fewer than 10 percent of governors were former members of Congress. During the most recent period, 1981 to 2011, that figure jumps to 18 percent. Almost one of every five governors left federal office and "came home" to become state governor. If we accept that politicians are progressively ambitious beings, then the implication of this move from federal office to state office is clear: states matter.

Interestingly, the increase in better-qualified people serving as governor has not been driven by the salaries paid to them. In 1959, the mean gubernatorial salary was $18,980, which was the equivalent of $142,540 in 2010. The mean salary actually paid governors in 2010 was $130,595. Gubernatorial salaries failed to keep up with inflation in twenty-seven states, with the biggest losers being governors in many of the largest states: New York, California, and Pennsylvania. Governors reaping the greatest real increases since 1959 are in moderate size states: Tennessee, Washington, and Georgia.[12] But even the best-paid governor in 2010, New York's at $179,000, made far less than many other state employees. Indeed, nine hundred New York state workers made more than the governor did.[13] Massachusetts governor Deval Patrick fared even worse: his $136,000 salary ranked 1,295th among state employees.[14] Clearly, pay is the not the cause of the improvement in the quality of state governors.

One positive change that has taken place over the last few decades is an expansion in the pool of potential candidates for the governorship. By the end of the 1960s, only three women had ever served as governor, each of them filling in, in one fashion or another, for her husband. Starting in the 1970s with Ella Grasso in Connecticut and Dixie Lee Ray in Washington, women who had worked their way up through the political ranks began winning the governorship on the basis of their own accomplishments. Similarly, by the 1980s, minority politicians in many states found the governorship open to them, further expanding the pool of possible contenders for the office. Allowing women and minorities to hold the office dramatically increases the prospects for electing high-quality candidates. Recent examples include Susana Martinez (Republican governor of New Mexico; graduate of the University of Texas, El Paso, law degree from University of Oklahoma; district attorney for fifteen years), Nikki Haley (Republican governor of South Carolina; graduate of Clemson University and former state representative), Maggie Hassan (Democratic governor of New Hampshire; graduate of Brown University and Northeastern Law School; former state senator), and Deval Patrick (Democratic governor of Massachusetts, undergraduate and law degrees from Harvard, assistant attorney general for civil rights in the US Department of Justice, and general counsel for both Texaco and Coca-Cola).

There are two other noteworthy developments that have increased the policy-making capacity of governors. As noted in chapter 3, gubernatorial terms of office have changed dramatically over time. Currently, all but two states—New Hampshire and Vermont—have shifted their governors to four-year terms of office. The move to four-year terms was motivated by a desire to spare the governor from perpetual campaigning and to allow for sufficient time to learn the job and to pursue complex policy agendas.

In many states, however, there are limits on the number of terms their governors may serve. At the most extreme, the Virginia governor may serve only one four-year term. Such a stringent limit makes it more difficult for a governor to fulfill his or her campaign pledges. The reason is that a one-term governor is quickly deemed a lame duck—an officeholder whose political power is weakened because his or her time in office is coming to an end. Because legislators and other government officials know that the governor cannot run for reelection, they have less incentive to cooperate with the governor's office. Most states sidestep this problem—or at least push it off for a few more years—by adopting a two-term limit. Indeed, thirty-five states mimic the Twenty-Second Amendment of the US Constitution and limit their governor to two four-year terms. (A handful of these states do allow a term-limited governor to again run for office after a specified period of time out of office.)

No limits on how many terms a governor may serve are found in fourteen states, although among these states, several have an informal norm that limits service to two terms. In recent decades a few midwestern states have had governors serve for more than two four-year terms. In Iowa, for example, Terry Branstad, a Republican, held the office from 1983 to 1999, and then was elected again by the voters in 2010. Such lengthy service affords a governor the best chance to leave his or her mark on a state.

The second significant development over the last few decades is that governors have come to sit atop a growing bureaucracy devoted exclusively to serving the governorship.[15] Staff is important, as will be argued again in discussing legislatures and the courts, because it expands an officeholder's reach. In this case, the more people the governor has working for him or her, the more information he or she has to use in making policy. In 1980, gubernatorial staffs ranged in size from just four in Texas to eighty-two in California. The mean size of gubernatorial staffs was twenty-eight. By 2010, staff sizes ranged from nine in Nebraska to 325 in Florida, with the mean being sixty-three. These numbers, of course, are likely supplemented by additional staff members commandeered by governors from state agencies on whose payrolls the staffers continue to appear. But the important point is that governors now have larger numbers of policy experts and other assistants, on whom they can rely to help them in making public policy, thereby increasing their policy-making capacity.

Bureaucratic Capacity

Has state bureaucratic capacity kept up with the policy demands being made on it? Over the last half century state governments have grown terrifically in size. There are, of course, a number of different ways to document this expansion.

The first, and most obvious, measure to examine is the number of people employed by state governments. Over the past fifty years, every state government has increased its number of full-time equivalent positions (FTEs). In 1959, the mean number of state FTEs was 27,100. By 2007 that number had exploded to 86,140.[16]

There are two things driving this growth. The first may be somewhat underappreciated. In 1960, there were about 180 million people resident in the United States. By 2010, the estimate was close 310 million residents. Obviously, the states were providing governmental services to far more residents, requiring some increase in the number of FTEs.

The second driving force in the growth of state government is, perhaps, more obvious: state government is being asked to do more than it was asked to do in the past. Evidence for this is provided by the dramatic expansion of state bu-reaucracies over the last half century, not just in the sheer number of agencies, but, more importantly, in the scope of their activities. As noted in chapter 3, in the 1960s, twelve additional agencies were present in thirty-eight or more states that had not been present the decade before. Among the agencies added were ones devoted to then emerging policy issues, such as air quality, community affairs, highway safety, and natural resources.[17] The next decade witnessed the emergence of twenty-nine more agencies appearing in most of the states, dealing with a series of new problems confronting state governments, including alcohol and drug abuse, historic preservation, Medicaid, occupational health and safety, and women's commissions. The 1980s and 1990s saw fewer new agencies being established across most of the states—sixteen total in the two decades—but again those that were created allowed government to respond to new policy concerns, for instance, groundwater management, hazardous waste, lotteries, mining reclamation, and crime-victim compensation. Admittedly, some of these new offices and functions were strongly encouraged by the national government, usually through new or expanded federal aid programs. Nonetheless, in the con-text of the discussion here, the addition of these new bureaucracies represents a significant increase in the capacity of state governments, giving them the ability to respond to a wide range of new issues.

The real capacity of government agencies, however, rests on the abilities of the people working within them. Importantly, the educational credentials of the top state bureaucrats have improved significantly over the last half century.[18] In 1964, 14 percent of top state administrators had only a high-school degree or less. In 2008, only 1 percent had such limited education. At the other extreme, by 2008, 75 percent had a graduate degree or had done graduate work, substantially above the 40 percent who had done so in 1964. Thus, the educational credentials of the people running state agencies have improved dramatically since the 1960s.

Current top administrators also are drawn from a substantially larger pool of potential candidates. In 1964, 98 percent of top state administrators were male and 98 percent were white. By 2008, 29 percent of leaders were female and 10 percent were minorities. Their experience levels have also improved. In 2008, administrative leaders averaged eighteen years in state government, and 44 per-cent of them had worked their way up through the ranks of the agency they led. In contrast, forty-four years earlier top administrators averaged eleven years in state government, and only 28 percent had held a subordinate position in their agency. Consequently, administrators today are drawn from a larger pool of potential candidates and have more agency experience than their predecessors several decades ago.

Overall, the evidence shows that state bureaucratic capacity has increased impressively over the last half century. States today have more people working in a wider array of specialized agencies making policies. The development of a professional, experienced bureaucracy has important implications for the conduct of federalism.[19] These policy experts defend the state interests and negotiate with federal bureaucrats as part of the process of policy implementation. This is an underappreciated but important relationship. It is a more nuanced assessment of federalism than the typical "winners and losers" approach. As law professor Erin Ryan points out, "Notwithstanding the rhetoric of zero-sum federalism, the boundary between state and federal authority is actually the project of ongoing negotiation."[20]

In almost all policy fields today, state and federal agency professionals share similar educational and career experiences. They have the same professional degrees, from the same institutions. They attend the same professional conferences. They know each other. They communicate regularly with one another, and they often negotiate the relative state versus national role in deciding and administering the policy details. And, to paraphrase an old observation, federalism is in the details. As Professor Ryan observes, "[C]ountless real-world examples show that the boundary between state and federal authority is actually negotiated on scales large and small, and on a continual basis."[21]

Administrative leaders are better educated and more experienced than in the past. All of this suggests that states are well prepared to implement the policies assigned to them. The question then becomes whether states are well equipped to make policy decisions.

Legislative Capacity

State legislatures, of course, play a central role in developing state policies. Thus, it is important to measure their capacity to make policy. Perhaps even more to the point, it is necessary to assess whether state legislators and the institutions in which they serve have improved their policy-making capacity at a time when the federal government has devolved more policies to state control.

The qualities of both the individual legislator and the legislative institution are relevant. In both instances the "reapportionment revolution" was a watershed period in the development of state legislative capacity. Prior to 1964, many state legislatures were malapportioned to the benefit of rural interests and the detriment of the growing urban and suburban populations. In fourteen states, less than one-fifth of the voters controlled a majority of seats in one or both houses of the legislature.[22] In their analysis of the impact of the reapportionment revolution, Stephen Ansolabehere and James Snyder note, "State legislatures did not represent their populations well, and as a result, neither the public within the states nor the national government viewed state government as true agents of the people. . . . In this climate, it made little sense to have a powerful, professional state legislature."[23]

As we discuss elsewhere, the reapportionment revolution came at the beginning of a significant transformation of state legislatures. These reforms led to a change in the qualities of the state legislators themselves. Given the trends that are already evident from the examinations of governors and top state bureaucrats, it should come as no surprise that state legislators today are, on average, better educated than were their predecessors a generation or two ago. Today, 75 percent of state legislators have graduated from college and 41 percent have earned a master's degree or higher. Only 11 percent have failed to advance beyond a high-school degree. Fifty years ago, far more state legislators had only a high-school degree, and a few had not even achieved that level of education.[24] State legislators today also are drawn from a much larger pool of potential candidates. In 1971, only 4.5 percent of the nation's state legislators were women; in 2013, 24.1 percent were women.[25] Similarly, the number of state legislators from various minority groups has increased substantially in recent decades.[26]

Legislators have also become considerably more experienced over the last century. Legislative experience is typically measured by the turnover rate, the percentage of new members coming in to a legislative chamber following an election. A high turnover rate translates into many inexperienced lawmakers and an increased likelihood that the legislature is not a powerful policy-making force. Longer-serving legislators gain a better understanding of the complexities and nuances of policy making. At the institutional level, a legislature with experienced members is better able to compete in policy making with the governor, the governor's staff, and the state bureaucracy.

There has been a noteworthy decline in the average turnover rate across state legislatures over the last century. In the 1930s, turnover each session averaged over 50 percent in state senates and almost 60 percent in state houses. But over the next five decades, there was a steady decrease in turnover rates. Just prior to the reapportionment revolution, the aggregate figures had declined to 34 percent—admittedly a troubling rate, but clearly not as high as the 1930s. In some states, however, the turnover rate was still extraordinary: 52 percent in Maine, 57 percent in Maryland, 58 percent in Tennessee, 59 percent in Alabama, 61 percent in Utah, and an astounding 67 percent in Kentucky.[27] But by the end of the 1980s, turnover averaged 22 percent in state senates and 24 percent in lower houses. Turnover in some states, notably Arkansas, California, Delaware, Illinois, New York, and Pennsylvania averaged 15 percent or less for each electoral cycle in the decade, figures comparable to those found in the US Congress.[28]

Since the beginning of the 1990s, turnover rates have continued to decline, if only slightly, in the states that have not imposed limits on the number of terms their legislators may serve. In the fifteen states that have term limits, however, turnover is creeping back up, as figure 4.1 shows. Since 1998, turnover in the lower chamber in term-limited states has never averaged less than 30 percent and is often much higher. Meanwhile in states without term limits, turnover is

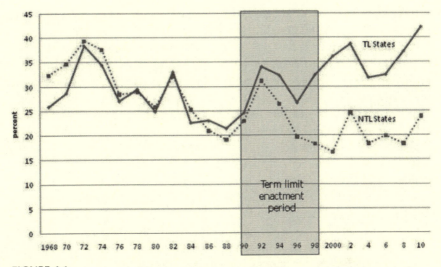

FIGURE 4.1
Turnover and term limits: Membership change in Houses. *Source*: Gary Moncrief,
Richard G. Nemi, and Lynda W. Powell, "Turnover in State Legislatures: An Update,"
Western Political Science Association, May 22–25, 2008, and Karl Kurtz, "Move
on Legislative Turnover." "The Thicket," June 12, 2012, at ncsl.typepad.com/the_
thicket/2012/06/more-on-legislative-turnover.html

much less—often under 20 percent. For the states that limit legislative service,
the benefits experience generates in terms of increased policy-making capacity
are largely sacrificed.[29]

The effect of term limits is conditioned by several factors. One of the most
important is the severity of the term limit law. There is a significant difference
between a six-year lifetime term limit, such as exist for the Arkansas or Michigan House of Representatives, and a twelve-year consecutive limit allowing for
legislators to return after a few years like the Louisiana limit.[30] In chambers with
the more restrictive limits, the effects on the institution may be substantial. The
increase in turnover appears to accelerate the heightened partisanship evident in
many legislatures and exacerbate the incivility and the inability to compromise.[31]
Recent research finds such behavioral consequences have important fiscal implications; for example, states with strict legislative term limits develop lower bond rat-
ings over time.[32] So, while state legislatures as a group are certainly more capable
policy-making institutions than they were a few decades ago, not all legislatures
have progressed at the same rate, and some may have even regressed a bit.

The evidence presented here shows that state legislators today are better
educated, more experienced, and drawn from a larger segment of the population than were their predecessors a generation or two ago. This suggests
that they are now better prepared to act as policy makers. The question then
turns to whether the institutions in which they serve have also changed. The

informational capacity of a legislature is usually measured by its level of professionalization.[33] Professionalization has three components: the salary paid
to legislators, the number of days the legislature meets in session each year,
and the staff provided. Legislatures that pay members well, meet for extended
periods, and have adequate staff resources are more professional, meaning that
they have a greater capacity to generate and process the information needed to
make policy. More professional legislatures are also better equipped to compete with the governor and bureaucracy in the policy-making process.

Indeed, professionalization impacts the sorts of policy decisions legislatures
make. The inclination to reform government practices and to adopt more
complex regulatory policies increases with professionalization.[34] Higher levels
of professionalization are associated with the adoption of more innovative approaches to new technologies and stronger environmental programs.[35] Professionalized legislatures are better able to mediate policy disputes, reducing the
motivation for interest groups to turn to citizen initiatives in the states that allow
them.[36] More generally, professionalized legislatures are better able to learn from
the policy successes of other states and to devise innovative policies of their
own.[37] Thus, the increased analytical capacity produced by professionalization
translates into a different set of policy choices.

How then, do contemporary state legislatures compare to legislatures several
decades ago on the components of professionalization? Table 4.2 compares state
legislatures in 2009 with state legislatures in 1979 on each of the three dimensions. It must be pointed out that 1979 is a point in time in which the significant
advances made in professionalization during the 1960s and 1970s had begun to
stall.[38] Perhaps it is not surprising that in terms of constant dollars, legislative
salaries have not really advanced much over the last four decades. The mean
salary has edged up by a trivial $281, while the median salary is lower by $2,292.
Both the mean and median salaries for 2009 are modest sums, well under the
national median household income of $49,777. These numbers, of course, mask

TABLE 4.2
Capacity Indicators for State Legislatures, 1979 and 2009

Indicator	1979	2009	Change from 1979 to 2009
Mean Member Salary	$27,949[a]	$28,230	+$281
Median Member Salary	$23,098[a]	$20,806	−$2,292
Mean Days in Session	62.4	70.9	+8.5
Median Days in Session	58.5	59.5	+1.0
Mean Staff per Member	3.7	4.8	+0.9
Median Staff per Member	2.7	3.9	+1.2

a. 1979 salary calculated in 2009 dollars

Source: Calculated by authors from data in various editions of *Book of the States.*

the great range in legislative salaries across the states. California lawmakers, for example, currently earn $90,526, a sum that represents a significant reduction from the $116,098 they were paid until late in 2009. In contrast, New Hampshire legislators are paid the same $100 a year the state has paid since 1889. Overall, in most states legislative compensation does not appear adequate to attract the best policy-making talent.

There has been a slight increase in the number of days state legislatures meet in session over the last four decades. The mean number of days in session in 2009 was 70.9, while the median was 59.5. The difference between the two numbers suggests that a few state legislatures meet for many days, thereby greatly increasing the overall mean. Indeed, that is the case. The National Conference of State Legislatures considers four state legislatures to be full-time institutions: California, Michigan, New York, and Pennsylvania. On the other end of the spectrum are a handful of legislatures that demand considerably less time from their members: Montana, New Hampshire, North Dakota, South Dakota, Utah, and Wyoming. Most state legislatures fall somewhere in between the two extremes, with sessions that last four or five months each year. Such sessions allow legislatures to play a role in the policy-making process, but it makes it more difficult for them to challenge the governor and executive branch, both of which are, of course, year-round institutions. Indeed, the challenge to keep up with the rest of the government is even more acute in the four states (Montana, Nevada, North Dakota, and Texas) that allow their legislatures to meet only every other year.

Perhaps the only hopeful sign for the increased policy-making capacity of state legislatures is found in the area of staff support. Both the mean and median numbers of staff per state legislator have increased appreciably since 1979. Again, some legislatures, such as California, afford their legislators greater staff support, while others, notably New Hampshire, provide very little assistance. Staff is important because it greatly increases the informational capacity of legislators to make policy by allowing them to uncover and analyze much more data than they could hope to do on their own. One saving grace for less professionalized legislatures may be the resources made available to them through the National Conference of State Legislatures and the Council of State Governments, which provides them access to detailed information about policies being developed across the nation. Conservative state lawmakers also benefit from legislative proposals developed by the American Legislative Exchange Council.

Overall, state legislators appear to be increasingly capable of making policy decisions, but the institutions in which they serve may lag a bit in that regard. This is, of course, in contrast to the increased capacities exhibited by the governor and the executive branch, both of which have made significant progress over the last several decades. The inability of state legislatures to keep up may signal a potential problem with shifting policy-making demands back to the states.

Judicial Capacity

The bulk of the judicial system in the United States is at the state level. While there are about 1,200 judges in the entire federal judicial system, there are more than thirty thousand judges in the state systems.[39] More judges are required at the state level because state judicial systems handle far more cases than does the federal court system. In 2009, for example, just over 1.5 million cases were filed with US District Courts and US Bankruptcy Courts. In comparison, that same year over 106 million cases were filed in state courts.[40] If someone comes in contact with the judicial system, it is far more likely to be at the state level than at the federal level.

Although controversy occasionally surrounds state courts and their legal decisions, most scholars accept the reality that they are, at least in part, policy-making institutions, particularly at the appellate level. But courts differ from other policy makers in at least one important regard: they cannot act as policy entrepreneurs surveying the political landscape for problems to solve, as legislators and executives can. Instead, the courts are inherently reactive, only solving problems that are brought to them. This means that they typically get involved with policy difficulties that the other governmental institutions have failed to adequately resolve, leaving some aggrieved party or parties to take their complaints to court.

The courts also differ in that the public has always assumed (if not actually required) their members to have attained a certain level of education. In the nineteenth century, this typically meant that aspiring lawyers had "read" the law and been trained by established attorneys. By the twentieth century, formal law schools had taken over the education of new lawyers.[41] And, of course, although it was not always spelled out in constitutions (including the US Constitution), the expectation was that judges would have the appropriate legal training. So, from an educational perspective, state courts have always had the capacity to render legal decisions because judges were expected to have attained a high level of education prior to being put on the bench. Thus, for example, while less than 60 percent of New Hampshire's state legislators have college degrees, all of their state judges have both bachelor's and law degrees.

The next question is whether states are willing to offer salaries sufficient to attract top talent to their benches. Here, again, the contrast with state legislatures is dramatic. In 2010, judges on state courts of last resort were paid a mean salary of $151,462 and a median of $146,917. The range of salaries was from California's $218,237 to Mississippi's $112,530. Keep in mind that Mississippi's judicial salaries are more than the highest state legislative salaries (recall that California's legislators are the highest paid, at $90,526). Even general (or trial) court judicial salaries are high relative to legislative salaries: in 2010 the mean salary was $136,030 and the median was $132,500, with a range from $104,170 to $178,835.[42] States are much more willing to invest in their judges than they are to invest in their state legislators. The most extreme example of this is New Hampshire. As noted earlier, New Hampshire state legislators are paid $100 a year, with no per diems. That means each year the state pays its 424 state legislators a total of $42,400. The five members of the New Hampshire Supreme Court each make $146,917, thereby costing the state $734,585 each year.[43] This is not to claim, of course, that judicial salaries are necessarily sufficient to attract top legal talent. There are ongoing battles in many states over judicial pay with judges decrying stagnant wages, but there is evidence that current salaries attract and maintain competent jurists.[44]

Like governors and the executive branch—and unlike most state legislatures—almost all state judges, and all appellate court judges, work full-time. As argued earlier, this time commitment enhances their policy-making capacity. State appellate judges also benefit from staff assistance, most importantly in the form of law clerks. Typically, clerks are recent law-school graduates with distinguished academic records. Their efforts greatly increase the judiciary's capacity. At the state-court-of-last-resort level, the number of clerks varies, from less than one clerk per justice in Alabama, to more than five clerks per justice in Pennsylvania. Once again, most states are far more willing to invest in assistance for judges than in assistance for lawmakers. In New Hampshire, for example, Supreme Court justices are each allowed two clerks. In contrast, each of the state's legislators enjoys only .42 of a staff member (including clerical support).

As with the other institutions of state government, state courts are also drawing on a larger pool of potential judges than in the past. Over time, more women and minorities have entered law school. In recent years this has translated into more of them making it onto the state bench. In 2011, women held 27 percent of state judgeships, with a high of 40 percent in Vermont and a low of 11 percent in Idaho.[45] Minorities have also increased their numbers. In 2010, a few states, such as New Hampshire, had no minorities on the bench, but other states, notably Florida and Maryland, had large contingents.[46] But no state has achieved population parity with either women or minority judges.

Thus, state courts are full-time institutions, populated by well-educated judges who in turn are assisted by very smart law clerks. Salaries are sufficient to attract and keep qualified people on the bench. All of this suggests that in terms of judicial capacity, state courts are currently well positioned to handle the tasks given them. There is strong evidence to support this assertion. Over the course of the twentieth century, state courts of last resort greatly reformed, restructuring to allow them to gain greater control over the cases they decided.[47] When modern state courts of last resort are compared to the US Supreme Court, they stack up well. Indeed, state courts of last resort in California and Pennsylvania are on the same level as the US Supreme Court in terms of salary, and the provision of law clerks. Overall, the typical state court of last resort is much more like the US Supreme Court in terms of its capacity, than any state legislature is like the US Congress.[48]

This brings us to one final question about state court capacity: are there enough state judges to meet the demand for their services? The number of residents per judge by state is presented in table 4.3. The number of judges is the combined count of those serving on the court of last resort, an intermediate appellate court (which exists in thirty-nine states), general jurisdiction courts, and limited jurisdiction courts, excluding magistrates and justices of the peace.[49] It provides a crude look at the ability of a state to meet the judicial demands made on it. Missing is any measure of caseloads, but these numbers give an important impression of capacity. There is a slight tendency for smaller-population states to enjoy a lower ratio of residents per judge. This is to be expected because in the American federal system, most legal cases fall under state law, requiring each state to create an extensive judicial system. Consequently, even small-population states have to have the same basic court structures that larger states have. In any event, almost every state has more judges than legislators, suggesting that the courts can largely meet the demands made on them.

TABLE 4.3
Judicial Capacity: The Number of Residents per Judge by State

State	Number of Residents per Judge	State	Number of Residents per Judge
ND	4,546	LA	11,986
AK	5,277	NE	12,382
KS	5,378	VT	12,938
NM	6,484	NH	13,030
WY	6,540	IL	14,024
MT	7,216	SD	14,230
AL	7,643	KY	15,138
MO	7,759	IN	15,329
OK	7,892	MA	15,810
AR	8,275	DE	15,873
IA	8,342	OH	15,931
RI	8,368	MD	16,097
OR	8,960	MI	16,108
CO	9,129	HI	16,304
MS	9,450	NY	16,503
GA	9,657	MN	17,171
SC	9,782	WA	18,396
TX	9,929	FL	18,532
CT	10,609	VA	18,542
WV	10,928	AZ	19,288
TN	10,942	ME	19,353
WI	11,035	CA	21,296
NJ	11,118	NC	23,829
ID	11,459	UT	24,873
PA	11,912	NV	28,261

Conclusions

Much is now expected of state governments. The pressure on them has come from two directions. First, the public wants them to be involved in a much wider range of policy areas than in the past. Second, the federal government over the last few decades has devolved many policy decisions to the states. The question we have tried to address is whether state governments are up to the varied tasks given them. By and large, we find that state government capacity has increased as more is being asked of it. Governors are better educated, more experienced, and supplemented with more staff than in the past. State bureaucracies are led by better educated and more experienced people drawn from a wider pool of candidates. State courts also appear to have increased their capacity.

Perhaps the only fly in the ointment concerns the capacity of state legislatures. Lawmakers are, like their counterparts in the rest of the government, better educated than in the past. Increases in member experience, however, have been forcibly truncated in the fifteen states with term limits. There are also doubts that the salaries offered in many states are sufficient to recruit the best and brightest to service. But the most troubling limitation involves staff support. Legislators are asked to respond to policy questions across a wide range of issues, taxing their own abilities to be competent in developing appropriate responses. Staff support is necessary to allow lawmakers to generate and digest the vast amounts of information they need to consume to make good public policy. Unfortunately, in a number of states legislators are not provided the assistance they need, leaving them to look to other parts of the government or to people and groups outside of government to give them the information they need. As the eminent legislative scholar Alan Rosenthal recently said of state legislatures, "They are probably the most unappreciated institutions in the country."[50]

In this chapter we have focused on the policy-making capacity of state officials. But we cannot leave this topic without noting that most policies also involve funding. And the funding, or fiscal capacity, of states is another matter entirely. It is clear that the federal budget deficit will impact states. This impact will be twofold. First, a reduction in federal aid to states and local governments (outside health care) is very likely. Second, the national government's "policy footprint" may shrink as the national budget is increasingly constrained. If so, then the states will have to decide which programs to fund on their own. Developing the fiscal capacity to do so is emerging as one of the major challenges for state officials.

5

Public Policy and the Role of the States in a Changing Federal System

---

States matter because:

- Significant issues are addressed in state legislative sessions every year.
- Innovative policy often begins with a single state and later gets adopted by other states and/or by the national government.
- States are the "default" setting of policy making.
- Gridlock at the national level increases the opportunity for state-based policy making.
- Concerns over the federal deficit will increase the opportunity for state-based policy making.

THE TITLE OF THIS CHAPTER can be read two ways. It can be read retrospectively, as a comment on the past, as in "because of the centralizing tendencies of the changes in the federal system the role of the states has changed." Or it can be read prospectively, as a prediction of the future, as in "fiscal exigencies at the federal level are going to require a recalibration of the federal relationship." We intend that it be read both ways, because federalism is indeed a dynamic relationship, ever changing.

There are those who see the states today as mere administrative outposts of the federal government.[1] In some policy areas that may, in fact, be close to the truth. But in most domestic policy arenas, states retain a large amount of discretion. And in other areas, they are still the dominant crafters of public policy.

If the states were not important actors, why would there be such interest and anticipation at the beginning of each new legislative session? Every year, in just about every major state media, one can find a major story about the issues to watch this year. A sample from January 2013, as many state legislatures were about to convene (with key issues in parentheses):

Denver Post: "FRESH FACES, HOT ISSUES WHEN COLORADO LEGISLATURE OPENS"
(gun control, fracking, education reform)

Minnesota Public Radio: "MINNESOTA LEGISLATIVE PREVIEW: 10 ISSUES TO WATCH"
(bonds, fracking, same-sex marriage, taxes)

San Antonio Express: "TEXAS' 83RD LEGISLATURE: ISSUES AND PEOPLE TO WATCH"
(water, higher education, abortion)

Lansing State Journal: "MICHIGAN LAWMAKERS: KEY ISSUES TO WATCH IN 2013"
(right-to-work, property-tax reform, transportation funding)

National publications such as *Governing* and *State Legislatures* identified the key state legislative issues for 2013 as public-education (K–12) performance; education funding; corrections reform; energy regulation; Medicaid expansion; public pension funding, and infrastructure needs, among others.[2] None of these issues is trivial. As Martha Derthick notes, absent concerted national action, "The states are the 'default setting' of the American federal system. To the extent that other levels of government lack the resources to act—authority, revenue, will power, political consensus, institutional capacity—the states have the job."[3]

In the previous chapter we showed how state governmental institutions, which were denigrated for decades, have become much more capable and professional over the past two generations. Today, state policy makers across the country are far more likely to share information and experiences about issues and how each state is addressing specific problems than their counterparts were in the past. But this does not mean that the states follow the same policy paths—far from it. The policy variation across the states may not be as wide as it once was, but it is still considerable. States continue to be the "laboratories of democracy," as Justice Brandeis once characterized them. Different states have taken the lead on a range of policy innovations. These states and policies are as varied as Minnesota (the first state to experiment with charter schools), Oregon (the first to permit doctor-assisted suicide for terminally ill patients), Florida (the first to require drug testing to qualify for public assistance), California (the first to create a carbon trading market), New York (the first to ban cell phone usage while driving) and Texas (the first to pass an in-state resident tuition policy for undocumented immigrant students). It was a Wisconsin policy requiring welfare recipients to be enrolled in school or training for a job (workfare) that became an integral part of the federal welfare law in 1995, and the Massachusetts health-insurance program was the model on which the federal Affordable Care Act law was based.

States approach policy problems in different ways. Variables such as a state's political culture and economic resources lead to policy variation. Dramatic changes in policy are often evident when a state shifts control from one political party to the other. Recent examples include the enactment of policies by Republican-dominated governments to weaken unions in Wisconsin and Michigan, states where labor has traditionally been strong.

In this chapter we discuss some of the important ways in which policies vary from one state to another. As one expert on comparative state politics notes, "Differences among the states abound," and a lot of these differences can be explained by a group of political, physical, and socioeconomic variables.[4] Some of these variables, like political-party control mentioned above, are obvious. Other, perhaps less apparent, variables include the level of competition between the two parties; the policy-making capacity of the legislative, executive, and judicial branches of state government; interest-group balance and strength within a state; public opinion; and the presence or absence of instruments of direct democracy such as the initiative process.

Public opinion and ideology appear to be especially important in a type of policy making that has come to be called "morality policy."[5] Morality policy is a type of social policy characterized by the appeal to "core values." It does not usually have significant economic impacts. The policy discussion surrounding morality policy is generally less technical and more about "right" and "wrong" than is the case in other policy areas. It is often highly salient and emotional. Because at least one side of the policy debate views the issue as about core values, there is very little room for negotiation and compromise. Religiosity is often strongly related to public opinion on morality policy.

Physical and socioeconomic factors are important because, as Virginia Gray points out, "These factors structure a government's problems and affect a state government's ability to deal with them."[6] State demographics are an example; the size and structure of the population are often important in determining the context in which problems are defined. For instance, in Utah a much larger proportion of the population is under eighteen years old than is the case in most states. This puts a special burden on the public-education system. Several states, including Arizona and California, have significant numbers of K–12 students who are from immigrant families with limited English-speaking skills. This also puts a burden on the state's public-education system, but in a different way.

A state's physical characteristics define some policy problems and solutions. Montana is a geographically large state with a small population, which means road and highway expenditures per capita are higher than in most states. The differences in terrain and climate from one state to another help define the role of such diverse economic sectors as agriculture and tourism. The presence of nonrenewable natural resources such as oil, natural gas, or coal, and renewable ones such as hydro, solar, and wind affect the nature of economic activity and the types of environmental concerns in a state. Sometimes, the economic future and the state budget outlook can change rapidly because of the discovery of oil or some other resource. Just look at recent events in North Dakota. Between 1930 and 2000, North Dakota had a net population loss of forty thousand people—an extraordinary statistic when one realizes that the overall population of the United States more than doubled during that period. But over the last decade the state has experienced a population boom, growing by 10 percent. Why this sudden change? It is largely because of the development of the oil- and shale-rich Bakken Formation in the western part of the state. North Dakota is now the second-biggest oil producer among the states, and the state's per capita income ranking leaped from thirty-eighth to seventeenth among the states between 2000 and 2010. The financial benefits to the state have been substantial: North Dakota is the only to state to have a state budget surplus in each of the past five years.

State economies play an important role in state policy making. First, the relative wealth or poverty in a state is a major factor in social welfare costs and the ability or inability to finance the service and regulatory activities of the state government. Second, the nature of the economy—agricultural, industrial, service, resource extraction—has a significant effect on the nature of the interest-group system in a state, and the ability of the state to adjust to changing economic realities.

While many policies vary from state to state, it is also true that states learn from one another. A good contemporary example is cell phone usage when driving. In 2001, New York became the first state to ban talking on a cell phone while driving. By 2013, nine additional states had done so, but forty states have not followed New York's example. Additional states ban texting but not talking; still others ban talking for young drivers (under age eighteen) only. Within the field of comparative state politics, there is a remarkably rich literature on policy innovation and diffusion.[7] Often policies begin in one state and are incrementally adopted by a few other states. A larger group of states then may adopt in rapid succession, while some states may never implement them. In these types of cases, if one were to graph the policy adoption by states over time, an "s-curve" pattern emerges.

At other times, one state develops a policy that then "breaks outs" and experiences "rapid and sudden adoption" across states.[8] "Amber Alert" laws are an example; first adopted in Texas, every state in the United States passed such a law within six years. The pattern of innovation diffusion depends in part on the type of policy being addressed. Some policy problems are highly salient to the public and the media, others are not. Some policy problems (and their potential solutions) are extremely complex, others are simpler. Research shows that the interplay between issue salience and complexity help define the degree and manner to which other states adopt the policy.[9]

There also is evidence that (1) some states are consistently more likely to be innovators (policy leaders) and (2) innovation often comes in "waves"—periods in which many states are adopting new policies.[10] Among the states that are innovation leaders are California, Colorado, Florida, Illinois, Minnesota, and North Carolina. Furthermore, we have been experiencing an extended "innovation wave" for the past quarter-century just as we might expect, given the growing capacity of state governments. Keeping in mind the political, physical, and socioeconomic factors and how they define the context of policy making, and how policies diffuse across states, we now turn to an examination of some of the most important policy areas for the states.

Public Education and the States

Along with public safety, education has long been considered the primary responsibility of the states and their local governments. Almost all state constitutions contain provisions to this effect, although the specific language varies considerably. For example, consider the mandate in the following state constitutions:

- Oklahoma: "The Legislature shall establish and maintain *a system of free public schools* wherein all the children of the State may be educated."
- New York: "The legislature shall provide for the maintenance and support *of a system of free common schools*, wherein all the children of this state may be educated."
- Minnesota: "It is the duty of the legislature to establish a general and uniform system of public schools. The legislature shall make such provisions by taxation or otherwise as will secure *a thorough and efficient system of public schools* throughout the state."
- Illinois: "The State shall provide for *an efficient system of high quality public educational institutions and services.*"[11]

The last two clauses appear to hold those states to a higher standard in the provision of public education than the first two. This is not a casual observation; most states (especially the state legislatures) have been sued at one time or another for not maintaining the public-school system at state constitutional standards. Whether the state constitution simply requires "a system of free public schools" or "a thorough and efficient system of high quality public educational institutions" may make a difference in the manner in which these lawsuits are decided by state courts.

There are many ways in which states matter in education policy. Here, we will emphasize four such ways: funding patterns, curriculum content, school choice, and higher education.

School funding: K–12 education funding is the single largest expenditure for the states (although health care is beginning to rival that position), accounting for about one-quarter of a typical state budget. It varies by state depending on how a particular state divides up the funding responsibility with its local school districts. Some states require most of the K–12 school funding to come from the local level, which means the primary funding source is the local property tax. Nebraska is one such state. Because of the heavy reliance on the local school districts, only 15 percent of the Nebraska state budget goes to public schools. In contrast, in Vermont very little of the K–12 money comes from the local governments and the state undertakes the primary responsibility, paying more than 80 percent of the total cost from the state budget. The consequence, therefore, is that public schools account for a much larger state expenditure in Vermont (one-third of the entire state budget) than in Nebraska.[12]

Regardless of how a state divides this revenue and spending function with its local governments, public education is ultimately the state's responsibility. The amount of total state and local spending on K–12 per student is quite variable, as shown in table 5.1. Utah spends the least amount per student (about $6,000) while its neighbor Wyoming spends about two-and-a-half times as much (about $15,000).[13] Some of the variation can be accounted for by differences in state wealth, the cost of living, the magnitude of the school-age population relative to total state population, and average class size. Education is a personnel-intensive endeavor, so most (about 75 percent) of the K–12 funding is spent on personnel costs—teacher and staff salaries and benefit packages. A recent study finds a "moderately positive correlation between per-pupil spending and education ranking."[14] The correlation is far from perfect; there are numerous variables that are important in determining the overall quality of education from one state to another, including the number of students for whom English is a second language. Nonetheless, of the ten states ranking highest in education quality, eight spent more than the average per child. Of the ten states ranking lowest in education quality, seven were below the average state spending per child. Consequently, lawsuits by citizens to force states to spend more on K–12 education are not uncommon.

The policy consequences of those lawsuits are quite different from one state to another. First, remember that most of these are lawsuits settled at the state supreme court level and not by the federal courts. With certain exceptions, the US Supreme Court has determined that K–12 school funding is largely a state function. So, while both the level and formula used to fund public schools in some states has been upheld, in others the courts have required dramatic changes. One recent analysis finds that since 1989 lawsuits based on "education adequacy

TABLE 5.1
Spending per Pupil K-12, FY 2010

State	Spending	State	Spending	State	Spending	State	Spending
AK	$15,783	IL	11,634	NC	8,409	SC	9,143
AL	8,881	IN	9,611	ND	10,991	SD	8,858
AR	7,848	KS	9,715	NE	10,734	TN	8,065
AZ	9,143	KY	8,948	NH	12,383	TX	8,746
CA	9,375	LA	10,638	NJ	16,841	UT	6,064
CO	8,853	MA	14,350	NM	9,384	VA	10,597
CT	14,906	MD	13,738	NV	8,483	VT	15,274
DE	12,383	ME	12,259	NY	18,618	WA	9,452
FL	8,741	MI	10,644	OH	11,030	WI	11,364
GA	9,394	MN	10,685	OK	7,896	WV	11,527
HI	11,754	MO	9,634	OR	9,624	WY	15,169
IA	9,763	MS	8,119	PA	12,995	US	10,615
ID	7,106	MT	10,497	RI	13,699		

Source: US Census Bureau, 2010 Annual Survey of Local Government Finances—School Systems, table 8.

liability" have been decided in forty-one states, and in twenty-six of those states the decision went against the state.[15] In most instances, "The funding systems were completely or partially overturned."[16] Kentucky and Michigan are two such cases, and in both significant changes were made to the state education system, including the manner in which they were funded. States, therefore, have become more and more involved in the funding of K–12 education.

States continue to grapple with the school-funding issue—both in terms of how schools are funded and the level at which they are funded. Lawsuits continue to be filed. This remains one of the key policy issues for states because they are the largest funder of public schools. Taking all states together, the source of funding for public schools is equally derived from state and local sources—about 45 percent from the state government and about 45 percent from local school districts. From 1995 until 2013, states were supplying a slightly larger share overall than the local districts (between 47 and 50 percent depending on the year), but many states cut their funding to local schools during the Great Recession. The federal government provides only about 10 to 12 percent of public-school funding, depending on the year. These figures vary considerably by state, of course. Northeastern states (Connecticut, Massachusetts, New Hampshire, New Jersey, New York, and Vermont) rely very little (2 to 4 percent) on federal funds while some southern states (Mississippi, Louisiana, and Virginia, at 15 percent or more) and Alaska (18 percent) are more dependent on federal money.[17]

Curriculum. High-school graduation rates diverge by state more than one might imagine. Recent reports show Nevada and New Mexico are on the low end at 62 and 63 percent respectively, while Iowa (88 percent) and Wisconsin (87 percent) had the highest rates.[18] There are many reasons for differences in graduation rates, including the percentage of students for whom English is not their native language.

Different states also have different curriculum requirements. While there is a voluntary effort among the states themselves to develop a "common core" of subjects and classes, there will remain some variation in what each state requires. For example, there are nine states that do not require students to take at least one course in American government or civics.[19] Recently, some education research-ers undertook to map the course content requirements in about a dozen states at several different grade levels. They found only moderate alignment of curricu-lum content requirements from one state to another, with minimal alignment between some states' requirements in certain subjects.[20]

Perhaps the most heated issue in regard to curriculum is the teaching of evolution and creationism in science classes. Most people are at least vaguely familiar with the "Scopes Monkey Trial," a 1925 case involving a prohibition against teaching evolution in Tennessee public schools. Fewer people know that Tennessee was not the first state to pass "anti-Darwin" legislation. The first to do so was Oklahoma in 1923, followed by Florida. Mississippi and Arkansas also passed such laws soon after Tennessee. The issue reemerged toward the end of the twentieth century. In Kansas, where the state board of education is an elected body, religious conservatives won six seats on the ten-member board in 2005 and the new majority voted to change the way evolution was addressed in the school curriculum. They required evolution be presented as a flawed theory and permitted "Intelligent Design" to be taught as an alternative theory.[21] By 2007, several of the conservatives on the state board had been defeated, resulting in a more moderate majority. The board subsequently repealed the 2005 policy. That action did not, however, end the controversy. In 2012, Tennessee passed a law that permits teachers to discuss alternatives to evolution in science class, claim-ing an "academic freedom" right to do so. Louisiana also passed such a law. A handful of other states legislatures are considering such measures, while other states have specifically rejected such policies.

The issue of teaching evolution and alternative theories in public schools is interesting because it is tied, in a broad sense, to state political culture and public opinion. Numerous polls find that, while a solid majority of respondents believe evolution should be taught in science classes, a majority also believes that creationism should be taught.[22] The belief that creationism should be part of the curriculum is especially strong among Evangelical Christians, a group that is particularly prevalent in the South. Many (but not all) of the states in which the public-school curriculum provides an alternative to evolution in science classes or at least a challenge to evolution are, indeed, southern states. As one report on this issue notes, "State evolution standards are strongly influenced by public opinion, which is itself strongly related to the number of Evangelicals and the number of advanced degree holders in the state."[23]

Another example of political culture influencing curriculum is sex education. About twenty states require public-school students receive sex education, while others do not, or leave it to the local school districts to decide.[24] Some states require abstinence be stressed in sex-education instruction; others make no such mandate.

School choice. One of the biggest educational movements in the past two decades has been the effort to allow parents and children more choice in the public schools they attend. By far, the largest component of this program is the charter school movement. The first state to authorize charter schools was Minnesota. According to the Minnesota Legislative Reference Library, "The basic charter concept is simple: a group of teachers or other would-be educators apply for permission to open a school. The school operates under a charter, a contract with the local school board or state." The charter school is exempt from most of the regulations required of traditional public school and is authorized to experiment with different types of curriculum or learning techniques. Students must still meet traditional graduation requirements and the school must demonstrate that it has accomplished the learning objectives stipulated in the charter. If the school has not met those objectives, it may lose its charter to operate. The idea is to introduce more innovation into the public-school system. The key, and the source of much of the initial resistance to charter schools in many quarters, is that the charter schools receive state tax dollars, generally in the same amount as traditional public schools. In addition, some charter schools are created and managed by private companies—another reason for resistance to them from some quarters.

Since the first charter schools were authorized in 1991, the system has expanded rapidly. Today there are almost six thousand charter schools enrolling close to 2 million students in forty states. Even with this rapid growth, however, charter schools remain a small part of the overall public-school system, comprising less than 6 percent of all public schools and enrolling less than 4 percent of all public-school students. There are ten states in which there are no charter schools.

The success of the charter school movement is very uneven. Research comparing student outcomes among charter school and traditional school students is mixed and inconclusive. Some have had their charters revoked for failure to meet state graduation standards or for mismanaging public funds. But others are innovative, popular, and successful, with long waiting lists of prospective students desiring to attend. Over half of the charter schools are in urban areas, and many serve minority communities for whom the public-school system has not succeeded. It is clear that charter schools are not a panacea for the ills of the public-school system. But, at their best, they offer the potential to experiment with learning strategies that, in the long run, may provide "best practices" that will advance the larger education system in many states.

While the overall assessment of the success of charter schools remains open, the concept of the charter school now seems to be accepted by a majority of the public. A recent Gallup poll found that two-thirds of the respondents favored the idea of charter schools.[25] The public is considerably less enthusiastic about the concept of using publicly funded vouchers to help pay for a student to attend private schools. Vouchers take the idea of school choice further. The idea is that under certain circumstances, students may take all or a significant portion of their public-school tax dollars with them as they move from public to private schools. Since most private schools in the United States are church-affiliated, many people are reluctant to see taxpayer funds used in this way. Fewer than half (44 percent) of the respondents to the Gallup poll mentioned earlier were in favor of permitting students to attend private school at public expense. Very few states allow such voucher programs. An exception is that about a dozen states do permit students with certain disabilities to attend private school and make use of publicly funded vouchers to pay all or part of the private-school cost. Otherwise, only a few states allow students to make use of public vouchers to attend private school: Arizona, Florida, Indiana, Louisiana, Maine, Ohio, and Wisconsin. Even in these states, the program is limited. For example, Wisconsin permits students in two cities (Milwaukee and Racine) to use vouchers (up to $6,442 in 2011) to attend a private school. Other states, such as Louisiana, only allow students to make use of vouchers if they (a) meet certain income eligibility requirements and (b) attended a public school that was poorly performing on the state school-assessment report. The Louisiana law was recently struck down by the Louisiana State Supreme Court. On the other hand, the Indiana Supreme Court recently upheld the Indiana voucher law.[26] Clearly, this is an issue that will be determined state by state.

Perhaps because of the public resistance to the idea that public funds should be transferred to private schools through a voucher system, some states have instead moved toward a "tax credit" program. Such programs allow taxpayers to reduce their tax liability by "donating" money to private schools for scholarships, similar to a tax credit for charitable contributions. But, because the taxpayer (i.e., the parent) can specify the scholarship recipient (their child) in some states, this program can become a "backdoor voucher" system. Ultimately, tax revenue that would have gone to the state is transferred to the private school as part of the private-school tuition. Currently, about a dozen states have some sort of tuition tax-credit program.[27] The first state to authorize such tax credits was Arizona, in 1997. The US Supreme Court upheld Arizona's law in 2011, and other states (most notably Georgia) have adopted an expanded version of this law.[28]

Another alternative to traditional K–12 schools is homeschooling, a phenomenon that is growing rapidly; by 2010 between 1.5 million and 2 million students were homeschooled.[29] This constitutes about 3 percent of all K–12 school-age children in the United States, only slightly fewer students than are enrolled in charter schools. Generally, it is up to the state legislature, the state board of education, or the state department of education to set standards for homeschooling.

As one might expect, these standards differ from one state to another. According to the Home School Legal Defense Association, six states (mostly in the Northeast) are "high regulation" states, requiring parents of homeschooled students to supply the state with achievement test scores, an approved curriculum, the teacher qualifications of the parent, and allowing home visits by state officials. At the other extreme are ten states that have no requirements. In these states, parents neither have to notify the state that they intend to homeschool their child, nor show any evidence of the students' academic progress.[30] Another fourteen states, mostly midwestern and western states, are categorized as having minimal requirements.[31] Most southern states are categorized as "states with moderate regulation" of homeschooling.[32]

The issue of school choice will remain a difficult one, as many states wrestle with issues of underperforming schools, the costs of public education, and the need to adapt to new technologies and circumstances. Like Minnesota (charter schools) and Wisconsin (vouchers), some states will be at the forefront of new, intriguing ideas in education. Different states will try different things; some will succeed and others will not. This is the essence of states as "the laboratories of democracy."

Higher education. Unlike many other federal countries, there are no national universities (with the exception of the military service academies) in the United States. For public universities in the United States, the direct support of teaching is provided through an appropriation from the state budget and student tuition.[33] Table 5.2 shows the tuition cost for in-state students in 2012–2013 at

TABLE 5.2
In-State Tuition 2012–2013

State	Tuition and Fees ($)	State	Tuition and Fees ($)	State	Tuition and Fees ($)
AK	6006	LA	6,989	OH	10,037
AL	9200	MA	13,230	OK	8,126
AR	7553	MD	8,908	OR	9,310
AZ	10,035	ME	10,594	PA	17,266
CA	12,874	MI	14,263	RI	12,450
CO	10,247	MN	13,549	SC	10,488
CT	11,242	MO	9,257	SD	7,704
DE	11,682	MS	6,282	TN	9,092
FL	6,143	MT	5,985	TX	9,792
GA	9,842	NC	7,694	UT	7,139
HI	9,404	ND	7,254	VA	12,006
IA	8,057	NE	7,897	VT	15,284
ID	6,212	NH	16,442	WA	12,428
IL	14,522	NJ	13,073	WI	10,384
IN	10,003	NM	6,049	WV	6,090
KS	8,926	NV	6,603	WY	4,278
KY	9,676	NY	7,989		

Source://trends.collegeboard.org/college-pricing/figures-tables/tuition-and-fees-flagship-universities-over-time.

the flagship public university in each state. The differences are substantial. There are a number of reasons for the variations. An obvious one is labor (faculty and staff) costs. These tend to vary by region, with the costs being higher in the East and lowest in the South. The state appropriation to higher education is another variable. If State A appropriates a larger share of the total higher education budget than State B, then, all other things being equal, tuition should be lower in State A. Of course, all other things are not usually equal from one state to another. Research shows that other variables that affect tuition costs include the amount of state financial aid awarded to students and the number of private colleges and universities in a state.[34]

Public universities are funded by a combination of sources: appropriations from the state budget, student tuition and fees, research grants and contracts, donations (gifts and endowments), and licensing and merchandising fees. The relative importance of these revenue streams to the public higher education system will diverge from state to state, and this makes generalizations a bit difficult.[35] But today most state flagship universities appear to receive between 20 percent and 30 percent of their total budgets from state appropriations, although in some cases it is as low as 6 percent.[36] As a proportion of total funds, this is a sharp decline over the past generation. In 1980, states contributed 46 percent of the public higher education budgets across the United States. By 2000, the figure was 36 percent.[37] Today it is around 25 percent. For some states, the decline is even more dramatic. According to the University of Michigan, appropriated state support for academic programs dropped from 87 percent of the university budget in 1960 to about 50 percent in 1980 to a mere 17 percent in 2012.[38] Higher education budgets took a major hit in some states during the 2008 to 2012 period as the effects of the Great Recession caused many states to cut back on appropriations. During economic downturns, when state finances suffer, higher education budgets are usually one of the first casualties because budget writers in the state legislatures know that universities can soften the blow by raising tuition. Thus, between 2007 and 2012, tuition and fees doubled in Arizona, California, Florida, and Hawaii.[39]

College tuition and fees rose rapidly in many states over the past decade or two. This is a topic clearly on the agenda of many state officials today, including governors, state legislatures, and university governing boards. States will be experimenting with a host of innovative education systems over the foreseeable future, including online delivery of instructional material, curricular changes, graduation requirements, and performance funding (state appropriations tied to graduate rates, for example).

The Police Power of the States: Public Safety, Crime, and Corrections

Despite the role of the federal government in ensuring due process and the rights of the accused, and in interpreting the "cruel and unusual punishment" clause of the Eighth Amendment, states retain substantial police powers. This includes state discretion in determining criminal definitions and penalties. States matter on a wide range of issues, from texting while driving laws to capital punishment.

Gun control laws are much in the news these days. As the struggle over the regulation of firearms continues at the national level, it is worth noting that a few states have adopted much more restrictive gun laws than others. Prior to 2013, California had the most restrictive laws. Hawaii and some northeastern states (Connecticut, Massachusetts, New Jersey, and New York) also had relatively strict laws, followed by Illinois, Maryland, Michigan, Pennsylvania, and Rhode Island. In contrast, most southern states and western states had very few restrictions.[40] But there are exceptions to this pattern. Following a series of mass shootings in Colorado, in 2013 the state passed a significant array of gun control laws limiting the size of ammunition magazines and requiring universal background checks on all gun purchases. And the Newtown massacre prompted Connecticut to pass the most stringent gun control laws in the country that same year.[41]

Gun laws are not static in the American federal system. Perhaps the most notable development over the last quarter century has been the spread of laws allowing people the right to carry a concealed weapon. In 1986, fifteen states did not allow private citizens to carry a concealed gun. State government officials were given discretion over the issuance of concealed carry permits ("may issue" laws) in another twenty-six states, essentially allowing them to give permits only to applicants who could demonstrate a need. Officials were compelled to give permits to applicants ("shall issue" laws) in only eight states. Vermont was in its own category, allowing anyone to carry a concealed weapon without any permit or license. Through a sustained campaign spearheaded by the National Rifle Association, over time resistance to concealed carry laws largely dissipated. By 2013, only Illinois continued to completely ban concealed carry—and its legislature passed a law allowing it that year. Alaska had joined Vermont in allowing anyone to carry a concealed weapon without restriction. Laws in only nine states fell into the "may issue" category. The much less restrictive "shall issue" mandate applied in thirty-eight states. A "shall issue" directive really does mean that virtually every permit request is granted. In the first two years following Iowa's switch to "shall issue" rules, 99.6 percent of permit requests were approved.[42] Thus, with the recent changes in the law across the states, far more people today have the right to carry a concealed weapon than was the case just a few years ago.

A related shift in state laws over the last few years has been in so-called castle and stand-your-ground laws. Castle laws, referred to initially as "make my day" laws, essentially allow people to do whatever they deem necessary, including using deadly force, to protect themselves in and around their home. Stand-your-ground laws, first passed in Florida in 2005, expand that right to any place a person feels threatened. Between 2000 and 2010, twenty-one states expanded their castle doctrine laws, always by removing a duty to retreat somewhere outside the home and usually by also removing any civil liability attached to one's actions.[43] Almost all of these states also adopted stand-your-ground provisions. These laws are most common in the South and Midwest. So in many states today, people are allowed to legally take actions against another person that they were not allowed to take in years past.

Dynamism and differentiation in the American federal system also surfaces in state laws governing police powers. Take, for example, marijuana laws, which, as suggested by the opening vignette in chapter 1, also vary both across the states and over time. In 2012, two states—Colorado and Washington—legalized possession of marijuana in small amounts. They are the first states to permit the use of marijuana for recreational use, although eighteen states had already legalized use of marijuana for medical reasons and at least another seven states are considering passing such a law.[44] While all of these provisions contradict current federal law in regard to marijuana use, the Obama administration has essentially said it does not intend to pursue the conflict. The laws in both Colorado and Washington were the product of the initiative process in which the voters approved the measures in a direct vote. It is likely that some of the other twenty-two states in which the initiative process exists will find this issue on their ballot soon. But most American states are unlikely to follow the path of Colorado and Washington, at least anytime soon. It is often the case that one or a few states innovate a policy and other states take a wait and see position. A common pattern is for policy innovations to diffuse slowly across the states, often on a region-by-region basis.

Consider, for example, the ban on tobacco smoking in public places (worksites, restaurants, and bars). In 1995, only one state banned smoking in restaurants (but not in the workplace). Not surprisingly, that state was Utah. In 2000, Delaware became the first state to pass a comprehensive ban on smoking in all three places (offices, restaurants, and bars). By 2005, four additional states (Massachusetts, New York, Rhode Island, and Washington) had passed comprehensive bans. But, only seven years later, twenty-five states had such comprehensive laws. None were southern states, where almost all the tobacco in the United States is grown.[45] Indeed, in 2012 there were still thirteen states in which there was no statewide ban on smoking in any of the public sites mentioned above.

The prison dilemma. One problem faced by all states in the past generation is prison overcrowding. Public concern over the rise in crime rates in the 1960s and 1970s resulted in "get tough" policies being put in place across the states. This was manifested in harsher sentencing laws, including mandatory and determinate sentencing. In particular, tougher mandatory sentences were imposed for nonviolent crimes such as illegal drug possession. One consequence of this policy decision was a dramatic rise in both the number of people incarcerated and the resulting cost of housing prisoners. Today, the United States has the highest incarceration rate of any country in the world and most of those prisoners are in state prisons, not federal prisons, county or city jails, or private correctional facilities. State prisons house about 60 percent of all incarcerated individuals in the country.[46] Approximately 1.4 million people are currently in state prison systems. Incarceration rates vary considerably by state; Louisiana has an incarceration rate six times greater than Maine's.[47] Nonetheless, virtually all states experienced a dramatic increase in the number of prisoners they house in the last generation. Since 1980, state prison populations have more than tripled. By 2008, five states were spending as much or more on their prisons than they were on higher education.[48] The reasons for this dramatic increase are several. The biggest contributor was a change in penalties for drug convictions. A second reason was the increase in the length of sentences. The consequences of these policy changes are substantial. State corrections budgets grew dramatically, straining state budgets.

A particularly interesting case of "policy innovation" in this area is the "Three Strikes and You're Out" (TSAYO) laws passed in the mid-1990s. These measures were adopted by some states in reaction to a particularly heinous crime in California committed by an individual who had been released after serving time for several violent felony crimes. The first state to adopt such a law was actually Washington, in 1993. California quickly followed in 1994, with a law passed by the legislature and subsequently confirmed by the public through the referendum process with over 72 percent of the voters approving it. Significantly, the California law made no distinction between violent and nonviolent felony offenses. A total of twelve states passed TSAYO laws in 1994 and another nine followed suit the next year. In a three-year period, almost half the states passed such laws, but virtually no state has done so since. Nonetheless, TSAYO laws remain quite popular in the states that passed them, and none have been repealed.

The details of these laws vary quite a bit. In most of the states that passed TSAYO laws, considerable discretion was left to prosecutors to determine whether or not to pursue penalties under the TSAYO provision. Consequently, TSAYO laws did not dramatically alter incarceration rates in most states that adopted them. The case of California, however, was another matter entirely. The TSAYO law in that state severely limited the discretion available to prosecutors and judges to consider mitigating circumstances, such as the nature of the "third strike" crime. Furthermore, the law allowed some crimes such as shoplifting, which is usually a misdemeanor crime, to be considered a felony if it was the third offense. Thus, California's law led to very lengthy prison sentences for some "three-time losers" even if their third conviction was for a minor or nonviolent crime. The law also mandated lengthier sentences for "second strike" offenders. Reviewing the impact of the law a decade after its passage, the California Legislative Analyst's Office estimated the additional costs directly attributable to the TSAYO law to be about a half-billion dollars per year, which is less than the original projections made when TSAYO passed in 1994.[49] However, one unanticipated consequence of the law is that TSAYO has contributed to an aging of the prison population. In 2012, half of the TSAYO prisoners in California were over fifty years of age.[50] The cost of housing aged prisoners is much higher than for most other prisoners, largely because of increased health-care costs.

In 2012, again through the initiative process, California amended its TSAYO law to permit the nature of the third-strike offense to be taken into account; a decision that permits minor crimes or nonviolent offenses committed by third-time offenders to be treated less harshly than under the original California TSAYO measure.

States differ considerably on sentencing philosophies, with some states taking stronger "get-tough" stances while others emphasize rehabilitation. Based on whether a state has adopted such policies as mandatory sentencing, the abolition of parole, TSAYO laws, and a required minimum prison term for six offender groups, an index of "sentencing policy toughness" has been constructed.[51] By this measure, the states with the toughest sentencing policies are California, Florida, Idaho, and Indiana. The states at the other end of the scale are New Mexico, Massachusetts, Kentucky, and Kansas. Generally speaking, "policy-liberal states tend to have more lenient sentencing practices and lower incarceration rates."[52] But the correlation is far from perfect and a few states, such as California and New York, which are generally considered to be liberal in policy outlook, have very tough sentencing requirements.

Further examples of how states vary in the application of their police powers include the institution of a death penalty and the willingness to turn over some corrections functions to "for-profit" corporations. Capital punishment is not imposed in eighteen states, most in the Midwest and East Coast. The trend in recent years has been to abolish the death penalty, as Illinois (2011), Connecticut (2012), and Maryland (2013) have recently done. Many southern states, however, have demonstrated little reluctance to impose and carry out death sentences. Of the ten states with the most executions since 1976, eight are southern states. As of March 2013, Texas (493 executions), Virginia (110), and Oklahoma (103) had executed the most prisoners since 1976.[53]

"Prison privatization" also has a distinct regional flavor. While only 7 percent of all state prisoners are currently housed in correctional facilities run by "for profit" companies such as the Correctional Corporation of America and the Geo Group (by far the two largest such companies), twenty states have no prisoners in such facilities. Indeed, in some states the law specifically prohibits such privatization. In contrast, over 30 percent of the state prison populations in Alaska, Hawaii, Idaho, Montana, and New Mexico—all western states—are incarcerated in for-profit facilities.[54]

The States and Social Issues

The states have traditionally controlled policies lumped together under the label of "social issues" or "morality issues." Currently, the most prominent and controversial of these involve marriage and abortion. Over time, the states have arrived at a number of different policies on these matters.

Laws regarding marriage have always been left to the states and there have always been differences across them on who can marry. For example, well into the twentieth century many states enforced laws banning miscegenation, or marriage between people from different racial or ethnic groups. A handful of states in the Northeast and upper Midwest never had antimiscegenation laws, and several others in those regions repealed the laws they had during the nineteenth century. But the largest movement to overturn antimiscegenation bans was initiated by a California Supreme Court decision, *Perez v. Sharp* (1948), which declared unconstitutional that state's law preventing blacks and whites from marrying.[55] Over the following two decades, other states in the West followed California's lead and swept aside their antimiscegenation laws. But it would take the US Supreme Court's decision in *Loving v. Virginia* (1967) declaring such laws to be unconstitutional to force southern and border states to allow such marriages.[56]

Attention today is focused on the question of same-sex marriage. In this case, there has been a dramatic shift in policies pursued by several of the states over a relatively short stretch of time. But, again, there is a federal dimension to the debate that may ultimately determine how this issue is resolved in all fifty states.

Serious political debate on the question of same-sex marriage first surfaced in 1993 when the Hawaii Supreme Court ruled that unless the state demonstrated that it had a compelling reason for denying same-sex couples the right to marry, the practice would be held to violate the state constitution. This led to a protracted political struggle over the issue. In 1998, Hawaii voters overwhelmingly passed Constitutional Amendment 2, granting the state legislature the power to limit marriage to only opposite-sex couples. The Hawaii Supreme Court subsequently dismissed the original lawsuit as being moot because of the voter-approved state constitutional amendment.

The decision reached by Hawaii mattered for the rest of the states because had that state recognized a right for gays and lesbians to marry in the mid-1990s, those marriages might have had to be recognized in the other forty-nine states because the US Constitution (Article IV, Section 1) requires that "full faith and credit shall be given in each state to the public acts, records and judicial proceedings of every other state." This clause can be read to mean that marriages performed in one state must be recognized as legal in other states. In response to the possibility of same-sex marriages being allowed in Hawaii, Utah passed a law in 1995 that denied recognition to all out-of-state marriages that do not conform to Utah law. This approach was essentially taken national in 1996 when Congress passed the Defense of Marriage Act (DOMA). The measure, which was signed into law by President Bill Clinton, barred federal recognition of same-sex marriages and permitted states to take no legal notice of same-sex marriages performed in other states where they might be allowed. In 2013 the U.S. Supreme Court declared DOMA unconstitutional, forcing the federal government to recognize same-sex marriages in the states that allow them. The Court's decision left the question of recognizing same-sex marriage to the states, at least for the moment.

Although Hawaii did not pursue same-sex marriage, debate on the issue continued across the states. As shown in table 5.3, Hawaii created domestic partnerships in 1997, a policy that gave same-sex couples limited rights. A few years later, Vermont became the first state to pass legislation allowing same-sex partners to establish a civil union, providing them almost the same legal rights granted to married couples under state (but not federal) law. The prospect of legislation creating civil unions led the Massachusetts state Senate in 2003 to seek an advisory opinion from the state's Supreme Judicial Court as to whether such unions would be legal under the Massachusetts constitution. The court's advisory opinion, handed down in February 2004, held that any law that fell short of allowing same-sex marriage would be unconstitutional because it would

TABLE 5.3
State Laws on Recognition of Same-Sex Relationships (as of June 2013)

| State | Domestic Partnerships | | Civil Unions | Same-Sex Marriage | |
	Some Rights	Most Rights		Court Decree	Passed by Legislature
Hawaii	1997		2011		
Vermont			2000		2009
Massachusetts				2004	
Connecticut			2005	2008	
New Jersey	2003		2006		
California		1999		2008, 2013	
New Jersey			2006		2012 *(vetoed, veto override pending)*
Iowa				2009	
Maine	2004				2009 (upheld by voters in 2012 referendum)
New Hampshire			2007		2009
Oregon		2007			
Nevada		2007			
New York					2011
Washington		2007			2012 (upheld by voters in 2012 referendum)
Wisconsin	2009				
Maryland					2012
Delaware			2011		2013
Illinois			2011		
Rhode Island			2011		2013
Colorado			2013		
Minnesota					2013

be discriminatory. The advisory opinion set the stage for allowing same-sex marriage in Massachusetts. The decision in Massachusetts pushed the issue of same-sex marriage back onto center stage in national politics.

The same day the Massachusetts opinion was handed down, President George W. Bush asked Congress to "promptly pass, and to send to the states for ratification, an amendment to our Constitution defining and protecting marriage as a union of man and woman as husband and wife." Although he was unequivocally opposed to same-sex marriage, the president recognized the federal dimension of American government by leaving open the possibility of accepting civil unions, saying that state legislatures should be left "free to make their own choices in defining legal arrangements other than marriage."[57] Although President Bush and many members of Congress backed the Federal Marriage Amendment, it failed to come close to passing in the Senate that year and it has made no headway since. Same-sex marriage opponents, however, enjoyed much greater success at the state level, with bans passing in all thirteen states where they appeared on the ballot in 2004, and two more states in 2005. But while bans passed in another seven additional states in 2006, the first cracks in opposition to same-sex marriage appeared that year when voters in Arizona rejected such a measure.

By 2008, forty-four states had either constitutional provisions or statutory laws on the books that prevented same-sex marriages. Only in Massachusetts and California were such marriages legal, and voters in the latter passed a state constitutional amendment to ban them that November. But public views about same-sex relationships had begun to shift, and that change started to show up in state laws. Civil unions had become more accepted after encountering some initial resistance. Connecticut had established them in 2005, followed by New Jersey in 2007, and Oregon and New Hampshire in 2008. Several more states adopted them by 2013.

The biggest change, however, came in same-sex marriage laws. State court decisions forced their acceptance in Connecticut and Iowa. Starting in 2009, however, state legislatures passed laws allowing same-sex marriage on their own volition, with such measures being adopted in Vermont, Maine, and New Hampshire. They were subsequently joined by legislatures in Delaware, Maryland, Minnesota, New York, Rhode Island, and Washington. In November 2012, referendums were held on both the Maine and Washington measures, and voters in each state upheld the statutes. The political tide that initially rolled so heavily against government recognition of same-sex relationships had clearly begun to recede.

Constitutional provisions and laws prohibiting same-sex marriage, however, remain in the vast majority of states. It is likely that the federal courts will have to confront the question of same-sex marriage recognition. Indeed, a decision by the California Supreme Court overturning the voter-passed state constitutional amendment against same-sex marriage was permitted to stand by the U.S. Supreme Court in 2013, allowing same-sex marraiges to resume in that state. Thus, while the states have taken the lead on the issue, it will remain for the federal government to determine if uniformity on the matter is required.

The second contentious social issue vexing state politics is abortion. Since the US Supreme Court handed down its decision in *Roe v. Wade* (1973), the landmark ruling that made abortion legal during the first trimester of pregnancy but recognized the "legitimate" right of the government to impose restrictions beyond that point, initially to protect the mother's health and later at viability to protect the life of the unborn child, controversy and passion have driven the debate over abortion policies at the state level.[58] Through a seemingly endless series of legislative and legal battles, the states have greatly reconfigured their approaches to regulating abortions. What is less appreciated is that even before the court's decision in *Roe*, the states had already begun to diverge in the ways they handled the issue.

During the course of the nineteenth century, states passed laws that outlawed abortions. Those laws largely carried over until the 1960s. In 1962 the American Law Institute's Model Penal Code recommended allowing abortions to protect the mental and physical health of the mother, and when there was a risk of birth defects. Colorado became the first state to liberalize its abortion laws along the lines of the American Law Institute model in 1967, followed shortly thereafter by California, North Carolina, and Oregon. By 1970, several other states pushed abortion rights even farther, with Hawaii allowing the abortion of nonviable fetuses as long as the procedure was done in a hospital. That same year New York adopted a law allowing all abortions during the first twenty-four weeks of pregnancy. Similar laws were passed in Alaska and Washington.[59]

By the time the court decided *Roe*, abortion laws actually varied a great deal across the states. Abortions for any reason were allowed in four states, thirteen states permitted them to protect the physical and mental health of the mother, and twenty-nine states to preserve the life of the mother. Women in Mississippi could get an abortion to preserve their life or if they had been raped. All abortions were banned in Louisiana, New Hampshire, and Pennsylvania.[60] Thus, the court's decision in *Roe* only forced most, not all, states to revise their laws.

In the forty years since abortion was largely legalized, a number of states have pursued policies that have narrowed the conditions under which one can be obtained. For the most part, these states have operated in the space granted by *Roe* and later decisions, notably in *Planned Parenthood v. Casey* (1992), to limit abortions toward the end of pregnancy.[61] By 2013, forty-one states had passed legislation to prohibit abortions in the latter stages except to protect the life or health of the mother. And "latter stage" has been interpreted differently across these states. Some set it at after twenty weeks, others at twenty-four weeks, and a few at the start of the third trimester. Over half chose to set it at "viability," an ambiguous standard that has entangled these states in drawn out legal battles. A few states have opted to push even harder on when abortions can be prohibited. In 2013, Arkansas passed a law to prohibit abortion after twelve weeks and North Dakota followed by adopting a measure to outlaw the procedure after six weeks. North Dakota then took a giant step toward outlawing abortion altogether by putting a "personhood measure" on the 2014 ballot. Among other things, the proposal would ban abortions under any circumstances. With all of these measures it is likely that the federal courts will have to sort out whether the various restrictions go too far. When he signed the North Dakota six-week bill into law, the state's governor admitted as much, saying, "Although the likelihood of this measure surviving a court challenge remains in question, this bill is nevertheless a legitimate attempt by a state legislature to discover the boundaries of Roe v. Wade."[62] Likewise, the courts have been heavily involved in determining whether the nineteen states that have forbidden so-called partial birth abortions have gone too far; the laws in a majority of the states that have these laws been enjoined by the courts, preventing them from going into effect.

Other regulations have been imposed on abortions. Counseling is mandated before the procedure can be performed in seventeen states. In five of those states, those seeking abortions must be told of a possible link between the procedure and breast cancer, twelve states require that they must be told that the fetus could feel pain, and eight states require that negative psychological effects must be discussed. Over half the states require a waiting period before an abortion can be performed, most setting it at twenty-four hours, but Utah imposes a seventy-two-hour wait in most cases. Parental involvement is required for minors getting an abortion in thirty-eight states, with roughly a third of them demanding that only notice be given and the rest mandating that a parent, or in some states both parents, give consent. Another political flashpoint has been over public funding. Public funds can be used for medically necessary abortions in seventeen states, while such funds are limited to situations where the mother's life is endangered or the pregnancy is the result of rape or incest in thirteen states.[63]

Thus, the obstacles a woman must overcome to secure a legal abortion can vary significantly across the states. In North Carolina, for example, an abortion must be performed by a licensed physician and, after twenty weeks, the procedure must be done at a hospital and not a clinic. More important, any abortion after twenty weeks is only allowed if necessary to save the life or health of the mother. In addition, any woman wishing to have an abortion in North Carolina is required to wait for twenty-four hours following required counseling and she must be told of possible negative psychological effects. In contrast, a woman in New Hampshire seeking an abortion faces almost no hurdles. She would not be required to have counseling or to wait for twenty-four hours and the procedure could be performed at a clinic by a clinician. These two cases not only highlight the substantial differences in an important social policy across the states, but they also reveal the dynamism of state politics and policies. When *Roe* became the law of the land four decades ago, New Hampshire was one of the few states where all abortions were outlawed. In contrast, North Carolina had been one of the states that had pioneered liberalizing abortion laws.

Health and Public Welfare Policies in the States

Traditionally, states have also controlled health and public welfare policies. But as noted in earlier chapters, over time the federal government has come to play a larger role in these areas. This is perhaps most obvious in the way government provides health care.

Currently, questions about government's role in health care are centered on the implications of the Patient Protection and Affordable Care Act, a measure signed into law by President Obama in 2010, and more commonly referred to as "ObamaCare." Among the many provisions in this law are requirements that businesses with more than fifty employees provide them with health-care coverage or pay a penalty, that individuals have health-care coverage or again pay a penalty—the so-called individual mandate—and that the states either set up and operate their own health-care exchanges or have the federal government operate one on their behalf or jointly with them.

Each of these provisions is controversial and there appears to be a widespread perception that they represent radical change. But each policy is rooted in programs that were already employed in some states. Indeed, people fail to appreciate the diversity of health-care laws that were in place across the country prior to the adoption of the Affordable Care Act. For instance, under a 1974 state law, employers in Hawaii have to provide health-care coverage for all employees who work at least twenty hours a week, a requirement that has greatly lowered the number of uninsured people over the years.[64] Health-care exchanges already operate in Massachusetts and Utah; in both states they had been pushed into law by Republican governors.[65] And, of course, the Affordable Care Act's individual mandate was modeled on a similar provision in the health-care law adopted by Massachusetts in 2006. As a consequence of its mandate and health-care exchange, Massachusetts has the lowest percentage of uninsured people among the fifty states.[66]

One other state-level health-care policy innovation passed at the same time the federal government adopted the Affordable Care Act. In 2010, Vermont established Green Mountain Care, a system that will eventually lead to the first statewide single-payer health-care system. The new program, which is intended to provide universal coverage for people in the state, is scheduled to be rolled out over the rest of this decade. It will, however, require waivers from the federal government under the Affordable Care Act to go into effect.

The federal government's involvement with health care did not begin with the Affordable Care Act. It actually became prominent with the passage of the law creating Medicare and Medicaid in 1965. Medicaid was designed to allow the federal government to assist the states in providing care for eligible needy people. It is a complicated program; the federal government establishes national guidelines, but eligibility and service standards are set by the states. Costs are split. Overall, the federal government covers at least half of the expense for Medicaid in each state, but the amount of money it contributes varies based on a state's per capita income. The wealthiest states receive the statutory minimum of 50 percent, leaving the other 50 percent of the program's cost for the state to cover. The federal government covers a greater share of the cost of the program for poorer states. In fiscal year 2014, fifteen states received the minimum 50 percent federal match, while Mississippi, the poorest state, received a match of 73 percent, leaving it to pay for only 27 percent of the program's cost.[67]

Given their control over Medicaid eligibility and service standards, it should come as no surprise that the program's details vary considerably across the states. As of 2012, eligibility for access to Medicaid and the Children's Health Insurance Program (CHIP) for low-income and moderate-income children was limited to families with incomes of less than 200 percent of the federal poverty line in Alaska, Idaho, North Dakota, and Oklahoma, while the standard was set at 350 percent of the federal poverty line in New Jersey, and 400 percent in New York. Eligibility standards for parents were much tighter: thirty-three states limit eligibility to those earning less than 100 percent of federal poverty lines, with seventeen of those states putting the limit at less than half of the federal poverty line. And only nine states provided full Medicaid coverage to other nondisabled adults.[68]

The Affordable Care Act provides financial incentives for the states to expand their Medicaid programs. The US Supreme Court's decision that found the Affordable Care Act to be constitutional allowed the states the option of whether or not to accept the incentives. The expansion decision has proven to be contentious and different states have arrived at different conclusions. As of March 2013, governors in twenty-five states, most but not all Democrats, support expanding Medicaid in their states, while fourteen governors, all Republicans and predominately in the South, have rejected it. Governors in the other eleven states had not yet fully committed one way or the other.[69] State legislatures, of course, also have to weigh in on the question and some governors may find that their state legislators disagree with them. In any event, it seems clear that some states will opt to greatly expand their Medicaid programs while other states will not. That outcome would mean that residents in some states will be much more likely to have health-care coverage than will residents of other states.

Similarly, the states have arrived at different decisions in regard to whether they wish to establish their own health-care exchange, partner with the federal government in creating one, or rely entirely on using an exchange built and run by the federal government. The question really revolves around state control versus federal control. Michigan Governor Rick Snyder, a Republican, calculated it this way, "The state exchange is something I'd ultimately prefer because, otherwise, if you have a federal exchange, you're going to have people at the federal government taking care of Michigan citizens and my preference is to have Michiganders helping Michiganders in terms of customer service."[70] Despite the governor's clear preference, the GOP-dominated state senate refused to allow the state to partner with the federal government, leaving Michigan to use the federal government's exchange. The same trend was found across much of the rest of the country; states controlled by the Republicans usually opted to have the federal government run their exchanges, while states under Democratic control either chose to partner with the federal government or to create their own exchanges. Both Massachusetts and Utah decided to stay with their own exchanges, although they have to make changes in them to meet the specifications of the Affordable Care Act.[71]

Perhaps the most significant instance of decentralization of power to the states from the federal government occurred in 1996, when Congress passed the Personal Responsibility and Work Opportunity Reconciliation Act. This legislation reformed welfare and created the Temporary Assistance for Needy Families (TANF) program, over which the states gained primary responsibility. Like Medicaid, TANF is funded jointly by the federal government and state governments and the states have considerable leeway over eligibility standards for receiving benefits from the program. As a result, the stringency of eligibility standards varies. In 2011, for example, a family with one parent and two dependent children could make, at most, $269 a month to be eligible in Alabama, while in Hawaii that same family could earn $1,740 a month and still be eligible. Benefits also vary. A family of three with no income would receive $215 a month in TANF benefits in Alabama, but $923 a month in Alaska.[72]

There are, of course, other important differences in TANF programs across the states. A central component of the program is an effort to move recipients into jobs. Indeed, most of those who receive TANF must participate in "work activities." States have devised a number of different approaches to fulfilling this requirement.[73] Occasionally, states adopt TANF policies that risk running afoul of federal regulations. Since 2011 at least seven states have passed laws requiring drug testing or screening of TANF applicants. As mentioned at the beginning of the chapter, Florida adopted a measure requiring all TANF applicants to submit to a drug test. Under the law the applicant is required to pay for the test. If the test turns out to be negative, the applicant is reimbursed through a higher TANF benefit. A positive drug result makes the applicant ineligible for benefits for one year, or for six months after the completion of a substance abuse treatment program. An injunction preventing the program from going into effect was granted by a federal judge and upheld by a federal appeals court. The program adopted in Missouri requires a drug test of only those applicants about whom there is reasonable suspicion of drug us. So far, that approach appears to pass judicial scrutiny.[74]

Health and welfare benefits vary across the states. But they do not always do so in the ways we might predict. A few decades ago, health and welfare benefits largely tracked each other, with states that were generous on one policy also being generous on the other policy. Today, that relationship has broken down. Wisconsin, for example, ranks high on the amount of money it spends per TANF recipient but low on money per Medicaid recipient. Additionally, there are no real regional differences in benefits. The only apparent relationship between health and welfare benefits and state characteristics is with state wealth: wealthier states tend to provide better benefits. Surprisingly, wealth is a much stronger predictor of benefits than is the prevailing political ideology of a state.[75]

The Responsiveness of State Policy Making

One of the underappreciated aspects of the American federal system is that states can, on their own initiative, respond to emerging issues. Indeed, with the federal government's policy-making capacity appearing in recent years to be paralyzed, states have had to fill the governing vacuum. Take, for example, policies on fracking, the use of hydraulic fracturing techniques to release oil and natural gas from formations deep underground. In 2010, Wyoming became the first state to force companies to reveal the chemicals they were pumping into the ground as part of the process. Colorado later adopted more stringent regulations. In 2012, nineteen states considered legislation to regulate fracking. It also comes as no surprise that given the financial difficulties in which the states have found themselves, the opportunity to tax oil and gas extraction associated with fracking is being pursued by a number of states.[76] On the flip side of environmental regulations, in recent years over half the states have adopted renewable-energy standards, forcing their utilities to secure more power from wind and solar sources.[77] All of these actions have come largely in advance of federal laws or regulations.

Indeed, the states have been active on a wide range of emerging issues. Since 2008, forty-nine states have enacted laws to prevent bullying. The laws passed have differed; some focused on cyberbullying, while other have centered on behavior in school.[78] But, as bullying rose on the national agenda, the states responded. Similarly, following the controversial acquittal of Casey Anthony on charges of having murdered her young daughter, at least eleven states rapidly enacted versions of "Caylee's Law," making it a crime to fail to report a missing or dead child within a specified time period.[79] And after concerns about child abuse escalated in the aftermath of the Penn State scandal, states began to seriously review their laws on reporting suspected abuse. In 2013, legislatures in thirty-three states were considering legislation on this matter. Montana moved first, enacting a law that "Authorizes the [Public Health and Human Services] department, upon request from any reporter of alleged child abuse or neglect, to verify whether the report has been received, describe the level of response and timeframe for action that the department has assigned to the report, and confirm that it is being acted upon."[80]

Legislative action does not always mean that the states are moving in the same direction on an issue. Following a series of horrific mass shootings in 2012, governments at all levels began to mull over changes to their gun laws. As noted earlier, within a few months Colorado and Connecticut passed several gun-control measures, something that New York had actually done first. A number of other states, however, were taking a very different approach to the problem, with legislative efforts not to control guns, but to allow the arming of teachers and others who might be in a position to possibly intervene during a shooting. South Dakota was the first state to pass such a measure in 2013.[81] Indeed, more measures to weaken gun control passed in 2013 than measures to tighten them. Similarly, while Arkansas and North Dakota were pushing to see how far they could go to limit abortions by passing prolife legislation, lawmakers in Washington were pushing to become the first state to require insurers to cover abortion costs. Commenting on all the action on abortion legislation in 2013, one lobbyist commented, "In the states things can happen very quickly."[82]

Government does not always move quickly, but in many cases the states are able to address policy problems faster than can the federal government. The states' policy responses are, however, apt to be varied. Indeed, occasionally the measures they pursue can seem extreme. Following Arizona's passage of several controversial bills during a one-week span in April 2010, comedian Jon Stewart jokingly referred to that state as "the meth lab of democracy."[83] But through the passage of a variety of different approaches to solving problems, states can begin to identify which among them are successful.

Conclusion

Although we tend to think that all policies flow from Washington, D.C., the reality is that there is vast space in the American federal system for the states to adopt different and distinctive approaches to solving problems. Thus, where you live makes a difference. Our attention in this chapter has been on very large policy questions. But keep in mind that these differences also appear on small matters. Take, for example, state laws on noodling. Noodling, or hand fishing, is an activity largely pursued in the rural South, where people use their hands to explore nooks and crannies in and around river banks to extract fish—usually catfish—from their hiding places. In recent years, a few states, among them

Georgia and Texas, have opted to make noodling legal. Other states, notably Missouri, have decided to keep noodling illegal in order to protect catfish populations from being over harvested.[84] These decisions matter because states that prohibit noodling enforce the law, as four noodlers in Iowa recently discovered.[85] So which state you live in will not only determine what sort of educational and health-care options you enjoy, whether you can marry a person of the same sex, if you can get a late-term abortion, or carry a concealed weapon, it will also dictate whether you can legally noodle.

6

Elections and Political Parties

States matter because:

- All elections in the United States, including the presidential election, are conducted at the *state* or local level.
- Almost all electoral rules of candidacy, qualifications, timing, and so on are *state* rules.
- Congressional districts are drawn by *state* officials.
- Candidates for federal (national) office often are former *state*-elected officials.
- Most *state* judges are elected, whereas no federal judge is elected.
- Instruments of direct democracy—the initiative, the referendum, and the recall—exist in many *states* but not at the national level. And these instruments have an important effect on public policy.
- The presidential nominees are chosen by delegates selected in a series of fifty separate *state* events.
- The mechanism by which we choose the president is the Electoral College, which is a *state*-based system.
- Political parties build their base at the *state* electoral level.

ONE OF THE ODDEST THINGS about the American electoral system is that there are no truly nationwide elections; none at all. In the United States, all elections are filtered through the states. For example, the president is not elected in a nationwide popular vote, but in a series of fifty-one elections (the fifty *states* plus the District of Columbia) all of which happen to be held on the same day. The purpose of these fifty-one separate elections is to choose a total of 538 individuals (called "electors") who, a month later, cast the actual votes for president. This is the procedure known as the Electoral College. The manner in which these "electors" are chosen is a matter for each state to decide. To reiterate: the president is not selected through a national popular vote, but by a group of intermediaries who in turn are chosen through a series of state elections.

What about the US Congress—the legislative branch? The 435 members of the US House of Representatives are elected in 435 separate districts distributed throughout the *states*. And, surprisingly, the rules for election are not the same in all 435 districts. This is because most of the rules are determined by each state, not the national government. And, of course, each *state* elects two individuals to represent it in the US Senate. And again, the rules by which each state chooses its two US senators are not necessarily the same.

To illustrate this point, consider the 2008 US Senate election in Georgia. Whereas most states only require a candidate to receive a plurality of votes to be declared the winner, Georgia requires a majority. In the general election held in November 2008, Republican incumbent Saxby Chambliss received 49.8 percent of the vote, Democratic challenger Jim Martin reaped 46.8 percent and Libertarian candidate Allan Barkley picked up 3 percent. Chambliss received a plurality (more votes than anyone else) but not a majority (50 percent +1). Under the circumstances, Georgia law requires a runoff election between the top two candidates. During the three week period between the general and runoff election, national attention was focused on the race. John McCain, Bill Clinton, and other national figures visited Georgia to campaign for their party's candidate. The two candidates and their parties spent millions of dollars. Independent organizations spent hundreds of thousands of dollars, running their own ads for or against the candidates. One newspaper reported that "national organizations are flooding Georgia with money. Much of it has been used to pay for a barrage of negative television ads."[1]

In the end, incumbent Chambliss won. Chambliss, who would have won in the general election under a plurality rule, was forced to spend millions of dollars more in the runoff. In other words, the electoral laws of the state of Georgia affected the process by which a candidate for federal office was chosen. And Georgia is not the only state to require a majority vote in elections (including federal elections).[2]

State electoral rules affect primary elections as well as general elections. In Texas, candidates seeking the party nomination for US Senate, US House, statewide races, and state legislative races must win a majority of the votes cast. If there is no majority winner in the primary, the top two vote-getters face each other in a runoff. In the 2012 Republican primary for US Senator, this rule became crucial (see table 6.1).

The primary was held in May. The key candidates in the race were Texas Lieutenant Governor David Dewhurst and first-time candidate and Tea Party favorite, Ted Cruz.[3] A well-known and long-time elected official in Texas, Dewhurst was the overwhelming favorite and, indeed, he received 145,000 votes

TABLE 6.1
How Electoral Rules Affect Outcomes: The 2012 GOP Texas Primary for US Senate

Candidate	Primary Vote	Primary Percent	Run-off Vote	Run-off Percent
D. Dewhurst	624,170	**44.6**	480,165	43.2
Ted Cruz	479,079	34.2	631,316	**56.8**
T. Leppert	186,675	13.3		
C. James	50,211	3.6		
G. Addison	22,888	1.6		
L. Pittenger	18,028	1.3		
Three others	18,400	1.3		
TOTAL	1,399,451		1,111,481	

more than the second-place finisher Cruz in the May primary. Dewhurst won over 44 percent of the vote compared to Cruz's 34 percent with the remaining 21 percent of the vote being split among seven other candidates.

But the electoral rule in Texas primaries is that the candidate must receive a majority of the total vote to win the nomination—and 44 percent is not a majority. In the subsequent runoff election held nine weeks later, Cruz won by a substantial margin. This race was viewed by many as a struggle between the "mainstream" and the "Tea Party" wings of the Texas Republican party. The outcome was interpreted as a show of strength for the Tea Party movement, as the *Wall Street Journal* indicated in a postelection story, quoting one source saying "Mr. Cruz's win 'is the biggest victory for the tea party to date.'"[4] The point is, if Texas used a plurality electoral rule rather than a majoritarian requirement, Dewhurst would have won and the significance of the event would have been interpreted quite differently. State electoral rules do indeed matter.

National Political Figures Come from the States

After the Democratic sweep in the 2008 national elections, one of the first topics for Republicans was where do they now look for leadership and potential presidential nominees for 2012? Some of the names most commonly mentioned were Haley Barbour, Charlie Crist, Mitch Daniels, Bobby Jindal, Sarah Palin, Tim Pawlenty, and Mark Sanford—the governors of Mississippi, Florida, Indiana, Louisiana, Alaska, Minnesota, and South Carolina respectively. The eventual GOP presidential nominee was Mitt Romney, a former governor of Massachusetts. After Romney's defeat in 2012, the early pool of GOP candidates for the 2016 presidential election included current governors such as Chris Christie (New Jersey), Rick Perry (Texas), Bobby Jindal (Louisiana), Nikki Haley (South Carolina), as well as former governors Mike Huckabee (Arkansas) and Jeb Bush (Florida).

It is no surprise that the "out" party—the party out of power at the national level—almost immediately turns its attention to the states in search of new leadership. Elected officials at the state level are sometimes characterized as the "farm teams" for national office. After all, about half of all members of Congress are former state legislators. Four of the last six presidents (Carter, Reagan, Clinton, and G. W. Bush) were former governors. Another (Obama) was a state senator. Of the last half-dozen US presidents, only George H. W. Bush never held state office. To put this another way, since 1976 the President of the United States was a former state elected official in all but four years.

This is not the case in all federal systems. In Canada, for example, provincial and national political careers are largely separate tracks; only a small proportion of the Canadian Parliament previously served in the provincial legislative assemblies. And in Germany, the flow of personnel often runs the other direction; state parliamentary leaders are drawn from the ranks of the national parliament. But in the United States, states provide both a "farm system" and a place for the out party to rebuild its strength. And sometimes, as in 2010, the out party can rebuild very quickly. The Republican Party lost its congressional majority in 2006, the presidency in 2008, and over five hundred state legislative seats in 2006 and 2008 combined. But in 2010 they gained about seven hundred state legislative seats nationwide, as well as regaining control of the US House of Representatives. The point is that these gains were made through elections at the state level.

But these days the flow of talent in the United States is not just in one direction. In 2013, twelve of the fifty governors in office were former members of the US Congress.[5] This is an important point, because it highlights the significance of the states. Strategic politicians do not voluntarily give up a seat in Congress to run for governor "back home" unless they perceive that being governor is a meaningful position. In other words, they recognize that states matter.

State Party and Electoral Systems

In this chapter, we discuss state electoral structures and state political party systems, and how they influence federal politics. Electoral laws and party systems are separate, but related, topics. The electoral structure affects the nature of the party system.

Because both the media and education establishments in the United States place a heavy emphasis on the role of the national government, many people are unaware of the variation in electoral laws and party strength across the states. More than most people realize, state electoral laws vary from one state to another. Here, we will focus on four of these differences: electoral rules, redistricting, direct democracy, and term limits.

We will also take a look at political party systems at the state level, and note how the state party systems interface with the national parties. Political parties are not equally competitive in all states. We will explore the consequences of this fact, from recruitment to policy impacts.

Finally, we discuss the ways in which national elective office in the United States is heavily influenced by state-based politics. This is clearly true in Congress, by virtue of the fact that its members are chosen from the states. It is also true because of that unique American mechanism known as the Electoral College. Born of a new federal system of government more than two centuries ago, the Electoral College is an important illustration that even national offices are heavily influenced by state politics—as was intended by the Founders. Indeed, an electoral-college-type mechanism was first used by Maryland to elect members of its state senate.

To emphasize the state-based nature of the national electoral system, we can point to the recent movement to repeal the Seventeenth Amendment to the Constitution—a movement that seems to be especially favored by Tea Party enthusiasts. As we discussed in chapter 2, originally the Constitution stipulated that United States senators were to be chosen by their own states' legislature. Obviously, this provision gave important power to state legislatures, and it remained in effect for 125 years. But corruption in some state legislatures in the late nineteenth century, coupled with the drive toward greater participatory democracy as embodied in the Progressive reform era, led to a widespread movement to have senators elected by the voters rather than chosen by state legislatures. This was achieved with the ratification of the Seventeenth Amendment in 1913.

Today, some contend that the states would be better served by repealing the Seventeenth Amendment and reverting to the system whereby state legislatures would choose senators. The argument centers on the notion that senators would be more sensitive to state than national interests if they were selected by state legislators. It is highly unlikely that such a movement will succeed, for a number of reasons. Nonetheless, the point remains that US senators are chosen through mechanisms that are located in the states. Again, there are no real national elections.

Electoral Rules of the States

As improbable as it may seem, there are more than five hundred thousand elected government officials in the United States.[6] And 99.9 percent of them are officials elected by rules established in the states. Even the 537 elected federal offices are influenced by state electoral laws—laws that define the way primary elections operate, for example. And the state electoral laws vary in many ways, among them voter eligibility, ballot structure, district magnitude, and timing of elections. Here we focus on five important ways that states matter when it comes to electoral rules.

1. The prevalence of single-member districts using plurality rules. For legislative bodies in a representative democracy, there are many ways to translate votes into seats. While there are a number of important decisions that go into creating an electoral system for translating votes to seats, two are paramount. The first is district magnitude; how many officials will be elected from each district? The choice ranges from one (a single-member district) to two or more representatives being elected in each district (multimember district) to the entire legislature being elected at large.

The second key decision is the allocation formula: on what basis do we decide who wins a seat? The choices are plurality, majority, and proportional (seats are allocated proportionate to the total votes received) or some combination thereof. This is not the place for a lengthy discussion of the fascinating variety of electoral systems that have evolved around the world, based on these two key decisions.[7] But it is important to recognize there are real consequences to the way the electoral system is structured—consequences for the party system, the nature of campaigning, and even the way we think about the job of the representative.

In the United States, the most common method is single-member, plurality (SMP) elections—known in many places as "first past the post." Under this system, one person is elected per district. The person elected is simply the one who received more votes than any other candidate. Like all electoral systems, SMP has certain characteristics. It is generally considered to be a system that reinforces a two-party political system, creates a substantial degree of incumbent stability, and fosters a direct link between constituents and their elected legislator. All of these features have implications for politics.

This system is so prevalent in the United States that we might mistakenly think it is the only one used. But there are a few American states that use other systems, at least for some offices. Seven states, all in the South, use a single-member district majority rule (also known as a double-ballot system) for primary elections. If no candidate receives a majority in the first election, a runoff between the two top vote-getters is held several weeks later. It is important to note that this majority requirement applies to primaries for congressional seats in these states as well. As noted earlier in this chapter, Senate contests in Georgia and Texas have required runoff elections in recent years.

Other states use multimember districts (MMDs) for state legislative seats. Fifty years ago, over forty states used MMDs for some of their legislative seats.[8] That number has declined considerably over the years. Currently, ten states use MMDs for all or some house legislative districts, while two states (Vermont and West Virginia) use them for the state senate.[9] The most common form is two-member plurality district. Each voter casts two votes, and the two candidates with the most votes win. In New Hampshire, as many as eleven members are chosen from a district, and in Vermont, as many as six state senators are chosen from a single district. At one time, some states used multimember districts to choose their members of Congress, but that practice ended by 1967.[10]

State law also applies to local governments, of course. And some states allow their local units considerable latitude in electoral design. Exotic (by American standards) voting systems such as the cumulative vote, limited vote, and instant runoff vote are used in some local jurisdictions in the United States. But, again, it is important to emphasize that this is all a matter of *state* law.

2. *The timing of the election.* Not all elections are held concurrent with the presidential contest. In fact, most states hold elections for their governors and other statewide officials (such as attorney general) in a year other than the presidential election year. The reason is obvious; the presidential election commands so much time, media focus and campaign resources. Within the last fifty years or so, most states moved the election for their own chief executives (the governors) to what is known as the "off-year"—the even numbered years in which the presidency is not on the ballot. Thus, while the presidential elections are 2012, 2016, 2020 and so on, thirty-four states hold gubernatorial and other statewide elections in 2014, 2018, 2022, and so on. Granted, there are still congressional races in those years, but these are really state elections, even though taken collectively they have national implications. A few states like New Jersey, Virginia, Kentucky, Louisiana, and Mississippi go even further and hold their state elections in odd-numbered years, when there are no presidential *or* congressional races at all. Perhaps the strangest arrangement of all is Kentucky's; the Bluegrass state holds the election for governor and other executive officers (secretary of state, etc.) in an odd year but the state legislative races in an even year. Focusing on statewide elections for governor, then, we find the following arrangements: two states (New Hampshire and Vermont) elect every two years; thirty-four states hold their governor's election every four years in the even-numbered nonpresidential years, and five states hold governor's elections in odd-numbered years.[11] Only nine states are on the same gubernatorial electoral cycle as the presidential electoral cycle.[12]

Sometimes, timing is everything. The 2010 election was hugely successful for the Republican Party—not only in congressional elections, but at the state level as well. They did especially well in the South, picking up legislative seats in eight southern states, including substantial gains in Alabama (a twenty-nine-seat increase), Arkansas (twenty-three seats), Georgia (fourteen seats), North Carolina (twenty-six seats), Tennessee (fourteen seats), and Texas (twenty-six seats).[13] Given the magnitude of the southern Republican wave in 2010, how can one explain that Republicans did not pick up a single seat in the Louisiana, Mississippi, or Virginia legislatures? The answer is that no state elections were held in those states in 2010.[14] It is a safe bet that Democratic officials in those states were thankful that their elections were not on the calendar that year.[15]

3. *Judicial elections.* Here's a major difference between the states and the federal government: as noted in chapter 3, no federal judge is elected but *most* state judges must win election in some way or another.[16] This includes state courts of last resort (state supreme court) judges in more than forty states.

Depending on the state and type of court we are examining, judges are chosen through one of three types of elections: partisan, nonpartisan, or retention. The most common is a retention election, a procedure whereby judges who were initially selected by the governor for an initial term of office must eventually stand for election for a full term.

The financing of judicial campaigns is currently a major topic of discussion in some states. A recent example that caught a lot of attention nationwide was the 2011 election for Wisconsin Supreme Court. Coming on the heels of the bitterly contested legislation to end public employee collective-bargaining rights in Wisconsin, the Supreme Court election was viewed as a referendum on Governor Walker's controversial policies. Over $3 million was spent on the judicial campaign.[17]

Such expenditures in court contests are not unusual. In 2000, two successful candidates running for the Supreme Court of Ohio spent $2 million *each*.[18] Even more dramatic was the level of independent spending outside the candidates' control; the Ohio Chamber of Commerce spent over $5 million in support of one of the candidates.[19] In 2008, two candidates for the Michigan Supreme Court spent $2.5 million between them, and interest groups allied with one or the other candidates spent another $3.8 million.[20] In Alabama, a 2008 supreme court race cost over $4 million.[21] In Iowa in 2010, three supreme court justices were voted out because of their decision in support of gay marriage. Interestingly, most of the money spent on the campaign to oust the justices came from out of state.[22]

The issue here is not that elections are expensive, but that some of the donors to the candidates, and virtually all of the groups engaging in independent spending, appear before the court in one or more cases. An episode in West Virginia in 2004 illustrates the situation. In a heated race between incumbent West Virginia Supreme Court of Appeals justice Warren McGraw and challenger Brent Benjamin, a private individual spent over $3 million to run an independent ad campaign in support of Benjamin's candidacy.[23] This private individual was Don Blankenship, the chief executive officer of Massey Energy, one of the largest coal companies in the country. West Virginia is a large coal-producing state, and Massey Energy's coal subsidiary in that state often appeared in cases before the West Virginia Supreme Court of Appeals. Aided by Blankenship's independent spending on his behalf, Brent Benjamin defeated Warren McGraw. When Massey Coal appeared before the court as a litigant against another coal company, Justice Benjamin chose not to recuse himself from the case, contending that the $3 million in independent spending had no effect on his ability to decide the case in an unbiased manner.

This case highlights the tension that may exist in a system that strives to be democratic and accountable by electing judges with the goal of an independent and unbiased judiciary.[24] Ultimately, the US Supreme Court determined that the amount of independent spending was so excessive in the West Virginia situation that Justice Benjamin should have recused himself.[25] But this does not resolve the issue in numerous other state judicial elections—at what point is the amount of independent spending excessive?

4. Rules for primary elections. One of the most obvious ways by which state electoral laws affect national politics is through the rules for nominating candidates—that is, deciding which candidate will represent each political party in the general election. The rules are rather complex, involving (a) who can vote in the primary, (b) when the primary is held, and (c) what constitutes a winner in the primary. Moreover, the rules may not even be the same for each party in the same state, especially in regard to who can vote. Finally, the rules may differ within a state for presidential nominations compared to other nominations. Indeed, the presidential and nonpresidential nomination systems within a state are different enough that we will discuss the presidential system by itself in a later section. For right now, we concentrate on the nomination system for offices other than president.

Each state decides when to hold its primary election: The primary calendar for 2010, a nonpresidential year, is shown in table 6.2. States decide for themselves when to hold their nominating events (primary elections, conventions, etc.). In 2010, state primary elections were spread over a seven-month span, from February 2 (Illinois) to September 18 (Hawaii). The most popular months for primary elections were June and August; fourteen states held primaries in each of those months. Ten states held primaries in May and eight states held theirs in September.

The timing of a state's primary can affect the national political agenda and the momentum of political organizations and ideas. For example, in 2010 the Tea Party movement was almost certainly aided by the fact that the group's message was especially popular in some states with early primaries. Rand Paul's win in the Republican senate primary in Kentucky in mid-May is an example. Once candidates with Tea Party backing were successful, the media were more likely to view the group as credible, helping legitimize it as a real political force. The legitimizing or delegitimizing effect of state primaries on the national electoral process is especially important in the presidential primaries, a topic discussed later.

Each state (or state party) decides who can vote in the primary election: Primary elections (or conventions, in a few states) determine the party nominees for the general election. One of the issues each state must address, therefore,

TABLE 6.2
Calendar of State Primary Elections in 2010

Early Months	*May*	*June*	*July*	*August*	*September*

Feb 2:
  Illinois
March 2:
  Texas
	4th:
	Indiana
	North
	  Carolina
	Ohio
		1st:
		Alabama
		Mississippi
		New Mexico
			20th:
			Georgia
				3rd:
				Kansas
				Michigan
				Missouri
				Tennessee
					14th:
					Delaware
					Maryland
					Massachusetts
					New
					  Hampshire
					New York
					Rhode Island
					Wisconsin

	11th: Nebraska W. Virginia	8th: California Iowa Maine Montana Nevada New Jersey North Dakota South Carolina South Dakota Virginia	27th: Oklahoma	10th: Colorado Connecticut Minnesota	18th: Hawaii
	18th: Arkansas Kentucky Oregon Pennsylvania			17th: Washington Wyoming	
		22nd: Utah		24th: Alaska Arizona Florida Vermont	
	25th: Idaho			28th: Louisiana*	

Note: Louisiana held congressional primaries on August 28. All other state primaries and runoff congressional primaries were held October 2.

is who should be allowed to vote in the primary election: anyone who is registered to vote in the general election or only those who are registered members of the political party. The parties themselves tend to argue that only those who are registered members of the party should be able to determine who the party nominees will be. For the state parties, it is a matter of the "right of association." Others, however, argue that the choices available in the general election are determined by the results of the primary election, and therefore everyone who is interested should have the right to help make those choices. These two arguments represent the philosophies behind the closed primary and the open primary. In truth, there are several shades of open and closed; in some states the primary is closed only to registered members of the other party but not to independent or unaffiliated voters. One authoritative source claims that only eleven states are truly open and another eleven are truly closed (see table 6.3).

The large category of "hybrid" systems masks a lot of variation among the states in this group. But the most important differences are twofold. First, how are unaffiliated voters treated? Most hybrid systems are closed to members of the opposition party but allow independents (usually called "unaffiliated" voters) to vote in the primary. Second, do both parties use the same rules? For states in this "hybrid" category, the answer is often "no." For instance, in a few states, only those who are registered Republicans can vote in the GOP primary, while those who are registered Democrats and unaffiliated voters can vote in the Democratic primary. In other words, the Republicans run a true closed primary while the Democrats run a semiclosed primary.

TABLE 6.3
Primary Election (Nominating) Systems

Truly Open	Truly Closed	Hybrid	Top-Two
Alabama	Delaware	Alaska	California
Arkansas	Florida	Arizona	Louisiana
Georgia	Kansas	Colorado	Nebraska*
Hawaii	Kentucky	Connecticut	Washington
Michigan	Maine	Idaho	
Minnesota	Nevada	Illinois	
Missouri	New Jersey	Indiana	
Montana	New Mexico	Iowa	
North Dakota	New York	Maryland	
Vermont	Pennsylvania	Massachusetts	
Wisconsin	Wyoming	Mississippi	
		New Hampshire	
		North Carolina	
		Ohio	
		Oklahoma	
		Oregon	
		Rhode Island	
		South Carolina	
		South Dakota	
		Tennessee	
		Texas	
		Utah	
		Virginia	
		West Virginia	

*For selected state office only.

Source: National Conference of State Legislatures, "State Primary Election Types" (updated September 2011), www.ncsl.org/legislatures-elections/elections/primary-types.aspx (accessed May 30, 2012).

Finally, there are a few states that use a system called the "top-two" primary (also known as the "Cajun Primary" since Louisiana was the first state to adopt it). In a "top-two" system, all the candidates for a particular office are listed to-gether on the ballot, regardless of party affiliation. The two top vote-getters, even if they are from the same party, face each other in the general election. Thus, it is possible to have two Republicans (or two Democrats) run against one another in the general election. All eligible voters, regardless of party affiliation, are permit-ted to vote in the "top-two" primary.

There are practical effects to this distinction between open and closed. Among those states that conduct truly open primaries for both parties, there is no reason to require voters to register by party. In these states, parties, groups, and candi-dates find it more difficult to target specific voters.[26] While they may have a list of who voted in previous primaries, they do not have a list of who voted in *which* primary (the Republican or the Democratic one). Consequently, communicat-ing with voters is less efficient (and therefore costlier). In a strictly closed system in which voters register by party, a ready-made list of contacts exists.

The open versus closed nature of the primary may also affect the nature of the message a candidate seeks to deliver. In a strictly closed primary, Republican can-didates may be more likely to take much more conservative issue positions, while Democratic candidates may espouse a particularly liberal point of view. After all, the eligible voters in a strictly closed primary are likely to be the more conserva-tive elements in the Republican primary and the more liberal in the Democratic primary. Since independents and others cannot participate, the candidates are, in essence, preaching to the choir—the party faithful. But in open or top-two pri-mary systems, the electorate represents a broader spectrum of policy positions. It was this assumption that led California voters to adopt the top-two primary in a 2010 ballot measure. The first election under the new system was held in 2012 and while it is too early to make definitive declarations, some analysts think the new system is already leading to a change in the way candidates present themselves to the electorate. As one political observer noted, "What we've noticed is candidates in California playing to a wider ideological audience as a result of the top-two pri-mary, instead of tailoring their message to a very narrow base."[27]

5. *Rules of voter eligibility and access.* In some ways, federal policies have diminished the amount of latitude that states have in determining eligibility. In particular, several amendments to the US Constitution were adopted to spe-cifically prohibit discriminatory practices of some states (e.g., the Fifteenth and Nineteenth Amendments, which prohibited the states from denying the right to vote based on race or sex respectively) or to establish a national standard (e.g., the Twenty-Sixth Amendment, which standardized the voting age requirement at eighteen years). The federal influence over voter eligibility and access certainly is not limited to the several constitutional amendments. Congressional actions such as the 1965 Voting Rights Act (and its subsequent renewals) and the 1993 National Voter Registration Act (commonly known as the Motor-Voter Bill)

are well-known examples of very significant federal mandates. The 2002 Help America Vote Act (HAVA), while not specifically targeted at eligibility and access, is another example of important federal action in the electoral process, in this case seeking to upgrade and partially standardize the mechanics and administration of voting in the states.

But in other important ways, the states remain in control over voting policy. A good example is the use of nontraditional voting procedures like early voting. States approach this in different ways. About two-thirds of the states currently allow "no-excuse" early voting, meaning the voter does not have to provide a justification for requesting an early ballot.[28] In most of these states, early voting can be done at centralized election offices or by mail, in others satellite voting facilities are allowed. There is something of a regional dimension; all the western states allow early voting, about half the midwestern and southern states permit early voting, but only a handful of eastern states do so. Oregon pioneered voting by mail ballot; all elections in Oregon have been conducted by mail now for over a decade. Washington now also conducts its elections by mail. Early (mail) voting has become the most common way to vote in several additional states. In 2012, large numbers of voters cast their ballots early in California, Florida, Ohio, and Texas.[29]

Whether or not a state encourages early voting (especially by mail) has important consequences. The consequence for the potential voter is obvious—it is much more convenient. The voter can read campaign material and fill out the ballot at her convenience, then slip the ballot in the privacy-protected envelope and drop it in the mailbox.

For the political parties and the candidates themselves, early voting adds to their planning and strategic burdens. In states where a lot of people vote early, candidates must time their campaigns to coincide with when the ballots are mailed to the voters—usually about three weeks prior to the actual Election Day. This means media buys and targeted mailings must be undertaken earlier, and presumably sustained for a longer period of time.

In June 2013 the U.S. Supreme Court effectively narrowed the scope of a key aspect (Section 5) of the Voting Rights Act, which required some, mostly southern, states to submit election law changes to the federal government for "preclearance" approval. The immediate effect of the Court's decision (*Shelby County v. Holder*) will be to increase the latitude that some states have in enforcing stricter voter identification laws. Indeed, by mid-summer 2013, several state legislatures were moving to do just that.

Redistricting

The American preference for single-member legislative districts and the "one person, one vote" conception of political equality means that redistricting is an important feature of state politics. Redistricting involves the redrawing of legislative district lines after each new census is released. It may seem obvious that the state is required to redraw those state legislative districts once new census data are available; after all, since the reapportionment revolution of the 1960s (discussed in chapter 4) we expect each legislative district to have about the same population as every other district within the state. But what may not be so obvious is this: states are also charged with drawing the *congressional* lines within the state as well. In other words, every ten years all congressional districts are redrawn by the states.[30]

In most states (currently there are thirty-five), the redistricting authority is the state legislature.[31] In other words, redistricting is achieved through statute—the legislature passes a bill laying out the boundaries of each legislative district and the governor signs the measure into law. Given the highly political nature of the issue, partisan control of the legislature and the governor's office are important advantages. If one party controls all three points of action—lower state house, state senate, and governor's office—that party is in a very strong position to implement a redistricting plan that is beneficial to its interests and harmful to the opposition party. And remember, these lines stay in effect for a decade—until the next census.[32] And also remember the state is drawing the lines for both the state legislature and the congressional districts within that state. For these reasons, state elections held in the "zero year" of a decade (2010, 2020, etc.) can have important consequences for partisan fortunes in both the state *and* Congress. Because the census data are made available in the "1 year" (e.g., 2011) and in most cases have to be used in redrawing district lines in the "2" year (e.g., 2012), the election in the "zero year" determines who will be in control of the redistricting process.

There are, however, about fifteen states in which the redistricting process is outside the immediate control of the legislature.[33] Here, the process is usually controlled by an outside (independent) commission that has been granted authority to draw the lines. While these independent commissions are still subject to political and partisan pressures (that is, they are not entirely "independent"), it is usually true that they are not as overtly partisan. In other words, in terms of the partisan implications for redistricting, the state election results in the "zero year" are not quite as important in those states with independent redistricting commissions.

Thus, the state elections held in 2010 had a significant impact on the political dynamics of redistricting in some states, as shown in table 6.4. Presumably, states listed in the first column are less sensitive to changes in partisan control of the executive and legislative branches, since primary responsibility for redistricting is initially controlled by outside commissions. The exception is Ohio, because in that state the five-person commission is comprised of three statewide elected officials (governor, secretary of state and state auditor) and two people chosen by legislative leaders.

Column 2 shows there are five states in which, prior to the 2010 election, Democrats had unified control (i.e., a Democratic governor and a Democratic

TABLE 6.4
The Effect of the 2010 State Elections on Who Controls the Redistricting Process

States with Redistricting Commissions	*BLUE TO PURPLE: Moved from Unified Democratic to Divided Control*	*PURPLE TO RED: Moved from Divided to Unified Republican*	*BLUE TO RED: Moved from Unified Democratic to Unified Republican*	*PURPLE TO BLUE: Moved from Divided to Unified Democratic*
AK	NH	AL	WI	CT
AZ	NM	IND		
AR	NY	KS		
CA	NC	MI		
CO	OR	OK		
HI		TN		
IA***		WY		
ID				
ME*				
MO				
MT				
NJ				
OH**				
PA				
VT*				
WA				

Note: States not listed are states in which there is no change in the partisan influence over redistricting (n=20, including Nebraska).

*Advisory Committee—legislature may accept alternative plan
** Ohio board includes governor, secretary of state, auditor, and one each chosen by political party leaders. All three statewide offices are now controlled by Republicans, giving them a 4-1 partisan advantage on the commission.
*** Iowa's is not actually an independent commission, but plans are drawn by nonpartisan legislative staff and legislature votes on the plan. It is included here under "commission" because legislature does not have direct control of drawing plans.

majority in both houses of the legislature) but in which the Republicans won a majority in at least one legislative chamber and/or the governor's office. In other words, the state went from unified party control to divided party control. The political implication is that the two parties must now negotiate and compromise in a bipartisan manner to reach consensus on a redistricting plan. If the Democrats had retained unified control, they would have largely controlled the redistricting process. Among the states that moved from unified Democratic to divided control were New York and North Carolina.

Column 3 represents states that moved from divided control prior to the election to unified Republican control after the election. These are states in which Republicans gained control over the process whereas previously—under divided control—they would have had to compromise. There are seven states in this category, including Michigan. Effectively, however, there are eight states in this category because of the way the Ohio commission is selected.

One state, Wisconsin, went from unified Democratic control to unified Republican control following the 2010 election (column 4). This represents a complete reversal of who controls the process. Finally, in one state (see column 5) we see an electoral gain for the Democrats, as Connecticut moved from divided control to unified Democratic control.

From table 6.4 we can conclude that, after the 2010 election, Democrats were in a worse position in fourteen states (if we include Ohio), and in a better position only in Connecticut. It is important to remember that the state legislature is responsible for redistricting the congressional districts within the state as well as the state legislative districts. That the Democrats were in a worse position to influence the drawing of congressional lines in New York, North Carolina, Michigan, Ohio, and Wisconsin is not a trivial outcome of the 2010 state elections or, for that matter, the 2012 congressional elections. There are those who believe the Republicans were able to maintain their majority in the US House of Representatives precisely because the GOP had gained majorities in so many state legislatures in 2010, and therefore were in a position to draw favorable congressional district lines in a number of states.[34] It is very likely that other factors were involved, but there is little doubt that the 2012 congressional elections were influenced by the 2010 shift in state legislative chambers.[35]

The States and Direct Democracy

In regard to political participation, the federal government has often taken a stronger position than many states in extending and protecting individual citizen's right to vote. Previously we discussed four amendments to the US Constitution that were designed to expand the right to vote to citizens who were being denied that right by some states. The discriminatory actions taken by some American states to discourage racial and ethnic minorities from voting are well-documented. We should remember, however, that African Americans were voting well before passage of the Fifteenth Amendment in some northern states; that women were voting in many western states well before passage of the Nineteenth Amendment; and that eighteen- or nineteen-year-olds could vote in Georgia and several other states well before passage of the Twenty-Sixth Amendment. Nonetheless, it is generally acknowledged that the federal government has done more than many states to extend and protect voting rights. For this reason, some observers are concerned about the recent U.S. Supreme Court ruling that limits the reach of the 1965 Votings Rights Act.

But in regard to other forms of political participation, states are often far ahead of the national government. This is especially true of those instruments of direct democracy known as the initiative, the referendum, and the recall. Virtually all states permit at least one of these instruments and almost one-third of the states allow all three forms. The national government allows none of them. One might say that the states are much more democratic than the federal government in the sense that at the state level the public has a greater ability to inform, direct or constrain the policy actions of elected officials.

The recall. Between March 2011 and June 2012, the biggest election story in the United States, other than the presidential campaign, was playing out in Wisconsin. It was quite a story—perhaps unprecedented in American history.

As part of the Republican electoral sweep in 2010, the Wisconsin Assembly (the House of Representatives), the Wisconsin Senate, and the Wisconsin governorship were suddenly all firmly in the hands of Republican officials. Under the leadership of the new governor, Scott Walker, the legislature made sweeping changes in the collective-bargaining rights and the benefits packages of the state's public-employee unions. The legislation did not pass without a fight; daily public demonstrations at the state capitol became national news. As the legislation was scheduled for a vote in the state senate, fourteen Democratic state senators actually fled the state to break a quorum and prevent action on the bill in the Senate. Meanwhile, as a report by the news agency Reuters stated, "Capitol police estimated 25,000 people, many carrying signs protesting the Republican plan, converged on the state Capitol building on Thursday, including 5,000 packed inside. The protests, which began on Monday, have grown in numbers every day this week, police said."[36] That scene in the Wisconsin State Capitol is shown on the cover of this book.

Ultimately, the Democratic senators returned and, amid emotional outcries from the crowds in and around the capitol, the legislation narrowly passed on strict party-line votes in both chambers and was then signed by the governor. Within days, petitions to recall some of the state senators were being circulated— under state law only those officials who had been in office for at least one year could be subject to a recall. By the summer of 2012, recall elections were held against thirteen state senators (ten Republicans, three Democrats), the lieutenant governor, and—most famously—Governor Scott Walker. Never had there been so many recall elections held in the span of a year than occurred in Wisconsin. Ultimately, only three of the fifteen officials were defeated in the recall elections—all were Republican state senators. A fourth Republican senator resigned rather than face a recall. After a brutal and expensive campaign that saw huge sums of money spent by individuals and organizations allied with each side, Scott Walker retained his office with 53 percent of the vote. Over $125 million was spent on the Wisconsin recalls, including at least $75 million on the governor's recall alone.

One of the reasons that so much attention and so much money were lavished on the Wisconsin recalls is that the issues in play had national implications. Collective bargaining, public employee retirement obligations and state budget constraints were issues playing out not just in Wisconsin, but in Indiana, Michigan and Ohio. In effect, the recall elections in Wisconsin served as a plebiscite on public policy in a way that only happens at the state level in the United States.

Recall elections can be held in eighteen states. The procedures vary among these states, but generally the requirement is that a petition calling for a recall election is circulated and a specific number of valid signatures must be gathered. If the petitioners meet this standard, a special election is called to remove the official from office. The process may be simple to comprehend, but it is rarely successful. Only twice have governors been recalled from office (the most famous example being the recall of Gray Davis in California in October 2003, resulting in the choice of Arnold Schwarzenegger as the new governor). Since 1990, only nine state legislators have been recalled over the years (Arizona, California, Michigan, and Wisconsin offering the most recent examples) and at least one other governor (Mecham, R-AZ) was facing a recall election when he was impeached by the state legislature.[37]

While it may be true that the recall is only occasionally successfully executed, the mere threat of its use can influence public policy. As one knowledgeable observer of politics in Michigan recently commented, "Make no doubt about it, threat of a recall has a tremendous impact on the State Legislature, in both parties."[38]

The referendum. While there are several versions of the referendum, the common element is that a policy proposal (a potential law or constitutional amendment) is submitted (referred) to the voting public for approval. It is also a common practice (indeed, it is constitutionally required in some states) to submit any proposal for bonded indebtedness to the public for a vote. None of this, of course, is allowed at the federal level.

The referendum process exists in all states—save, perhaps, for Delaware—most commonly for adoption or rejection of amendments to the state constitution.[39] Note that at the federal level, constitutional amendments are not submitted directly to the public for a vote. In about half the states, members of the public can directly challenge a law passed by the state legislature by requiring a *popular referendum* on the law. This requires the gathering of signatures on a petition and, if the threshold for the required number of signatures is surpassed, the issue is put to public vote in the next election. As one authority on state politics notes, "The popular referendum is effectively a public veto of a law."[40]

Granting the right of approval or rejection, through a referendum vote, is an important form of direct democracy that does not exist at the federal level. In this sense, state governments afford their citizens the ability to have a direct impact on public policy in a way that does not exist nationally. Indeed, about 30 percent of the items brought forth by referendum are rejected by the citizens. For example, in 2011 Maine voters used the popular referendum—called the "People's Veto" in that state—to repeal a law passed by the state legislature abolishing Election Day voter registration. In 2012, a total of twelve public referenda made state ballots, the highest number in many years. Of these proposed laws, five were rejected, including three in Idaho and one in South Dakota in which voters rejected laws passed by their legislatures that would have put strict limits on teachers' unions.

Again, a state referendum can carry considerable weight nationally. In 2011 Ohio voters rejected a bill (Senate Bill 5) that the Ohio Legislature had passed earlier in the year. The measure was similar to the one that had passed in Wisconsin that led to the recall frenzy discussed earlier. In the Ohio case, the bill limited the collective-bargaining options for public-employee unions, eliminating the mandatory payment of union dues and requiring public workers to contribute more to their pension funds—provisions similar to those that had passed in Wisconsin.[41] But, instead of pursuing recall elections of the officials involved—which was not an option under Ohio law—Ohioans sought to repeal the law through the popular referendum process. They were wildly successful, striking down the law by 62 percent to 38 percent. As in Wisconsin, huge sums were spent on the referendum election—about $54 million dollars.[42]

Ohio voters had the ability to pursue a straightforward path of holding a referendum election on the antiunion bill. Why did their counterparts in Wisconsin take the recall route on their antiunion bill, a process that required a series of elections strung out over more than a year? The answer is simple: the popular referendum does not exist in Wisconsin. Thus, the only immediate avenue open to challenging the law in Wisconsin was an attempt to recall the public officials involved in passing the law. Rules matter and different states have different rules.

The initiative. There are several versions of the initiative, but the most important point is that in some states the initiative can be a powerful instrument of direct democracy. As one expert source on the subject proclaims, initiatives "are the most potent form of direct democracy."[43] Indeed, some of the most important and controversial public policies today—same-sex marriage, immigration, abortion, and gun control—are the result of the initiative process in one state or another. Tax limitations and expenditure mandates are also common topics addressed through the initiative process.

Only about half the states (twenty-four, to be exact) provide for the direct initiative. About 150 million people, just under half of the total population in the country, live in states with the direct initiative. In this form, sponsors of a proposal must gather the requisite number of signatures on petitions in order to get their proposal on the ballot in the next regularly scheduled election. The direct initiative, therefore, is an instrument of political participation that allows the public to bypass the legislative process altogether.

Elizabeth Garrett uses the term "hybrid democracy" to describe the initiative states.[44] We think this an apt term; it captures the idea that these states have a policy-making process that combines the traditional American penchant for representative government by elected officials with the element of direct democracy through the initiative. Clearly, the policy process has the potential to be very different in these states.

The ease or difficulty by which initiatives can be employed is quite variable; in states like California, Oregon, and North Dakota it is much easier to use than in Illinois or Wyoming.[45] The most important difference is the proportion of valid signatures that must be gathered. In some states the requirement is 5 percent of the number of votes in the last statewide election (for governor, for example). In other states the requirement is 10 percent, or even 15 percent. In a few states there are requirements that the signatories must be geographically dispersed (a certain number of signatures must come from a certain number of counties, for example), which increases the difficulty of meeting the standards for acceptance onto the ballot. Because of these variables, the use of the initiative as a method of policy making is much more likely in some states than others. For example, over a recent ten-year period in California an average of fifteen measures qualified for the ballot every two-year election cycle; Oregon averaged thirteen, while Colorado and Washington each averaged about eight.[46]

In about sixteen initiative states the instrument can be used to amend the state constitution; while in the remaining eight initiative states it can only be used to create statutory law. This is an important point. Any changes made to the state constitution through the direct initiative can only be altered or overturned by the courts. But initiatives that simply create statutory law can be changed by legislative action.

Donovan and his colleagues provide a useful summation of the role that instruments of direct democracy play in the political environments of some states. They note, "[D]irect democracy—specifically, the initiative process—has important effects where it is used. It . . . may alter participation levels and the issues voters use when evaluating candidates. There is some evidence that direct democracy may lead state policies to be more representative of what voters in a state prefer."[47]

There are both positive and negative aspects of direct democracy in the states, and they are debated and discussed frequently among political practitioners and academicians alike. But the point is that the discussion takes place in the context of state politics, not national politics. There are no instruments of direct democracy at the national level in the United States. At the state level, as states appear to be realigning or sorting on the basis of political ideology and culture, the initiative, referendum, and recall may be especially useful in fostering innovative or unusual policy differences in different states. They are, in effect, important instruments in the laboratories of democracy. Very different policies in regard to same-sex marriage, the use of marijuana, end-of-life decisions, abortion, environmental regulation, and the definition of animal cruelty exist between states in part because of the initiative and referendum procedures in the states.

Term Limits and the States

Around 1990, a movement began to limit the number of terms legislators could serve in office. The trend began with the passage of initiatives in California, Colorado, and Oklahoma in November 1990. Two years later, again through the initiative process, limits were placed on legislative terms in Arizona, Arkansas, Florida, Michigan, Missouri, Montana, Ohio, and South Dakota. By the end of

1994, term limits were in place in nineteen states. Almost all of these laws were the product of the initiative process in the various states.

In important respects, the term-limitation laws that were adopted differed from state to state, with some states imposing stricter limits on state legislative service than other states. But one thing that all the term-limit initiatives contained was a term limit on congressional office as well as on state legislators. Here, then, is a case in which almost 40 percent of the states (and about 80 percent of the states with the initiative form of direct democracy) used a state-based process to define a federal office. While the precise nature of the term limits on state legislatures differed from state to state, almost all of them placed the exact same limit on the their members of Congress: six years (three terms) in the House of Representatives and twelve years (two terms) in the Senate. Few people recall that the original term-limit laws passed in the states included provisions limiting congressional terms as well. This has been largely forgotten because, in 1995, the US Supreme Court struck down that part of each of the state initiatives that imposed limits on members of Congress, finding that states cannot impose an additional qualification for federal office beyond those in the U.S. Constitution.[48] Thus, what was viewed by many as an effort to limit congressional terms through the use of a state-based instrument of direct democracy ultimately had no direct effect on the federal office, but a substantial effect on state legislative office in some states.

Nonetheless, it would be a mistake to assume that state legislative term limits have no effect on Congress; one report finds that members of Congress from term-limited states are more likely to be former state legislators than members from non-term-limited states: 61 percent of members who represented states with legislative term limits were former state legislators compared to only 46 percent of members from non-term-limited states.[49] The presumption is that term-limited legislators who do not want to end their political careers are forced to seek other offices for which to run, and a congressional seat would be an obvious next step.

Because term-limit laws differ, the effect of the law is not the same for all the states that impose them.[50] In those states where the limit is generous (twelve years in Louisiana, Nevada, and Oklahoma), the effects are different than in states where the limit is especially stringent (six years in the lower chamber in Arkansas and Michigan). A very strict term limit can actually accelerate the already substantial effect of a "wave election," such as that experienced in 2010. A good example is Michigan; when the state legislature convened in January 2011, 54 percent of the state representatives and 76 percent of the senators were newly elected—an extraordinary level of turnover by any standard.

Party Systems

It is axiomatic that the United States is a two-party political system. But there are many ways to define or measure party strength. One way is to look at the party identification of the American public. Periodically, Gallup conducts large-sample surveys of voting-age Americans. From these polls, Gallup measures the proportion of the population that identifies with each party, or that "leans" toward each party. Between January and June 2010, Gallup conducted such a poll, randomly surveying over 175,000 adults (eighteen years and older).[51] More importantly, for our purposes, is the fact that the survey results are broken down by state.

A scatter plot diagram of party identification in the states is given in figure 6.1. The vertical (Y) axis represents the proportion of respondents in each state that said they identified or leaned toward the Democratic Party, and the horizontal (X) axis depicts the percentage identifying or leaning toward the Republican Party. States toward the bottom right-hand corner of the diagram are states in which many more citizens identify themselves as Republicans; states toward the upper left-hand corner are states with substantially more Democratic identifiers.

Nationwide, a slightly larger proportion of adults identified with the Democratic Party, but the gap was small (44 percent to 40 percent). For our purposes here, the main thing to note is how the states are spread out on the scatter plot, indicating substantial variation among them in terms of partisan identification. By this measure, Utah was the "reddest" state (58 percent Republican and 26 percent Democrat), followed closely by Wyoming, Idaho, and Alaska—all western states. At the other end of the spectrum, Vermont was the most Democratic state (53 percent Democrat and 27 percent Republican), followed by Maryland, Massachusetts, and several more East Coast states.

These are very real differences in party identification and support from one state to another and they clearly translate into real differences in political power through electoral office. For example, look at figure 6.2, which plots the states based on the percentage of Democrats and Republicans in the legislatures.

As one might expect, most of the states that appear in the corners of figure 6.1 also appear in the corners of figure 6.2. For example, Utah, Wyoming, and Idaho are in the extreme lower right-hand corner of both figures. Not surprisingly, states with strong one-party identification often result in strong one-party legislatures.[52] But there are some anomalies. For example, Hawaii had the most lopsided partisan majority of any state legislature in 2011–2012—at 88 percent Democratic (figure 6.2). But there are at least seven states with a larger Democratic advantage in partisan identification (figure 6.1). The scatterplot in figure 6.2 will look slightly different, however, from one election to another.

Partisanship is also clearly related to ideology but, again, it is not a perfect relationship. A 2010 survey by Gallup found that five southern states appeared on a list of the ten most conservative states, but only one of those states also appeared on the list of ten most Republican states.[53] The historical ties to the Democratic Party in the South still has relevance to some southern citizens, but the strength of those ties have eroded substantially and are likely to erode

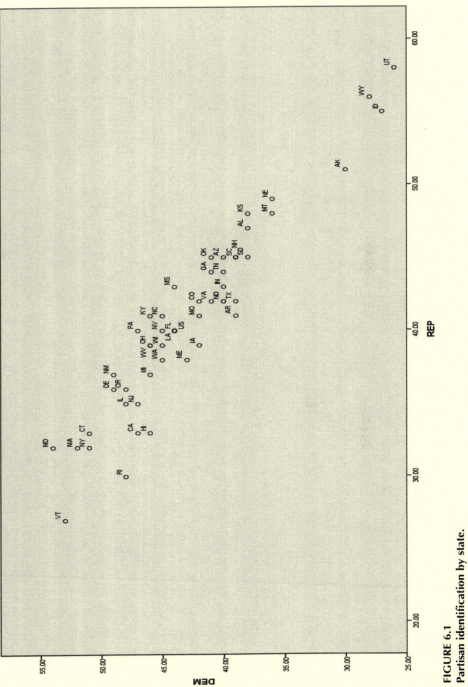

FIGURE 6.1
Partisan identification by state.

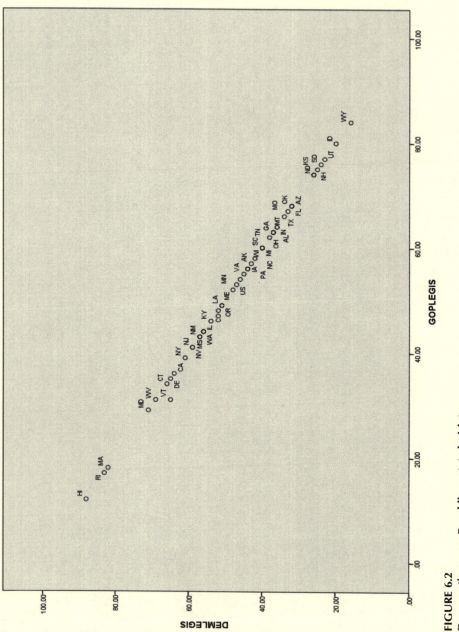

FIGURE 6.2
Democratic versus Republican state legislatures.

even further. Another way to say this is that party strength in a state is not just about ideology, but about a complex set of variables including historical and cultural antecedents.

For many years now, political scientists have devised ways to measure the partisan differences between the states. The best-known is the Ranney Index, which classifies states on the basis of interparty competition for executive and legislative elections within a state over a period of years. Essentially, the index takes into account which party wins, and by how much, over a series of state elections. Because the index is comprised of multiple election years, the effect of a highly unusual election such as 2010 is muted. For precisely the same reason, the index may underestimate real change in partisan strength. Nonetheless, because the Ranney Index makes use of data on multiple offices and years, it is regarded as a reasonable measure of party strength. The most recent calculation of this index identifies five states as Democratic, twelve states as Republican, and the remaining thirty-three states as "two-party competitive."[54] The point, of course, is that the strength, competitive position, and policy-making role of the two major parties are not the same in all the states.

The Presidential Election and the States

The method by which Americans choose their chief executive is unique. Some might even characterize it as bizarre. It consists of two distinct and very different phases—the nomination phase and the general election phase. The two phases evolved separately. But each, in its own way, emphasizes the role of the states in choosing the national executive.

The presidential primaries. The first step—the nomination phase—is actually a series of steps defined by a combination of national party rules, state party rules, and state election laws. There is no mention of the nomination phase in the US Constitution. The system has evolved over time and the current process bears almost no resemblance to the system of 1800, and only faint resemblance to the system of 1900 or even 1950. Indeed, the nomination phase does not seem to change, rather it morphs (see table 6.5). For our purposes, the key things to understand about the current nomination system are the following:

1. Each state party is allocated a certain number of delegates by the national party. Most of these delegates are pledged to support a particular candidate, and they are authorized to attend the national nominating convention and vote for that candidate. There are several ways that delegates may be selected, the most common of which are caucuses or primary elections. In 2012, about a third of the state parties used a caucus nominating system, like Iowa. But in most states primary elections are held.

2. The decision about how many delegates can participate at the nominating convention is a matter for each national political party to decide. In 2012, the Republican convention had 2,286 delegates while the Democrats decided on a larger convention, with 5,556 delegates.

3. The manner in which the delegates are allocated to each state is different for each party and it is not based solely on state population. The Democratic Party, in particular, tends to allocate additional delegate seats to those states that tend to vote for its candidates—basically, a reward for voting for the party in the past. To a lesser extent, the Republicans do this also.

4. The manner by which delegates within a state are allocated to various candidates also differs. For the most part, the Democratic Party requires that the delegates within a state be divided proportionally by the primary vote: if candidate A received 30 percent of the vote in the primary, she would receive roughly 30 percent of the delegates from that state. In contrast, the Republican Party allows each state Republican Party to determine for itself how its delegates will be allocated. Many of the state Republican parties decide on a winner-take-all allocation.[55] For example, in the 2012 Florida Republican presidential primary, Mitt Romney received 46 percent of the vote; Newt Gingrich, 32 percent; Rick Santorum, 13 percent; and Ron Paul, 7 percent. But Romney received all fifty Florida delegates. Gingrich got almost one-third of the primary vote but none of the delegates. Under the rules used by the Democrats, the outcome would have been different. Take, for instance, the 2008 Virginia Democratic presidential primary: Barack Obama received 64 percent of the vote while Hilary Clinton got 35 percent of the vote. Obama was awarded fifty-four delegates and Clinton received thirty-five delegates. Clearly, this is not a "winner-take-all" arrangement.[56] Because many state Republican organizations opt for the "winner-take-all" system, some GOP candidates are knocked out of the running early. In 2012, more state GOP parties chose a proportional or semiproportional system than in the past. We will have to wait until 2016 to see if this becomes a trend or just a one-election anomaly.

5. Since 1972, the first two nominating events are the Iowa caucuses, followed within a few days by the New Hampshire primary elections. Because they host the first events in which delegates are allocated, Iowa and New Hampshire attract a substantial amount of money and time from the candidates and the media. Any candidate who does better than projected in Iowa and New Hampshire is bestowed instant credibility and the appearance of momentum. Any candidate who does worse than expected may find it difficult to recover. In effect, these two small states exert disproportionate influence on the presidential nomination system. In this regard, an important observation is that, in some respect, Iowa and New Hampshire are not particularly reflective of the national electorate because they have much smaller racial and ethnic minority populations.[57]

TABLE 6.5
Growth in States' Use of Primary Elections to Select Delegates to the Presidential Nominating Conventions

Year	Number of States Holding Primary*	Percent of Delegates Chosen through Primaries**
1948	14	36%
1968	15	39
1988	36	72
2008	42	75

*This represents the larger number between the number of states holding Republican primaries and the number of states holding Democratic primaries. In 1948, fourteen state Democratic parties held primaries while twelve state Republican parties did so.
**Calculated as the average of the Republican and Democratic Party Delegates chosen through primary elections

Source: Authors' calculations based on data in Harold W. Stanley and Richard Niemi, eds. *Vital Statistics on American Politics, 2009–2010.* CQ Press, 2009, p. 55.

Each state, usually through legislative statute, determines when it will hold its presidential nominating event, sometimes ignoring national party desires. And within a state, the two parties might not share the same primary date or even method of selection. For example, in 2012 Arizona Democrats held a caucus on March 31 while Arizona Republicans held a primary election on February 28.

Starting in the 1980s, many states have moved their primaries or caucuses to an earlier date, hoping to increase their influence on the nomination process. And as one state moved forward, other states would subsequently move their events even earlier on the calendar. A sort of "calendar creep" occurred, a process known as "frontloading." Increasingly, we see states moving their primaries to the early months of the presidential election year (from say, April to February). Calendar creep has changed the dynamics of the presidential nominating process. In 1976 only 10 percent of the delegates were selected by early March; in 2008 over 70 percent had been chosen by then.[58]

In 2008, eighteen states moved their nominating procedure (either primary or caucus) forward on the calendar. Two particularly nettlesome cases were Florida and Michigan, two states that defied the national party organizations' stipulation for when they could hold their primaries. Frontloading was not quite as dramatic in 2012 as in 2008, but nonetheless remains a problem that pits the national party organizations against the state parties because the former's interests may not always coincide with the latter's interests.

One can see that the nomination phase is really a series of state-based political events. And each state (or the state party organizations, in some cases) makes important decisions about the manner and timing of its particular nominating events. As one well-known textbook on political parties and elections notes, "Front-loading remains a larger problem than ever; the calendar is determined by the whim of state legislators."[59] Moreover, some states, like

Iowa and New Hampshire, exert special influence in the process although they are far from "typical" or representative states in terms of national demographics. Clearly, states matter when it comes to establishing rules for choosing presidential nominees.

The General Election and the Electoral College. In the presidential selection process, the nomination phase and the election phase are distinct. As Sandy Maisel and Mark Brewer note, "The general election is separate from the campaign for nomination. The opponent is different, the rules are different, the strategies are different, and the length of time one is campaigning is different."[60] But what is not different is the strategic role of the states. As Darrell West notes, "[C]andidate behavior is conditioned by the rules of the game. Presidential elections in the United States are determined by the state-based Electoral College. . . . This electoral structure has enormous implications for advertising strategies. Most candidates . . . focus on the fifteen to twenty states that swing back and forth between the two major parties."[61]

At the beginning of this chapter we noted that the president is not elected by a nationwide popular vote but in a series of fifty-one concurrent elections (each of the fifty states plus the District of Columbia). The purpose of these concurrent elections is to choose each state's electors for the Electoral College. The number of electors from each state is equal to that state's congressional delegation (seats in the House of Representatives plus two senators). Thus, the more populous states like California (fifty-five) and Texas (thirty-four in 2008; thirty-eight in 2012 due to population growth and reapportionment) have many more electors than New Mexico (five) or West Virginia (five).[62]

One might expect presidential candidates to spend far more time, money, and effort in the large states like California and Texas, since there are many more electoral votes in those states. So why is it that the past few presidential elections the candidates have spent about as much time in New Mexico and Nevada as they have in California and Texas? It is because of a combination of three things: (1) a competitive presidential election, (2) a series of noncompetitive state elections, and (3) something called the "unit rule." The unit rule is the same thing as "winner-take-all." It is up to each state to decide how to allocate its Electoral College votes, and all but two states choose to assign all their electors to the winner of the popular vote in the state.[63] Thus, the plurality winner in a state gets 100 percent of the electoral votes. Note that the allocation of presidential electors is a state decision.

One of the closest state contests for president in 2012 was in Florida, where Obama received 4.23 million votes to Romney's 4.16 million. Obama wound up with 50 percent of the popular vote while Romney received 49.1 percent. With more than 8.4 million votes cast in Florida, the difference between the two candidates was about seventy-three thousand votes. But because Florida allocates its electors using the unit rule, Obama received 100 percent of its Electoral College vote, all twenty-nine electors.

States use the winner-take-all rule because they think it increases their Electoral College clout. But this is only true in those states where the popular vote is expected to be close. If the popular vote in a state—even a large state like California—is expected to be one-sided, then the candidates will not spend much time or effort there. For one candidate the state is a given, for the other it is a lost cause. Either way, why spend precious resources pursuing a sure thing or a lost cause when there are states still up for grabs? And in an election in which the Electoral College vote is expected to be close, every state and its unit of electoral votes (even New Hampshire's paltry four votes) can be important. Washington state (twelve electoral college votes) and Virginia (thirteen electoral college votes) have almost identical value in Electoral College math. So why, according to a *Washington Post* report, did presidential candidates Obama and Romney make a combined forty-seven trips to Virginia and only three trips to Washington between June and November of 2012?[64] The answer is obvious: Washington was considered a safe Democratic state while Virginia was one of the prized battleground states. In presidential electoral politics, some states matter more than others because they are competitive.

Recently, Republicans in some states have questioned whether the winner-take-all rule works to their disadvantage, prompting them to consider trying to change the way their Electoral College votes are allocated. They note that the GOP currently controls legislatures in Ohio, Michigan, Pennsylvania, and Virginia but lost the presidential vote in all four states (providing seventy-one total Electoral College votes to the Democratic candidate Barack Obama and no Electoral College votes to the Republican candidate Mitt Romney). Whether anything becomes of this effort in any of these states remains to be seen.

The other, oft-noted, aspect of this system is that it is possible for a candidate to receive more overall popular votes nationwide and still lose in the Electoral College. Indeed, this happened at least four times, the most recent instance being the 2000 election in which the Democratic candidate, Al Gore, received slightly more popular votes nationwide but the Republican George Bush won slightly more votes in the Electoral College. And it is the Electoral College vote that matters.[65]

Many people call for an overhaul of the way we elect our president in the United States. Most of them would abolish the Electoral College and replace it with a direct national popular vote. But there are others who defend the unique contrivance of the Electoral College, arguing that it is an important reflection of a federal system of government—one in which the states play a key role in the selection of a federal office.[66] Indeed, it is likely that elected officials who consider the various proposals to reform the system will always calculate whether their state wins or loses under any changes.

Conclusion

It is a curiosity of the American federal system that each level—national and state—has been at the forefront of "democratizing" the political system, but in very different ways. Generally speaking, the national government has led the way in opening the franchise—the right to vote—to more classes of people. One need only think of the effects of the Fourteenth, Fifteenth, Nineteenth, Twenty-Fourth, and Twenty-Sixth Amendments to the US Constitution and the effects of the 1965 Voting Rights Act to understand how the national government expanded the definition of citizenry, in terms of who could vote, beyond what the states (or at least, some states) were willing to do.

Many states have allowed their citizens greater opportunities to directly influence public policy than what is permitted at the national level. One need think only of the instruments of direct democracy available at the state levels that are not available at the national level, to appreciate the difference. A multitude of judicial elections at the state and local level, in contrast to the manner in which federal judges are chosen, are another example of significant differences.

The main theme of this chapter is the variety of ways in which electoral rules and procedures that are defined at the state level impact on the way politics plays out at the national level. All federally elected office-holders are chosen under rules influenced by the states. Rules matter, and certainly this is true of electoral rules. And electoral rules among the states are something of a hodge-podge. They differ from one state to another in one or more of the following ways:

- Who can vote (voter eligibility)
- How they vote (ballot structure, absentee/mail voting)
- For whom they can vote (open versus closed primaries, which offices are elected)
- When they vote (presidential year, off-year, odd-year)
- How often they vote (term of office)
- For what they can vote (just candidates, or candidates and issues)

States also differ, rather dramatically, in terms of the relative strength of each the two major political parties. While, nationally, the two parties are currently roughly equal in strength, that is certainly not the case in many states today. Some states are heavily Republican, some are heavily Democratic, and a smaller number are very competitive and highly contested between the two parties. At the intersection of these two issues—state party strength and state electoral rules—we find the Electoral College and the campaign for the presidency. In numerous ways, some obvious, others less so, state electoral and party systems matter.

7

State Fiscal Systems

States matter because:

- About 10 percent of the average citizen's income goes to pay state and local taxes.
- The way a state puts together its tax system determines which citizens carry more of the tax burden.
- The ability of local governments to tax and spend is controlled by state policy makers.
- Public education in the United States is largely funded by the states and their local governments.
- The sales tax is almost exclusively a state tax.
- Unlike the federal government, states have balanced-budget requirements.
- State fiscal systems are procyclical, which magnifies the effects of economic cycles.
- Underfunded public-employee pension funds pose a significant future problem.
- State fiscal systems are likely to become more reliant on their own revenue sources in the coming years.

IN 2009, *USA TODAY* ran a story entitled, "Federal Aid is Top Revenue for States."[1] According to the article, it was the first time this had ever happened. It happened again in 2010.[2] Note that this does not say that most of the revenue that states received was from the federal government; it says that federal aid was the largest single source of revenue; in 2010, federal aid accounted for 26 percent of all state and local revenue, while sales taxes produced about 21 percent, property taxes yielded another 21 percent, income taxes contributed about 18 percent, and other taxes and sources comprised 14 percent. In other words, while state and local governments rely on numerous sources of revenue for their budgets, in 2009 and 2010 they relied on federal aid more than on the sales tax or on the property tax. This is unlikely to happen again—at least not in the foreseeable future.

To understand why this occurred, why it is not likely to happen again anytime soon, and the consequences of each outcome, we must examine state and local fiscal systems. There are three broad topics to cover: public budgeting cycles, revenue sources, and expenditures. And, as always, there are differences in the way states handle each of these matters.

A key issue in the future for the states will be their degree of financial independence. As we have noted several times throughout this book, the fiscal problems of the national government will have a trickle-down effect on the states. What federal fiscal aid exists in the future will be largely consumed by the entitlement category—especially Medicaid. This means states will likely have to go it on their own in even more policy areas than they have in recent decades.

Types of Budgets and Budget Cycles

There are several ways to distinguish budgets. One of the most common is the division between operating budgets and capital budgets. For states, most of the expenditures are payments to personnel or to purchase goods or services. These are part of the operating budgets—think of them as the price of ongoing government operations. But some types of expenditures are for long-term projects involving the acquisition of property and the building of something on that property. Thus, capital budgets are about physical items—highways, bridges, university campus buildings, and so on. For the most part, capital budgets involve onetime items—once a building is built, it's no longer in the capital budget. But operating budgets are ongoing. Once a program is started, the personnel have to be paid every year. For states, one of the most important distinctions between operating and capital budgets is that states can only go into debt (that is, borrow money through government bonding) for capital budgets, not operating budgets.

General Fund and Total Funds Budgets. But when talking about state budgets, there is an even more important way to distinguish between types of budgets, and it has to do with the control the state has over the way the funds are allocated. There are two of these, and in most states they are called the general fund budget and the total budget. In most states, the general fund budget makes up 40 to 50 percent of the total budget. Although it is roughly only half of the total budget, the general fund is the one that gets most of the media attention. The reason is simple enough; the general fund is *discretionary* money—meaning it can be spent in a variety of ways. *Nondiscretionary* funds are monies that are "locked in"—they must be spent on specific programs or items. There is no

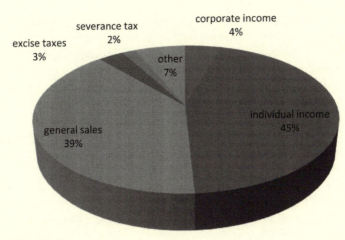

FIGURE 7.1
General fund revenue, Kansas FY 2012.

choice in how the money is allocated. It is mandated by the state constitution, state legislative statute, judicial court order, or in the case of federal grants-in-aid, by the federal government. For example, in most states, revenue from the state gasoline tax (more formally known as the "motor fuels tax") must go to the state transportation department or state highway department. This money cannot be diverted or reallocated by the legislature or the governor to schools or prisons or something else. Given that there is no discretion, there is no argument over who (what department) gets the money. Figures 7.1 and 7.2 show a typical state (Kansas, in this case) general fund budget and total fund budget.

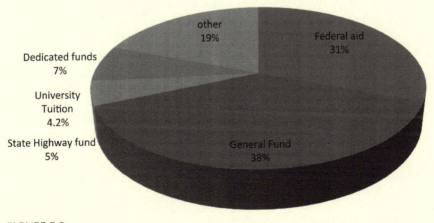

FIGURE 7.2
Total fund budget, Kansas FY 2012.

Discretionary funds can be moved from one account to another. Consequently, there is almost always an argument in the legislature over who gets what share of discretionary, general fund money. Thus, the media focuses almost entirely on the fight over the general fund appropriation; it is often characterized as "slices of the (budget) pie" and who is getting a larger or smaller piece. Some types of programs and interests tend to be funded through nondiscretionary funds (e.g., highways) while others (e.g., public education) are mostly financed through discretionary, general funds. From the point of view of program beneficiaries, nondiscretionary funds are more desirable than discretionary funds.

Federal aid—also known as fiscal federalism, or federal intergovernmental transfers—is an important component of the nondiscretionary part of the total state budget. Almost all of these funds are accompanied by mandates—rules and regulations on how the money is to be spent. We will say more about fiscal federalism later in the chapter.

Fiscal Years and Budget Cycles. For most of us, the major annual time-referent is the calendar year: it begins January 1 and ends December 31. So, when someone makes reference to the year "2014," we know that to mean January 1, 2014, through December 31, 2014. But there are other "years." There is the "academic year," which begins in August or September of one year and ends in May or June of the following year. And then there is the "fiscal year." The fiscal year is when the budget expenditures start anew. Anyone who has served in the military, or otherwise been employed by the federal government, knows that the federal fiscal year begins October 1. Thus, for the federal government, fiscal year (FY) 2014 begins on October 1, 2013, and ends on September 30, 2014.

Almost all states operate on fiscal years that run from July 1 to June 30. For these states, FY 2014 begins July 1, 2013, and ends on June 30, 2014. Only four states do not operate on this fiscal year schedule. Alabama and Michigan use the same fiscal year as the federal government (beginning October 1), while New York begins the fiscal year on April 1, and Texas begins on September 1.[3] The overlap of fiscal years with the legislative session and the calendar year in a "typical" state is depicted in figure 7.3. Most states have legislative sessions that begin in January and run three or four months. There are numerous exceptions, however. A few states have legislatures that operate full-time—essentially for the entire year. And a few states meet only every other year, or begin their session in March rather than January. But most states operate in the time cycle depicted in figure 7.3.

CALENDAR YEAR 2014											
Jan	Feb	Mar	Apr	May	June	July	Aug	Sept	Oct	Nov	Dec
2014 Legislature in Session				End of FY 2014		Beginning of FY 2015					

FIGURE 7.3
Calendar years, fiscal years, and legislative sessions.

In terms of the budget process, what this means is that the governor and the legislature are setting the fiscal year 2014 budget in the early part of calendar year 2013. Thus, in January through about March of 2013, policy makers are projecting revenues for a period about sixteen to eighteen months in the future—until June 30, 2014. Because budgets are always forecasts, they are prone to being in error and almost never correct. How could they be? State revenues are sensitive to economic trends and the best that policy makers can do is make an educated guess as to what the condition of the economy will be a year or a year and a half in the future. The truth is, the forecasts of future revenues are usually reasonably accurate although the forecasts are often colored by political considerations (fiscal conservatives will use more pessimistic forecasts than fiscal liberals, for example). For states, the revenue forecasts are especially important because of balanced-budget requirements. The important point is that spending is conditioned by revenue forecasts.

When economic conditions change rapidly, the state budget process can become chaotic. A particularly dramatic example of this is the Great Recession of 2008–2010.[4] The recession began just as most state legislatures were, in early 2008, beginning work on their FY 2009 budget. And the data they used to make the FY 2009 forecasts were from 2006 and 2007—years of economic growth. Thus, their revenue projections, and the budgets based on those projections, for FY 2009 turned out to be inaccurate. Of course, this was not known for some months. As the National Conference of State Legislatures (NCSL) later reported, "Lawmakers were aware of the slowing economy when drafting their FY 2009 budgets, but none could have foreseen a collapse of the magnitude that has stricken state finances."[5] By the time state legislatures reconvened in early 2009 (halfway through the 2009 Fiscal Year), they were facing, collectively, a budget shortfall of $110 billion dollars.[6] Some states were hit especially hard; Alabama reported a FY 2009 shortfall of 12 percent; Arizona, 15 percent; and California, 14 percent. Other states reporting shortfalls of 10 percent or more were Georgia, Nevada, New Hampshire, South Carolina, and Tennessee.[7] The FY 2010 shortfalls turned out to be even worse, approaching $200 billion. The decline in revenues in 2009–2010 was unusually large; we can get a sense of the magnitude of the fiscal shock by comparing the "trough" between 2009 and 2010 to the one between 2002 and 2003, which was a more typical recessionary period (see figure 7.4).

The situation surrounding the Great Recession required drastic action in some instances. For several fiscal years, California had to cope with budget deficits totaling $100 billion. As one observer noted, some of the spending cuts they had to adopt were "downright breathtaking in size and scope," including eliminating some child care programs, cutting assistance for the elderly, and eliminating $1 billion dollars in appropriations to state universities.[8]

FIGURE 7.4
Year-over-year percentage change in state and local government tax receipts. *Source:*
www.gao.gov/special.pubs/longterm/state/fiscalconditionsfaq.html.

The states' budget situation would have been even more severe if the federal government had not provided $68 billion in relief aid to the states in FY 2009 (as part of the American Recovery and Reinvestment Act—ARRA—perhaps better known as "federal stimulus money"). Federal stimulus funds also helped soften the blow of budget shortfalls in FY 2010 ($59 billion in ARRA funds were sent to the states). These federal funds were no longer available by 2012. It is also the case that many states were able to lessen the budget blow in FY 2009–2011 by transferring money from their "rainy day funds"—basically state government savings accounts. But, like the ARRA funds, these state savings accounts were largely depleted by the end of FY 2011. The dramatic economic downturn meant that state policy makers were faced with severely cutting back on program expenditures, raising taxes to make up the shortfall, or some combination of the two approaches. By FY 2013, most states were reporting that their budget situation had stabilized.

Balanced-Budget Requirements. One of the key ways in which the national government and states differ is their approach to matching spending and revenue. The federal government regularly engages in "deficit spending," but the ability of states to do so is quite limited.[9] It was not always this way. In the early nineteenth century, states engaged in deficit spending on a regular basis. The problem was severe enough that by 1840 "some states teetered on bankruptcy from excessive debt" and at that point state constitutions were amended to place limits on state spending and debt.[10] Except for Vermont, all states require a balanced operating budget, although it should be noted that not all balanced budget rules are the same. The enforcement mechanism to require a balanced budget is weak in some states and stringent in others.[11] In about half the states, if policy makers cannot agree on a balanced budget, a partial shutdown of government functions is required.[12] A recent example occurred in Minnesota in July of 2011 (the beginning of the 2012 fiscal year), when many services deemed "nonessential," such as state parks, road construction, and child-care services, were closed for three weeks, until a balanced budget was finally passed.[13] It was the second time in five years that Minnesotans had experienced a state government shutdown. But generally, the mere threat of a shutdown is enough to bring state budget makers to some agreement on balancing the budget. Because the consequences of not reaching an agreement can be serious in many states, policy makers have a strong incentive to balance the budget.

Direct Democracy and Fiscal Policy. One of the unique features of some state electoral systems, as described in chapter 6, is the existence of the direct initiative. This is a process by which the public (or some segment thereof) can propose a law or state constitutional amendment to be decided upon by a vote in a subsequent election. Among the most prevalent types of propositions are tax limits or spending mandates, known collectively as TELs (Tax and Expenditure Limitations). The most famous such TEL is California's Proposition 13, which passed in 1978 and put a strict limit on property taxes. That measure precipitated the "tax revolt" in numerous states during the 1980s. Some of these propositions involve a requirement that a certain percentage of the state budget be dedicated to a specific expenditure (such as K–12 public schools). While more than half the states have one or more TELs in place, they are especially prevalent in states that permit the direct initiative. In addition to California, Colorado, and Washington are two such states. States with TELs are constrained in their fiscal policies in ways not found in states without them. There is evidence that TELs and other budget rules such as strict balanced-budget requirements constrain the growth in state government spending and reduce the year-to-year volatility in state expenditures.[14] But they also hamper the choices and actions available to state officials during times of economic stress.

A Note about Variation. State and subnational fiscal systems are complicated because they experience variation in three important ways. First, there is variation *between* levels of government: the revenues and expenditures at the state level look different than the revenue and expenditure patterns at the local government level. Second, there is variation *within* a particular level of government: for example, no two states generate revenue or spend money in precisely the same pattern. And certainly this is true at the local government level—cities, counties, school and special districts and townships are local governments but they have very different fiscal fingerprints. Finally, there is variation *over time* in the way state and local fiscal systems operate. This is largely due to changes in the supply and demand structure of public fiscal systems; where they get their money (supply) and how they must spend it (demand) change over time. With these variations in mind, we turn to an explanation of the revenue structures for state, and then local, governments.

State Revenues

For the most part, states must balance their budgets; expenditures cannot exceed revenues. So government spending is shaped by the revenue generated. And the revenue is generated in many ways. Most of the revenue sources are different types of taxes: personal income, general sales tax, tobacco tax, and so on. Lotteries generate revenue. Federal aid is yet another source. Because states need to balance their budgets, their ability to spend money is constrained by the revenue they obtain. During an economic downturn like the Great Recession, revenues decline and, as a consequence, expenditures must be cut. The Great Recession was a particularly difficult period for state and local governments; as noted earlier, many states saw revenues drop by 10 percent or more, and, as a result, substantial cutbacks occurred in state spending. Over six hundred thousand state and local employees were lopped off government payrolls.

While most state and local revenue sources are sensitive to economic conditions, some are more so than others. The general sales tax is affected by the economy, because when the economy slows, people tend to cut back on discretionary spending; they stop buying expensive items like hot tubs, big-screen televisions, and automobiles and they reduce spending on dining out and weekend getaways. This means government collects less sales tax money. The personal income tax is also affected by the economy. During robust economic times, unemployment is low; most everyone is working, making money, and paying income taxes. And because many states tax higher incomes at a higher rate, the income tax captures a higher percentage of economic activity in good times than in bad times. These two revenue sources are especially important contributors to the general fund budgets of most states. It is these features of state fiscal systems, along with the balanced-budget requirement, that make state fiscal systems procyclical. During a recession, when the economy slows, states must either raise taxes or cut programs (or both). Since these actions negatively affect spending and employment, they further slow the economy. Katharine Bradbury, an economist with the Federal Reserve Bank, sums up the macroeconomic situation succinctly, "Tax revenues, which are generated by economic activity, tend to move pro-cyclically; as a result, budget-balancing by state and local governments tends to amplify national business cycle swings."[15]

States have an array of revenue sources available to them—and to their local governments. Over time, each state has made decisions about which particular revenue sources to use, and how much to rely on each of them. Each state's revenue package is a product of numerous decisions by public officials over many years. Some of these decisions involved hard-fought, well-publicized struggles over the imposition of a particular tax, or the raising of a specific tax rate. Other decisions were made incrementally, as short-term adjustments to economic upturns or downturns. Consequently, each state has a rather unique fiscal fingerprint (see table 7.1 for a summary of the tax rates on various state and local

TABLE 7.1
Various Tax Rates in the States

1 State	2 Personal Income Tax Rates (percent)	3 Corporate Income Tax Rate (percent)	4 State Sales Tax (percent)	5 State and Local Sales Combined (percent)	6 Gasoline Tax (cents per gallon)	7 Tobacco Tax ($ per pack of cigarettes)	8 Total State and Local Tax Rate (rank in parentheses)
AL	2.0–5.0	6.5	4	8.3	18	0.425	8.5% (40)
AK	0	1.0–9.4	0	1.8	8	2.00	6.3 (50)
AZ	2.59–4.54	6.97	6.6	9.1	19	2.00	8.7 (38)
AR	1.0–7.0	1.0–6.5	6.0	8.6	21.8	1.15	9.9 (14)
CA	1.0–9.3	8.84	7.25	8.1	41.2	0.87	10.6 (6)
CO	4.63	4.63	2.9	7.4	22	0.84	8.6 (39)
CT	3.0–6.7	7.5	6.35	6.35	25	3.40	12.0 (3)
DE	2.2–6.75	8.7	0	0	23	1.60	9.6 (23)
FL	0	5.5	6.0	6.6	16.6	1.34	9.2 (31)
GA	1.0–6.0	6.0	4.0	6.8	20.4	0.37	9.1 (32)
HI	1.4–11.0	4.4–6.4	4.0	4.4	17	3.20	9.6 (22)
ID	1.6–7.8	7.6	6.0	6.0	26	0.57	9.4 (28)
IL	5.0	9.5	6.25	8.2	20.1	0.98	10.0 (13)
IN	3.4	8.5	7.0	7.0	18	0.995	9.5 (25)
IA	0.36–8.98	6.0–12.0	6.0	6.8	22	1.36	9.5 (24)
KS	3.5–6.45	4.0	6.3	8.3	24	0.79	9.7 (19)
KY	2.0–6.0	4.0–6.0	6.0	6.0	27.8	0.60	9.3 (30)
LA	2.0–6.0	4.0–8.0	4.0	8.8	20.125	0.36	8.2 (42)
ME	2.0–8.5	3.5–8.93	5.0	5.0	30	2.00	10.1 (9)
MD	2.0–5.5	8.25	6.0	6.0	23.5	2.00	10.0 (12)
MA	5.3	8.0	6.25	6.25	21	2.51	10.0 (11)

(continued)

TABLE 7.1
(continued)

1 State	2 Personal Income Tax Rates (percent)	3 Corporate Income Tax Rate (percent)	4 State Sales Tax (percent)	5 State and Local Sales Combined (percent)	6 Gasoline Tax (cents per gallon)	7 Tobacco Tax ($ per pack of cigarettes)	8 Total State and Local Tax Rate (rank in parentheses)
MI	4.35	6.0	6.0	6.0	19	2.00	9.7 (21)
MN	5.35–7.85	9.8	6.875	7.2	28.1	1.23	10.3 (7)
MS	3.0–5.0	3.0–5.0	7.0	7.0	18.4	0.68	8.7 (36)
MO	1.5–6.0	6.25	4.225	7.5	17.3	0.17	9.0 (34)
MT	1.0–6.9	6.75	0	0	27	1.70	8.7 (35)
NE	2.56–6.84	5.58–7.81	5.5	6.8	27.6	0.64	9.8 (15)
NV	0	0	6.85	7.9	23.805	0.80	7.5 (49)
NH	0*	8.5	0	0	19.625	1.68	8.0 (44)
NJ	1.4–8.97	9.0	7.0	7.0	14.5	2.70	12.2 (1)
NM	1.7–4.9	4.8–7.6	5.125	7.2	18.875	1.66	8.4 (41)
NY	4.0–8.82	7.1	4.0	8.5	25.8	4.35	12.1 (2)
NC	6.0–7.75	6.9	4.75	6.8	39.15	0.45	9.8 (16)
ND	1.51–3.99	1.7–5.2	5.0	6.4	23	0.44	9.5 (26)
OH	0.587–5.92	—	5.5	6.7	28	1.25	9.7 (18)
OK	0.5–5.25	6.0	4.5	8.7	17	1.03	8.7 (37)
OR	5.0–9.9	6.6–7.8	0	0	30	1.18	9.8 (37)

	Individual Income Tax[2]	Corporate Income Tax[3]	Sales Tax[4]	State and Local Sales Taxes[5]	Motor Fuel Tax[6]	Cigarette Tax[7]	State–Local Tax Burdens[8]
PA	3.07	9.99	6.0	6.3	31.2	1.60	**10.1 (10)**
RI	3.75–5.99	9.0	7.0	7.0	33	3.46	**10.7 (5)**
SC	0–7.0	5.0	6.0	7.1	16.75	0.57	**8.1 (43)**
SD	0	0	4.0	5.8	24	1.53	**7.6 (48)**
TN	0*	6.5	7.0	9.4	21.4	0.62	**7.6 (47)**
TX	0	—	6.25	8.1	20	1.41	**7.9 (45)**
UT	5.0	5.0	5.95	6.7	24.5	1.70	**9.7 (20)**
VT	3.55–8.95	6.0–8.5	6.0	6.1	26.13	2.62	**10.2 (8)**
VA	2.0–5.75	6.0	5.0	5.0	17.5	0.30	**9.1 (33)**
WA	0	0	6.5	8.8	37.5	3.025	**9.3 (29)**
WV	3.0–6.5	7.5	6.0	6.0	33.4	0.55	**9.4 (27)**
WI	4.6–7.75	7.9	5.0	5.4	32.9	2.52	**11.0 (4)**
WY	0	0	4.0	5.3	14	0.60	**7.8 (46)**
						average	**9.8 %**

*New Hampshire and Tennessee tax income on dividends and interest only

Sources for data in each column:
1. "State Individual Income Taxes" as of January 1, 2012. Federation of Tax Administrators, January 2012
2. "Range of State Corporate Income Tax Rates" as of January 2012. Federation of Tax Administrators, February 2012.
3. "State Sales Tax Rates" as of January 2012; Federation of Tax Administrators, January 2012
4. "State and Local Sales Taxes in 2012." Tax Foundation, February 12, 2012; *Tax Foundation Fiscal Fact No. 291.*
5. "State Motor Fuel Tax Rates" January 2012, Federation of Tax Administrators, July 2012
6. "State Excise Tax Rates on Cigarettes" as of January 2012; Federation of Tax Administrators, January 2012
7. "State–Local Tax Burdens, All States, 2009." TaxFoundation.org; *Tax Foundation Special Report No. 189*

taxes). We now turn to an examination of the revenue sources that most or all state and local governments employ.

Personal Income Tax. Only seven states (Alaska, Florida, Nevada, South Dakota, Texas, Washington, and Wyoming) do not rely at all on a personal income tax. Another two states (New Hampshire and Tennessee) tax personal income from interest and dividends, but not from wages, so they are taxing a much narrower income base. For the remaining forty-one states, the personal income tax is an important source of revenue; in many states it is the single most important source. But even among these forty-one states, there are substantial differences in how the tax is applied. A few states tax all personal income at a flat rate (e.g., 3.4 percent in Indiana; 5 percent in Illinois and Utah); this is known as a "proportional tax" in that everyone pays the same proportion of their income to the state.[16] Other states have a graduated income tax structure, applying a higher tax rate at higher income levels. This system, known as a "progressive tax," means that people who make the most money are paying a higher tax rate than others. For example, New Jersey has six separate tax brackets, beginning at 1.4 percent for those making $20,000 and going up to almost 9 percent for those making over $500,000.

General Sales Tax. Historically, the general sales tax (also known as a "consumption tax") has been an important revenue source for states. And while the sales tax is not as unpopular as some other taxes, it is increasingly a difficult tax upon which to rely. Most states that impose a general sales tax do so for physical goods (products) but not services. In this sense, a good or product is a tangible item, like a computer. A service is an activity or intangible good, such as legal representation by an attorney. Increasingly the American economy is service-oriented more than product-oriented. Consequently, over time a particular sales tax rate (say, 4 percent) captures less and less of the overall economic activity as more and more of the economic activity is service-oriented and therefore not subject to the sales tax. Furthermore, states find it difficult to monitor and recoup sales taxes on products purchased on the Internet. The rapid expansion of e-commerce, therefore, represents another problem for states that rely on the general sales tax.

For the last half of the twentieth century, the sales tax was the primary revenue source for most states, generating about one-third of all state revenue.[17] But, as the sales tax became less efficient at capturing revenue as the nature of the economy changed, the personal income tax surpassed the sales tax as the primary revenue source in many states. As one analyst notes, "Public finance experts generally believe that personal income tax revenue will continue to grow as a percentage of state tax revenue, while sales tax revenue will continue to decline."[18]

Another problem with the sales tax is that it tends to be a regressive tax, meaning the tax burden falls disproportionately on people in lower income levels.

This is because poorer people must spend virtually their entire income on food, clothing, and other items that are subject to the sales tax, while people at higher incomes can save or invest some of their income, and those funds are not captured by the sales tax. High-income earners are also more likely to spend money on services, which usually are not subject to the sales tax.

In other words, the sales tax is actually a tax on spending rather than on income, and it is an inefficient tax on spending because it usually only captures one type of spending—goods, not services. A few states (Alaska, Delaware, Montana, New Hampshire, and Oregon) do not have a general sales tax at all. For the other states, a general sales tax between 5 and 6.5 percent is typical, although seven states impose a sales tax of only 4 percent while five states charge 7 percent or more. In order to lessen the sting of regressivity, virtually all states exempt purchases of prescription drugs from the sales tax, and about half the states exempt food purchases as well. It is also worth noting that some states that do not have a state sales tax, such as Alaska, allow their local governments to impose one.

Excise Taxes. Also known as "product taxes" and sometimes called "sin taxes," these excise taxes are sales taxes on specific items or goods (thus, "excise" taxes are distinguishable from a "general sales" tax). The most common excise taxes are the motor fuels (gasoline) tax, the tobacco tax, and various alcohol (beer, wine, distilled spirits) taxes. In many states these taxes are "earmarked," or dedicated, for specific expenditure funds; gasoline taxes are usually set aside for the highway or transportation department. Therefore, the contribution of these revenues to the state general fund is usually quite limited. Moreover, the tax rate is highly variable by state. For example, in 2012 the gasoline tax was 14 cents per gallon in Wyoming but 37 cents or more per gallon in California, North Carolina, and Washington. The state-by-state disparity in the tobacco excise tax rate is even greater: 17 cents per pack of cigarettes in Missouri to $4.35 per pack in New York.[19]

Corporate Income Tax. For the most part, the same states that impose a personal income tax also impose income taxes on corporations that do business in the state. In the case of the corporate income tax, most states use a flat rate rather than a graduated (progressive) structure. A typical flat rate is around 6 percent, but it is as low as 4 percent (Kansas) and almost 10 percent in Minnesota and Pennsylvania. In recent years, many states have reduced their corporate income tax rate.[20]

Severance Tax. This is a tax on the extraction or depletion of a nonrenewable natural resource, usually a resource associated with energy production. A few states—Alaska and Texas are the obvious traditional examples—have substantial underground reserves of oil or natural gas. Coal is another such resource. States that are fortunate enough to have such resource supplies tax the "producer"—the coal or oil company—for extracting the resource from the state. The producer, of course, will eventually pass this tax on to the consumer as part of the total cost of the good. For a few states, this is an important part of the revenue stream. In West Virginia, over $400 million dollars (representing about 11 percent of the state budget) is derived from severance taxes on coal and natural gas.[21] The severance tax generates the majority of budget revenue in Alaska—so much so that Alaska does not usually tax general sales or personal income. Recently, almost half of the North Dakota general fund budget comes from the severance tax on its new western oil patch. This recent and large "oil boom" means that North Dakota is the only state that consistently had a budget surplus over the past few years. Only about six or seven states, however, can count on as much 10 percent of their budget from severance taxes. For the vast majority of states, the severance tax generates very little revenue.

Charges and Miscellaneous Revenue. User fees, license fees, and fines are often lumped together under this category. These sources tend to be regressive because they are usually a flat amount ($50 for vehicle registration, for example) rather than a percentage of income. But there are exceptions; some states charge a higher license or registration fee for luxury cars, for example. Moreover, the states vary a lot in what they charge. In the state of Washington, vehicle registration and title fees amount to $35 while in Montana it can cost up to $339 to register the same vehicle—almost ten times as much.[22] The same is true of fines; failure to wear a seat belt can cost the driver $110 in Oregon but only $10 in Kansas or Wisconsin.[23] User fees include highway or bridge tolls, camping fees at state parks, tuition at state colleges and universities, and a host of other charges. During the 2008–2009 recession and the subsequent serious budget shortfalls, many states increased user fees to help close their budget gaps.[24]

Lotteries, Gambling, and Other Revenue Sources. State-authorized lotteries were common in the nineteenth century but became increasingly contaminated by fraud and corruption. Interstate lotteries were outlawed by Congress and most states banned lotteries within their borders. By 1900 there were no state lotteries. This remained the case until 1964, when New Hampshire authorized a state lottery. Once New Hampshire opened the door, other states followed— New York in 1966 and New Jersey in 1970. By 1975, fifteen states had reintroduced lotteries. The modern-day adoption of state lotteries basically followed a regional pattern; once one state in a region introduced a lottery the neighboring states created their own lotteries within a few years. In 2009, Arkansas became the forty-third state to establish a lottery.[25] Lotteries do not generate nearly as much revenue for the states as sales and income taxes, but almost all states have adopted them, in part to capture these gambling dollars for the state. If a state does not sponsor its own lottery, its citizens who are attracted to this type of gaming will simply take their dollars across the border to the nearest state with a lottery. A vivid example of this phenomenon occurs in the intermountain region of the United States. Neither Wyoming nor Utah has a lottery but Idaho does. The stores with the highest volume of lottery sales in Idaho are in the sparsely populated southeast corner of the state—close to the Utah and Wyoming borders. One recent analysis found that Utahans bought almost 20 percent of traditional lottery tickets purchased in Idaho.[26]

Among the states that do maintain a lottery, there is a lot of variation in the way the lotteries are administered. Typically about 62 percent of the ticket sales are returned as prize money, about 5 percent goes to administering and advertising the lottery games, and 33 percent is retained as revenue for the state. Overall, the states netted a total of about $18 billion dollars on sales of $53 billion dollars.[27] But there are big differences in the payout margin by state. Massachusetts (76 percent) and Minnesota (73 percent) return the highest percentages of total sales as prizes, while Louisiana, North Dakota, and Oklahoma return less than 55 percent. In other words, if you are inclined to play a state lottery, it is a better deal to play in East Grand Forks, Minnesota, than across the river in Grand Forks, North Dakota. Of course, by paying out more, Massachusetts and Minnesota retain a relatively low percentage of the revenue from lottery sales for the state coffers (around 20 percent), while Oklahoma keeps over 40 percent.

A related source of state revenue that has gained in popularity in recent years is casino gambling, which generates money for states from licenses and taxes on the profits. For many years, gambling was illegal in every state except Nevada (which legalized it in 1931). In 1976, New Jersey legalized gambling in Atlantic City as part of an effort to revive the downtrodden resort community. In 1989, Iowa responded to budgetary problems by permitting gambling on riverboats plying the rivers along the state's borders. Riverboat gambling quickly became adopted by several other states along the Mississippi River as they too searched for new revenue streams. By 2013, twenty-two states had legalized commercial casino gambling, generating $7.9 billion in tax revenue.[28] In addition, twenty-eight states have agreements allowing American Indians to operate casinos on tribal lands, generating another $2.4 billion in tax revenue.[29] Only Hawaii and Utah do not allow any form of wagering.

The states have other miscellaneous revenue sources, among them state-run enterprises such as state liquor stores (in some states) and insurance trust funds. North Dakota owns its own state bank. For the most part these are not major revenue generators and the funds they produce are usually earmarked for specific expenditure accounts (and therefore are not part of the discretionary general fund account).

Federal Aid. For generations now, federal grants in aid to states and, to a lesser extent, to local governments, have been an important part of the total subnational revenue package. The first significant transfer of funds from the national to subnational governments began during the Great Depression of the 1930s.[30] As figure 7.5 shows, the proportion of federal aid to states has increased over time, but not in a monotonic manner. This figure shows federal aid to state/local governments as a percentage of the revenue generated by subnational govern-

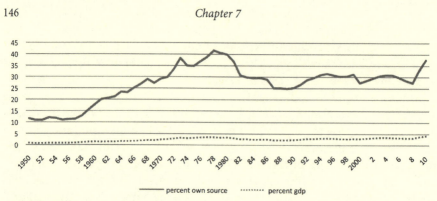

FIGURE 7.5
**Federal aid as percent GDP and percent state/local own revenue. *Source*: US
Office of Management Budget, table 431: "Federal Grants-in-Aid to State and Local
Governments." www.whitehouse.gov/omb/budget. Internet release data September
30, 2011.**

ments from their own sources. In the 1950s, for example, the amount of federal
aid received was only 10 percent to 12 percent as much as the revenue that state
and local governments were generating themselves, from their own tax systems.
Beginning about 1960, we see a dramatic and fairly steady increase in federal aid,
peaking around 1979 when federal aid to the state/local governments was as high
as 41 percent of what the subnational governments were generating through
their own means. To put it another way: for every $100 that state/local govern-
ments generated through their own tax structures, they received an additional
$41 from the federal government.

Under the Reagan administration, there was an effort to roll back the magnitude of the reliance on fiscal federal dollars—in part because of the president's
desire to reverse the growing state dependence on the federal government but
also because of growing concerns over the size of the federal deficit. This effort
was successful; by 1988 federal aid relative to state and local own-source revenues had dropped from 41 percent to 25 percent. Over the next twenty years,
the federal aid figure was relatively stable, generally hovering around 30 percent.
But this changed again with the advent of the Great Recession. By 2010, federal
aid relative to state and local own-source revenue was again up to 37.5 percent.
We will discuss federal aid in more detail later in the chapter.

Changes in the State Revenue Structure

State fiscal systems are not static. They change over time as they adapt, often
somewhat slowly, to changing economic circumstances. For example, look at
table 7.2, which shows the adoption of income, sales, and gasoline taxes and lotteries by the states over time. Almost all states adopted the gasoline tax between

TABLE 7.2
The Number of States Adopting Revenue Sources in Each Decade

Decade	Income Tax	General Sales Tax	Gasoline Tax	Lottery
1900–1909	1			
1910–1919	9		4	
1920–1929	5		44	
1930–1939	17	23	1	
1940–1949	1	5	1	
1950–1959		5		
1960–1969	7	11		2
1970–1979	4			11
1980–1989				18
1990–1999				6
2000–2009				6

Source: Authors' calculations.

1910 and 1929, as the automobile became more and more prevalent and the demand for paved roads became stronger. The personal income tax became a primary revenue source in the early decades of the twentieth century; thirty-two states adopted the income tax between 1900 and 1939. Adoption of the general sales tax occurred slightly later; forty-four states adopted the sales tax between 1930 and 1969. Finally, lotteries became a common revenue source in the later part of the twentieth century as thirty-seven states established state-authorized lotteries between 1960 and 1999.[31]

One of the reasons that states seek new or altered revenue sources is because the revenue generation ability of some older sources changes over time. A case in point is the general sales tax. As noted earlier, most states tax sales on goods (products), but not on services. This was fine when most of the economic activity in the United States was goods-oriented. But over the last half century, the economy has increasingly shifted toward the service sector. This means that less and less of the overall economic activity is captured by the goods-oriented sales tax. This is one of the reasons that so many states have increased the sales-tax rate over time—to make up for the revenue "lost" to the service sector. A related problem is the development and expansion of e-commerce. Increasingly, when goods are purchased they are bought "online" and states find it extremely difficult to capture sales-tax revenue from online purchases. It is estimated that by 2012 states were losing a combined $11.4 billion dollars in sales-tax revenue due to e-commerce sales. By this estimate, a typical state lost over $220 million in sales tax receipts.[32] Since a few states do not rely on a general sales tax, they obviously are not particularly affected by the shift to online purchases. But some states are affected greatly. It is estimated that California lost about $2 billion in 2012—that's a little over 2 percent of the general fund budget for FY 2013.[33]

Due to these factors, the relative impact of the general sales tax as a revenue source has declined over the past quarter century. In 1977, this tax accounted for 31 percent of all state general revenue. By 2009, it accounted for less than 24 percent.[34] During that same period corporate income taxes have declined from about 5.5 percent to 3.5 percent. Meanwhile, reliance on charges and miscellaneous revenues has increased from about 12 percent to 19 percent. Clearly, the relative contribution of various revenue streams changes over time. As we shall see later, the same can be said on the expenditure side—over time spending changes. Both the supply and demand sides of state fiscal systems are in constant flux.

Local Revenues

Across the United States, the amount of revenue generated by the states is about equal to the amount of revenue generated by local governments. But all of these funds—whether at the local or state level—are authorized by the states. States determine what taxes and other revenue sources their local governments can use, the types of expenditures for which their local governments are responsible, and the relative mix of state revenues to local revenues and expenditures. Different states handle this in very different ways. In some states, the bulk of the revenue and expenditures are processed at the state level. In Arkansas, 75 percent of the revenue is generated at the state level and only 25 percent at the local level. In Vermont, almost 85 percent of the funds are state revenues. In contrast, in Florida less than half of the revenue is generated at the state level. In other words, the relative fiscal magnitude of state governments to their local governments varies quite a bit from one state to another.[35]

The ability of local governments to generate their own funds depends on what revenue tools the state allows them. Moreover, different types of local governments within a state may have very different revenue sources. Counties may be allowed to impose a local sales tax but cities may not. School districts may be allowed to tax property at a higher rate than special districts. Consequently, any figures discussed in this section are simply averaged for all types of local governments in all states. Remember, however, that there is in fact quite a bit of variation from state-to-state and type of local government.

Generally, the biggest revenue streams for local governments are the property tax, miscellaneous revenue (charges, user fees, licenses, fines), and intergovernmental transfers (direct state aid and some federal aid passed from states to local governments). Overall, these revenue streams account for 90 percent of local funds nationwide, but there are large differences in these figures from state to state. For example, two-thirds of the total local revenues in Vermont are from intergovernmental transfers, while only 10 percent in Hawaii are from these state- and federal-aid accounts.[36] Moreover, there are big differences by type of local government. In most states, about half of all the revenue received by public-school districts is state aid—money appropriated by the state legislature and sent to local school districts. But much less state aid is sent to special districts, and even less to cities or counties. Because of the wide array of state and local fiscal practices, the discussion below is based on general arrangements and trends.

Property Taxes. For most local governments in most states, the property tax is by far the largest own-source revenue generator. All types of local governments—school districts, special districts, townships, counties, and cities make use of the property tax. The degree to which they use the property tax is determined by the state. This usually means that the state sets a maximum percentage that a particular type of local government can impose.

The actual amount of property tax paid is determined by two things: the property-tax rate and the assessed value of the property. Using data on the median property tax paid on owner-occupied homes and the median home value, the Tax Foundation estimates that the typical property tax ranges from 0.18 percent in Louisiana to 1.89 percent in New Jersey.[37] By this particular metric, Louisianans pay about one-tenth as much as New Jerseyans.[38]

Local governments have been hit hard in the last few years because of their reliance on the property tax. One of the primary causes of the recent economic recession was the collapse of the housing market, which caused property values to decline precipitously in many areas. Home prices dropped nationwide by about 20 percent, and in states like Nevada and Arizona the drop was far more substantial. With the decline in property values, there was a significant drop in the revenue produced by the property tax. By 2010, property-tax collections had suffered the largest decline in thirty years.[39]

Charges and Miscellaneous Revenues. Just as states make use of fees, charges, and fines, they permit their local governments to do so as well. In the case of some types of local governments—cities and special districts in particular—this is often a major source of revenue. In Pennsylvania, for instance, such charges account for about 45 percent of all the revenue generated by cities.[40] Many special districts (also known as special purpose districts) rely primarily on such fees and charges. Common examples include airport districts and public-utility districts like water and sewer districts.[41] During the Great Recession, many subnational governments increased various user fees to help fill some of the budget holes created by declining revenues.

Local Option Taxes. While these are called "local-option" taxes, let us not lose sight of the fact that ultimately it is the state that regulates their use. In other words, some states permit their local governments (if the local government so chooses) to impose such taxes, but other states do not allow them. Nationwide, these local option taxes represent a much smaller proportion of total local revenues. But in some states, they may account for a large proportion of local revenue—especially for cities or counties. According to the National Conference of State Legislatures, thirty-eight states allow for local option sales taxes.[42] A much smaller number of states permit local option income or payroll taxes. Where such taxes are permissible, they are usually collected at the county level, although in some states they may be imposed by municipalities (cities). Where these taxes are permitted and where the state does not impose a strict cap on such taxes, they may become significant. Compare, for example, columns 3 and 4 in table 7.1. Column 3 reports state sales tax rates, while column 4 shows the combined rate for the state sales tax and the local option sales tax. In Alabama, for example, the sales tax jumps from 4 percent (state) to about 8 percent when we include the local-option sales tax. The same is true in the state of New York. Similar increases occur in Colorado, Louisiana, Missouri, and Oklahoma—suggesting a heavy reliance on local option taxes in these states.

The Regressive Character of State and Local Tax Systems

As mentioned earlier, the way a state structures its overall tax system—and that of its local governments—defines several fiscal consequences. How the tax burden is spread among the citizens of the state is one of these. As any introductory textbook on macroeconomics will point out, tax structures may be progressive, proportional, or regressive. A progressive tax is one that takes a larger percentage as income rises; a proportional tax takes the same percentage from all income levels, and one that is regressive taxes people with lower incomes at a higher rate than wealthier people. The focus here is on rate, or percentage, not on the total amount the tax generates. Even a regressive tax will often mean a wealthier person is paying a greater amount than a poor person, even if the wealthy person is paying a lower percentage. For example, if Person A makes $100,000 and pays 5 percent toward taxes and Person B makes only $10,000 but pays 15 percent toward taxes, A pays $5,000 while B pays $1,500. Person A paid more in actual dollars ($5,000 to $1,500) but considerably less as a percentage of her income (5 percent compared 15 percent for B). Nonetheless, the discussion about the regressive, proportional, or progressive nature of the tax structure is a common one because it is ultimately a discussion about what "share" of one's income goes to taxes, and what amounts to a "fair share" across various income levels. To illustrate how the tax structures of states can affect the citizens, consider figure 7.6. The state of New York has a tax structure that is basically proportional, and even slightly progressive at least when we compare the tax burden of the lowest quintile (lowest 20 percent of income earners) to the highest quintile (highest 20 percent of income earners). The lowest quintile pays 9.6 percent if its income as state/local taxes while the highest quintile pays 10.5 percent. The middle class (represented as the third quintile) actually pays a

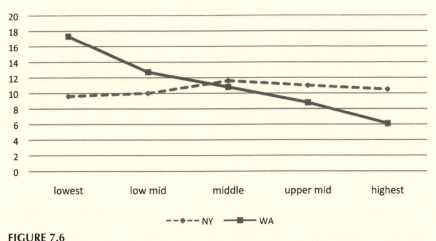

FIGURE 7.6
Comparing tax burden of income groups in NY and WA (percent of income that goes to state/local taxes).

slightly higher (11.6 percent) portion of its income to state and local taxes, so the New York system is not perfectly progressive. It looks, however, very different from the state of Washington's situation, in which the lower income groups are paying a much higher percentage (17.3 percent) of their limited income to state and local taxes while the wealthiest quintile is only paying 6.1 percent. This is a dramatically regressive tax structure.

The fact of the matter is that almost all state and local tax structures are regressive. The reason is that most excise taxes, licenses and user fees, and sales taxes are regressive. For example, a $100-per-year automobile registration fee is a larger percent of the income of someone making $5,000 a year than it is of someone making $50,000 a year. In this case, the tax is a flat fee of $100, regardless of income. A sales tax is also regressive because it is based on the purchase of goods (consumption) rather than income. Most state and local governments rely heavily on fees, sales, and excise taxes. For the most part, the only tax that can be designed as truly proportional or even progressive is the income tax. Thus, the degree of regressivity of a state and local tax structure is largely a matter of how much that state relies on a progressive income tax structure instead of a general sales tax or user fees. Table 7.3 shows the regressive nature of most state and local tax structures. The states with the most regressive tax structures are Washington, Florida, Wyoming, Texas, and Tennessee—all states without a personal income tax, and therefore states that rely more heavily on sales and excise taxes and user fees, all of which are regressive.[43] New York has a slightly progressive tax structure (at least when comparing the poorest and wealthiest quintiles). Several states have state and local tax structures that approach proportionality: South Carolina, Vermont, Wisconsin, Maine, and Minnesota are examples.

TABLE 7.3
State Tax Burdens for Different Income Groups

State	Tax Burden for Lowest Quintile (lowest 20% in state)	Tax Burden for Middle Quintile (middle 20% in state)	Tax Burden for Highest Quintile (highest 20% in state)	Measure of Regressive Tax Structure*
AL	10.2%	9.5%	6.1%	67
AK	7.0	4.0	3.2	119
AZ	12.5	9.1	6.1	104
AR	12.1	11.7	8.4	44
CA	10.2	8.1	7.6	34
CO	10.2	8.2	6.0	50
CT	12.0	9.9	8.1	48
DE	6.0	5.4	5.0	20
FL	13.5	9.0	5.2	160
GA	11.7	10.3	8.1	44
HI	12.2	11.2	7.5	63
ID	8.6	8.2	7.3	18
IL	13.0	10.1	7.7	69
IN	11.9	10.4	7.6	57
IA	11.0	9.6	8.4	31
KS	9.2	9.0	7.7	19
KY	9.4	10.8	8.3	13
LA	10.4	9.8	6.9	51
ME	9.5	9.8	9.1	4
MD	9.9	9.8	7.8	27
MA	10.1	9.6	7.4	36
MI	8.9	9.5	7.7	16
MN	9.2	10.0	8.7	6
MS	10.8	10.7	7.5	44
MO	9.6	9.2	7.3	32
MT	6.1	6.0	5.2	17
NE	11.1	10.3	8.0	39
NV	8.9	6.4	4.1	117
NH	8.3	6.3	4.3	93
NJ	10.7	8.6	8.0	34
NM	10.8	9.9	7.1	52
NY	9.6	11.6	10.5	−9
NC	9.5	9.4	7.7	23
ND	9.4	7.9	5.8	62
OH	12.0	10.6	8.5	41
OK	9.9	9.0	6.6	50
OR	8.7	7.9	7.3	19
PA	11.2	9.1	6.7	67
RI	11.9	10.1	8.3	43
SC	7.1	7.6	7.0	1
SD	11.0	7.8	5.0	120
TN	11.7	9.3	5.3	121

State	Tax Burden for Lowest Quintile (lowest 20% in state)	Tax Burden for Middle Quintile (middle 20% in state)	Tax Burden for Highest Quintile (highest 20% in state)	Measure of Regressive Tax Structure*
TX	12.2	8.5	5.4	125
UT	9.3	8.6	6.7	39
VT	8.2	9.4	8.0	2
VA	8.8	8.4	6.7	31
WA	17.3	10.8	6.1	183
WV	9.7	9.3	8.2	18
WI	9.2	10.6	8.8	4
WY	8.3	6.1	3.6	131
MEAN	10.9	9.4	7.2	51

*Calculated by authors as percentage difference between the lowest quintile and highest quintile ((HQ-LQ)/HQ). Higher values represent more regressive tax structures.

Source: "Who Pays? A Distributional Analysis of the Tax Systems in All 50 states." Institute on Taxation & Economic Policy, November 2009. Calculated using data after federal tax offset.

Fiscal Federalism: Federal Aid to States (and Localities)

Fiscal federalism is a touchy subject for the states. On the one hand, state officials (especially state elected officials) assert the independence, sovereignty, and innovation capacity of their state. On the other hand, the same officials are willing to accept federal financial assistance during tough times. As mentioned earlier in the chapter, in 2009 ARRA provided a substantial infusion of federal funds to help the states weather the worst of the recession.[44] Those funds were used by the states in many ways, but principal among them was to help the states pay their share of Medicaid costs and to extend unemployment benefits for longer periods than usual.[45] ARRA funds also helped many states avoid cuts (or avoid deeper cuts) in K–12 and higher-education funding and to continue or start a number of infrastructure construction projects (e.g., road building and other "shovel ready" infrastructure projects). Without this additional assistance from the federal government, there is little doubt that state and local governments would have suffered even greater program cuts than they did. Of course, there was the requisite partisan posturing first. Several governors, among them Republicans Bobby Jindal of Louisiana and Mark Sanford of South Carolina, announced that their states would not accept some of the "bailout" funds. Ultimately, however, the legislatures in both states passed bills that accepted virtually all the money available to them.[46] It is hard for a state to walk away from federal money.[47]

But this particular example of fiscal federalism (ARRA) occurred under unusually severe economic circumstances. Most federal aid is ongoing, annual transfers of money from the federal government to state or local governments with very specific conditions and guidelines ("strings attached") for the use of those funds. Federal grants, therefore, are not part of the state "general fund" budget but rather are part of the nondiscretionary part of the budget over which states have considerably less control. Moreover, most federal grant-in-aid programs require that states share in the cost by using some state funds to pay for part of the program, as with the Medicaid and TANF programs discussed in chapter 5. This is known as the "match" or "cost-share" that the state must contribute. As David Brunori observes, "In this regard, the amount of federal funds received by states is deceiving. State governments generally cannot spend federal monies as they wish. Thus, aid from the federal government lessens state control over the underlying policy program."[48]

Some of the programs mandated by the federal government (perhaps especially environmental and health-care programs) might go unfunded in some states without the federal mandate. As previously discussed, figure 7.5 shows federal aid to the states and illustrates that while it has increased over the long term, it does fluctuate. Overall, of the money state and local governments spend, over the last several generations a larger proportion of it has come from the federal government. And if the money comes from the federal government, it almost always comes with conditions. The consequence is that the state loses some control over policy making, as the federal "strings" require states or local governments to do certain things.

As a result of the growing concerns over the federal debt, it is very likely that some types of federal aid to the states will diminish. If reductions come to pass they will pose additional difficulties for the states and their local governments, as the programs currently funded in part by federal grants will have to be pared back, eliminated altogether, or funded by an increase in state revenues, likely necessitating an increase in state taxes. None of these are politically attractive alternatives; nonetheless, this is the reality facing state (and local) officials.

While figure 7.5 shows the proportion of state revenues received through federal aid over the years, what it does not show is how the nature of that aid has changed. At one time, the largest federal aid program was physical infrastructure needs—especially the construction of the interstate highway system. Over time, the federal aid emphasis has shifted away from infrastructure to social programs, especially health care in the form of Medicaid (see figure 7.7).

In 1960, there was no Medicaid (health care, largely for lower-income groups) program at all. Highway grants were the largest federal aid program (accounting for 43 percent of federal aid), followed by income security ("welfare," primarily Aid to Families with Dependent Children at 38 percent), and education and unemployment (8 percent). Those three functional areas accounted for almost nine out of every ten dollars of federal aid.

By 1980, federal aid was flowing to the four functional areas of health care, welfare, education/unemployment, and transportation in a roughly equal manner, and federal aid was increasing modestly for all four functional areas. As

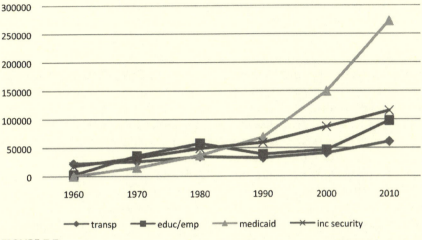

FIGURE 7.7
Federal aid by functional area. *Note:* Dollar figures are in constant dollars.

figure 7.7 shows, this trend changes dramatically after 1990. Medicaid, which had been created in 1965, had become the driving force behind the increase in federal aid, and by 2010 it accounted for virtually half of all fiscal federalism.

To look at this point from another angle, consider that most grant money goes to one of two purposes: costs to provide for individuals and costs to build or maintain physical infrastructure. In 1960, only 35 percent of all federal aid went to payments for individuals (health care, welfare, unemployment, etc.). About half of all federal aid was for "physical capital" (i.e., infrastructure).[49] By 2011, payments to individuals accounted for 64 percent and infrastructure costs accounted for only 16 percent. In other words, between 1960 and 2011 "human costs" went from about one-third to about two-thirds of all federal aid dollars. In a half century, the broader purpose behind federal assistance to the states and their local governments had shifted from infrastructure to social services. What this suggests is that any reduction in federal aid will have a human face attached to it—meaning that the decisions about what the state should do about these programs will directly affect some citizens of the state. Sequestration (the so-called fiscal cliff much discussed at the beginning of 2013) provided a glimpse into this future. The congressional sequester of funds mandated $54 billion in cuts. A significant portion of those cuts were in the federal aid programs to the states. Certain programs, such as Medicaid, were protected, but many others were not. Analysts estimate that almost 20 percent of the grant funds were subject to across-the-board cuts, including aid to K–12 education; Women, Infants, and Children (WIC, a program to provide nutrition to low-income women and children); and low-income housing programs, among others.[50]

State (and Local) Expenditures

The first point to emphasize is that the services and regulatory actions performed at the local level—by cities, counties, and so on—are ultimately the responsibility of the state government. States delegate some of their governmental responsibilities to local governments because it makes sense to do so. But exactly which responsibilities they delegate, and to which local governments and to what extent they are delegated—these are questions that are answered differently by each state. It is, in other words, a complex situation. We will try to simplify it by using the term "subnational" to refer to actions of both the state and local governments, when appropriate. Public education, for example, is clearly a subnational responsibility—one shared and funded by both state and local governments. While K–12 education is delivered at the local government level, state constitutions generally hold the state government responsible for providing primary and secondary education.

As noted in chapter 5, historically, the largest state and local expenditure is public education. In 1980, almost 40 percent of all subnational expenditures were for education. This includes public schools (K–12), community and vocational-technical colleges, and state universities. Expenditures in other functional areas in 1980 were pretty evenly distributed between health (13 percent), welfare and social services (10 percent), public safety (10 percent), and transportation and economic development (11 percent). A generation later, in 2010, the expenditure pattern had shifted (see table 7.4). State and local expenditures on health care have increased substantially, now accounting for over 20 percent of all spending for subnational governments. The only other area in which in which state and local governments are now spending a greater share of their funds than in 1980 is public safety. This is largely due to the increase in spending on corrections (prisons). Relatively speaking, the biggest loser in the past thirty years is public education; its share of spending has dropped from 39 percent to 33 percent.

Public education remains the single largest subnational expenditure, by a substantial margin. And, just to be clear, the actual total dollars spent on education

TABLE 7.4
Combined State and Local Expenditures, 1980 and 2010
(as percentage of total expenditures)

Functional Area	1980	2010	Increase/Decrease
Public Education	39	33	−6
Health	13	22	+9
Social Services	10	8	−2
Public Safety	10	13	+3
Transportation and Development	11	8	−3

Source: General Accountability Office, "State and Local Governments' Fiscal conditions: Frequently Asked Questions." www.gao.gov/special.pubs/longterm/state/fiscalconditionsfaq.html.

have not declined; in fact, they have increased substantially. But the relative position of public education compared to other functional areas—especially health care—has clearly eroded. Most of this decline is in state support for higher education, not for K–12 schools. While public colleges and universities have seen their relative slice of the state budget pie diminish slowly for several decades, the cuts were substantial in some states during the Great Recession. In three years, the University of Washington saw its state support drop from $400 million to $200 million.[51] The University of North Carolina has experienced a drop of $230 million during the same time period.[52]

Expanding health-care costs are a major concern, especially for state-level officials. The reason is that Medicaid costs continue to absorb an ever-increasing share of the state budget.[53] Medicaid costs to the states have increased an average of 7 percent per year over the past decade—that means the costs have basically doubled in ten years.[54] Indeed, the National Association of State Budget Officers (NASBO) recently reported that Medicaid is the single largest expense now for state governments (23.6 percent), surpassing K–12 spending (20.1 percent).[55] Moreover, Medicaid costs increase during an economic downturn. As more people become unemployed and lose job-related health-care insurance, they become eligible for health-care benefits through Medicaid. So the demand for Medicaid benefits increases but the supply of state revenue to fund those benefits decreases (since the unemployed pay less in taxes). It is, in other words, a procyclical effect. For example, the Medicaid caseload in Colorado grew by 19 percent as the Great Recession took effect.[56]

An increasingly significant expenditure for subnational governments is their contribution to public-employee pension funds. As the National Conference of State Legislatures notes, "State pension funds have been impacted by underfunding of obligations and by the severe economic recession."[57] Historically, retirement packages for many state and local employees included "defined benefit" plans, meaning that recipients would receive a specific, defined, annual retirement benefit based on their years of service and the salaries they earned. These benefits (pensions) are paid from a fund the state and local government maintains. In most instances, this retirement fund relies on income from three sources: contributions from the public employee, direct appropriations from the state or local government budget, and revenue generated by investments of pension funds. Today, many of these pension accounts are underfunded; they do not contain enough money to meet their obligations as public-employee baby boomers begin to retire. In part, this problem was caused by the Great Recession, which caused pension fund investments to perform poorly. But it is also the case that many states opted not to make their required contributions, using the money instead to fund other priorities. The public-employee pension problem is especially acute in California, Connecticut, Illinois, and Rhode Island, but at least another half-dozen states are also seriously underfunded. The Pew Center on the States has referred to this as "the trillion dollar gap" and it is a looming demand side (expenditure) problem for many states.

One result of this situation is a movement to change the way public-employee pensions are funded in the future. Many states are instituting "defined contribution" plans for the newly hired, where the employee and employer both contribute to a retirement account that the employee controls. Once the state makes its contribution, however, it is no longer on the financial hook in the manner it is with a traditional "defined benefit" plan. The financial risk is transferred completely onto the employee.

Conclusion

In this chapter we have discussed a number of factors that, in combination, bode ill for state fiscal systems. The balanced-budget rules and heavy reliance on income and general sales taxes as revenue sources mean that state fiscal systems tend to be procyclical. To exacerbate the situation, economic downturns trigger a higher demand for state social services (unemployment benefits, health care, and the like). Furthermore, federal aid to the states is likely to diminish as the national government grapples with its own very substantial fiscal problems. As two public finance experts note, "While the federal government has recently provided antirecession assistance to states and localities in the short term, escalating deficits in the short and long term will sap the flexibility and capacity of the federal government to play its time-honored role as the equalizer in public finance."[58] Meanwhile, many states are facing public-employee pension obligations that are not fully funded, and the baby boomers who work for the states are about to retire.

To compound the situation, many states are experiencing an infrastructure system that is rapidly deteriorating. Well-publicized bridge collapses in Minnesota and in the state of Washington are dramatic contemporary examples of the situation. Recently, the American Society of Civil Engineers graded the quality of American infrastructure—the roads, highways, bridges, and levees—as "D+." Much of the responsibility for dealing with the sorry state of the infrastructure will fall to the states. Interestingly, some Republican governors—usually extremely reticent to discuss tax hikes—are pushing to raise gasoline taxes or automobile license fees as a way to generate money for road and highway upgrades.[59]

It will be necessary for states to face these issues head-on. "State's Rights" also means "state's responsibilities." It may also mean "opportunities for the states." Given the extent of the federal deficit, and given that most federal aid now and in the future will have to be spent on health care, now is the time for states to think about their role and responsibility in the other policy arenas. This includes the way in which states allow their local governments to address problems at the community level.

8

Why States Matter Now

I N THE PREVIOUS CHAPTERS, we have made the case that states continue to matter in the American federal system. They are important because many significant policy decisions are made at the state level. They are important because federal policy is often administered through state agencies. They are important because states are often innovative policy makers, in some cases well in advance of the national government. They are important because they offer a greater role for the individual citizen through the instruments of direct democracy. They are important because the states are the electoral source of all national elected officials. They are important because they generate and spend billions of dollars on their own and determine how local governments operate. In a recent interview, Thomas Gais, director of the Rockefeller Institute of Government, pointed out that,

> A lot of people don't realize that state and local governments carry out the great bulk of domestic policies in the United States. The federal government administers some big domestic programs such as Social Security, Medicare, SSI and a few others. For the most part, however, when you're talking about the domestic programs, state and local governments make them happen. Out of eight people working for governments in the United States, seven of them are on the state and local payrolls. My guess is that states will continue to acquire more and more responsibilities.[1]

States in an Ever-Evolving Federal System

The American experiment with federalism was just beginning as the eighteenth century was ending. It was a new political system for a nascent nation, and there was much uncertainty about exactly how the new arrangement would work in practice. For the nineteenth century, historians and political scientists often characterize the arrangement that developed as "dual federalism," meaning that each level of government had its own sphere of operation, and the national level did not intrude very much into what was considered the state sphere. This characterization is, of course, a simplification. In fact, there was considerable disagreement about the proper roles to be played by each level.

As we noted in earlier chapters, the New England states resisted some of the federal government's actions surrounding the War of 1812, as illustrated by the Hartford Convention. John C. Calhoun, of South Carolina, ardently defended slavery and states' rights and was a central figure in the 1832 Nullification Crisis. He argued that states not only had the right to nullify odious federal laws, but that they also had the right to secede from the Union. By 1861, Southern efforts to leave resulted in the Civil War. More than six hundred thousand soldiers died in that war—more not just as a percentage of the population but also in raw numbers than any other war in American history.[2] Perhaps "Duel Federalism" is a more apt description of the period than "Dual Federalism."

During the latter half of the nineteenth century and continuing in to the twentieth century, the nature of the relationship between the national and state governments changed. Some of the changes were wrought by the European wave of immigration prior to World War I, the rapid population growth, and the transition from a rural to an urban society brought on by industrialization. Recall that at the beginning of the twentieth century the US population stood at about 100 million. By the close of the century it was about 300 million. In 1900, the majority, about 60 percent of Americans, still lived in rural areas. By the close of the century about 80 percent lived in urban and suburban areas. A huge transformation of American society had occurred. Many local governments, especially cities, adapted and expanded their service and regulatory functions.

Meanwhile, after two world wars and a severe economic depression, the national government emerged as a much stronger presence. Thus, both the national and local levels of government adjusted to modern times. Meanwhile, many states languished. Still geared toward a rural society, many of them resisted making the transition. One journalist lamented "the shocking depth to which state government has sunk in the United States."[3]

As the country was urbanizing, many legislatures remained dominated by rural interests, largely due to lingering malapportionment. One observer proclaimed that "state legislatures may be our most extreme example of institutional lag. In their formal qualities they are largely nineteenth century organizations and they must, or should address themselves to twentieth century problems."[4] As Stephen Ansolabehere and James Snyder note, "Over the course of a century, the state legislatures evolved from the wellsprings of American government into political backwaters."[5] The president of the US Conference of Mayors in 1949 wrote that "American cities are under the control of unsympathetic state legislatures dominated by agricultural oligarchies."[6]

By mid-century, then, there was growing pressure to "do something" about state governments generally, and about state legislatures in particular. The American Political Science Association commissioned a study, and the Council of State Governments created committees to make reform recommendations.[7] Several other organizations aimed at modernizing state governments were active. One of these organizations was the National Municipal League, which had become frustrated with what they saw as unsympathetic views of the states toward their own cities and urban problems.

Thus, at roughly the same time of the "reapportionment revolution" there began a concerted effort to upgrade and modernize the institutions of state government. California was at the forefront of this movement, but others followed quickly. The Eagleton Institute of Politics at Rutgers University provided an institutional locus, often with funding from benefactors like the Carnegie Corporation and the Ford Foundation. The Eagleton Institute provided commissioned analyses of state legislatures in at least eight states. Meanwhile, many states pursued their own reform agendas; commissions to review and recommend changes to state legislative practices were created in Pennsylvania, West Virginia, Iowa, Illinois, Idaho, Oregon, and Washington.[8] As we discussed in chapter 4, similar modernization efforts were made on behalf of the executive and judicial branches. Moreover, numerous states transformed their fiscal systems during the last few decades of the twentieth century. By 1980, states had emerged as stronger and more capable partners in the federal system. Their metamorphosis has been called a "quiet revolution," a "resurgence," and "a phoenix-like resurrection of federalism."[9]

Getting Beyond "Zero-Sum Games" and the "Alabama Syndrome"

Reemergence of the states is not a topic that is well understood. First, there is the proclivity to view developments in federalism as a zero-sum game. As Alison La-Croix states, "the debate is nearly always framed in terms of a binary confrontation" in which either the national government wins or the states win.[10] We have tried to show that federalism in today's world is much more complicated than that simple characterization.

Second, even today, despite the irrefutable progress made by states as policy making and administrative units over the past forty years, there is a lingering tendency to judge states by their lowest common denominator. This phenomenon has been called "the Alabama syndrome" and refers to the reluctance of the federal government decision makers in the 1960s to give any latitude to state administrators in administering new federal policies like Medicare or the

"War on Poverty" for fear of what a "George Wallace would do" with that sort of power.[11] For some, that period still colors their perception of the relationship between the national government and the states. As one expert on the subject wrote, "The tenacity and violence of southern resistance to changes in race relations gave federalism a very bad name."[12]

Clearly, not all states are the same. We have sought to document that fact in this book. Some states are leaders and some states are laggards on any given policy. Perhaps we are reluctant to embrace an expanded role for the states precisely because we lack confidence in some states to "do the right thing," whatever we perceive that to be on any given policy.

Most people are inconsistent in their views of the proper federal–state relationship. Members of both political parties are guilty on this score. People favor a national or state approach depending on the particular issue, the relative position of the national government and any given state on that issue, and their own opinion on that issue. Politicians, in particular, use varying positions on what federalism "ought" to look like as an "expedient tool," according to David Brian Robertson, who points out that "federalism has been used by and against Republicans as well as Democrats, liberals as well as conservatives and innovators as well as those who resist change."[13] In this regard, people are focused on generating their preferred policy outcome and are less concerned about the process that produces the result they want. When it comes to federalism, we are all hypocrites. So federalism gets something of a black mark against it because everyone seizes on the policies that some states produce that they do not prefer.

States and the Task Ahead

As one expert on federalism notes, "The most appealing reason for courts to enforce limits on Congress and to preserve the role of autonomous states is the prediction that states will in fact experiment with new policies, looking for new ways to serve the public good."[14] This comment, of course, harkens back to Justice Brandeis' "laboratories of democracy" argument. The notion may be particularly pertinent today, for several reasons. First, the federal deficit will almost certainly require cutbacks in federal aid, especially outside the health-care area. Second, changes in technology and communication are such today that states are imminently aware of the policy choices undertaken by other states. Policy makers and administrators in one state talk to their counterparts in another state. They are aware of the options available, especially as some associations, policy groups, think tanks, and others provide such information to state policy makers. Finally, there is a strong argument to be made for allowing states some latitude to pursue their own preferences, as it is clear that states still differ in terms of political culture. The party realignment, or sorting, that began in the 1960s and

1970s is complete, and many states appear to be "more red" or "more blue" today as fewer states are experiencing divided government. As Ann Althouse succinctly states, "There are times for the national government to stand back and let policies emerge at the lower level of decision making."[15] This is likely to be one of those times.

Recently, the venerable British newsmagazine *The Economist* published a special report on how the states were leading the way in search of innovative policies to reinvigorate the United States. The article was aptly entitled, "Let 50 Flowers Bloom" and noted that "[A]merica's 50 states are consciously and vigorously competing to find the best formula for regulation and taxes and introducing sweeping reforms to that end. . . . Whether or not Congress puts aside its fiscal vendetta long enough to help with any of this, progress is being made around the country."[16]

The challenges for state governments, and for their local governments, will be great. The biggest challenge will be the financial one, as many states are likely to face, in the words of one observer, "prolonged fiscal austerity."[17] Alice Rivlin, former head of the federal Office of Management and Budget (OMB), argues that the combination of the current federal deficit and the aging of the population results in a long-term structural imbalance that is unsustainable.[18] As the federal budget problems continue, there will be a tremendous incentive for national policy makers to simply push the cost of administering programs down to the state level. Indeed, this has been happening for some time. The National Conference of State Legislatures estimates that the administration of George W. Bush off loaded over $100 billion in program administrative costs onto the states. Such unfunded mandates may help the federal government's books, but it poses major fiscal problems for the states.

Increasingly, state officials will have to make hard choices between paring back or eliminating programs or raising taxes and fees. In a recent review of American federalism, the authors observed that "Mounting concern about federal debt, partisan politics, and legislative gridlock at the federal level has also contributed to the need for states to step up and take matters into their own hands."[19] Demography and economics are conspiring to force the states to the policy fore.

The Public's Responsibility

The first task of the public citizen is to be better informed of the role that states play. While states remain essential partners in the American federal system, they are not often presented as such. For one thing, from the media's point of view, there is rarely a natural state constituency. News is usually viewed as being either national or local in scope.[20] Over time, there are fewer and fewer reporters covering the "state capitol beat."[21] A recent survey found that newspapers were assigning one-third fewer reporters full-time to the state capitol than they had just a decade earlier. As the report notes, "State governments have more power and more money than ever before. . . . Everyone—political parties, academics, trade organizations, labor unions, corporations—has discovered this. Everyone, that is, except the press."[22]

Even when there is coverage from the state level, it is almost always just about a particular state. In this sense, there is very little comparative reporting occurring. This is understandable, since most consumers of the news are only interested in what is happening in their own state—if they are interested at all![23] But without a comparative perspective, we miss most of the trends in state policy making, and we miss the bigger picture of the changes in the federal relationship. There are, however, a few excellent sources of comparative state political news available, such as *Governing* magazine and stateline.org. Unfortunately, these sources are not well known to the general public. They should be. One gains a greater appreciation for the vitality of the states through such venues.

It is only through a comparative framework that we can truly appreciate the advantage of a federal system. The public needs to understand that states only matter if they have the freedom to try a variety of approaches to solving public problems and that they have the ability to do so within the political and cultural context of each state. There are limits to such variation, of course. In a compound republic, both individual rights and state's rights have a place. "State's rights" is an easy phrase to toss about, especially when one is frustrated with the national government. But with rights also come responsibilities to the citizens of the state, and not just the citizens who form the majority. There is a cost to having the states continue to matter as we enter a period of austerity. It may be a cost in the form of reduced services or the entire elimination of programs in some instances. It may be a cost in the form of higher state and local taxes in order to replace federal aid. It may well be both. The most important task of the citizen is to understand there are hard choices ahead and the value of having a variety of policy options explored.

Notes

Chapter 1

1. We are not the first to point out the policy differences affecting the residents of these two cities. See James Gimpel and Jason E. Schuknecht, *Patchwork Nation* (Ann Arbor: University of Michigan Press, 2004), 7.

2. The 1790 Pennsylvania Constitution actually required free public education for those who could not afford it on their own, but legislation creating such public schools did not pass for some years.

3. US Census Bureau, "1790 Fast Facts," www.census.gov/history/www.through_the_decades/fast_facts/1.

4. "Biggest US Cities by Population," www.google.com/url?sa=t&rct=j&q=&esrc=s&source=web&cd=8&ved=0CE8QFjAH&url=http%3A%2F%2Fwww.biggestuscities.com%2F&ei=Shd7UK7uCObtigLos4HwDQ&usg=AFQjCNHxmog_dU1pRYE146_KMD_KN3C-Ng.

5. Belle Zeller, *American State Legislatures: The Report of the Committee on American Legislatures* (New York: Greenwood Press, 1969 [reprinted with permission of Thomas Y. Crowell Company 1954], v.

6. Martha Derthick, *Keeping the Compact Republic: Essays on American Federalism*. (Washington, DC: The Brookings Institution, 2001), 3.

7. Derthick, *Keeping the Compact Republic*, 3

8. The quote is from Daniel Webster, as cited in Samuel Beer, *To Make a Nation: The Rediscovery of American Federalism* (Cambridge, MA: The Belknap Press of Harvard University Press, 1993), 12.

9. For a thoughtful summary of these events and the changes they wrought, see Martha Derthick, "Federalism," in Peter H. Schuck and James Q. Wilson, eds., *Understanding America* (New York: PublicAffairs, 2008), 121–45.

10. Terry Sanford, *Storm Over the States* (New York: McGraw-Hill Book Company, 1967), 21.

11. Robert Allen, "The Shame of the States," in Robert S. Allen, ed., *Our Sovereign State* (New York: Vanguard Press, 1949), i.

12. Allen, "The Shame of the States," iii.

13. Jon C. Teaford, *The Rise of the States* (Baltimore: The Johns Hopkins University Press, 2002), 2

14. See especially Teaford, *The Rise of the States*.

15. Alan Rosenthal, *Heavy Lifting: The Job of the American Legislature* (Washington, DC: CQ Press, 2004), 7–8, and Donald Herzberg and Alan Rosenthal, eds. *Strengthening the States* (Garden City, NY: Anchor Books, 1972), ix.

16. The Pew Research Center, "Growing Gap in Favorable Views of Federal, State Government." April 26, 2012, www.people-press.org/2012/04/26/growing-gap-in-favorable-views-of-federal-state-governments/. Also see Gallup, "Trust in Government, September 2012," www.gallup.com/poll/5392/trust-government.aspx.

17. As noted in chapter 4, states are not required to allocate their Electoral College votes in a "winner-take-all" manner. But all states except Maine and Nebraska do so.

18. Andrew Gelman, David Park, Boris Shor, Joseph Bafumi, and Jeronimo Cortina, *Red State, Blue State, Rich State, Poor State* (Princeton, NJ: Princeton University Press, 2008), 21–22.

19. This point is often made in the context of the growing polarization in the U.S. See, for example, Alan Abramowitz, *The Disappearing Center* (New Haven, CT: Yale University Press, 2010).

20. Bill Bishop, *The Big Sort: Why the Clustering of Like-Minded Americans is Tearing Us Apart* (Boston: Houghton Mifflin, 2008), 5.

21. Not everyone agrees with Bishop's "big sort" argument. For another view, see Samuel J. Abrams and Morris P. Fiorina, "The 'Big Sort' That Wasn't: A Skeptical Reexamination," *PS: Political Science and Politics* (April 2012): 203–10.

22. Gimpel and Schuknecht, *Patchwork Nation*, 9

23. Daniel Elazar, *American Federalism: A View from the States* (New York: Thomas Crowell Co., 1966), 6.

24. Gross state product is from the Department of Commerce, Bureau of Economic Analysis, www.bea.gov/newsreleases/regional/gdp_state/gsp_newsrelease.htm. Gross National Product is taken from the World Bank, databank.worldbank.org/databank/download/GDP.pdf.

25. Frank Newport, "State of the States: Importance of Religion," www.gallup.com/poll/114022/state-states-importance-religion.aspx.

26. Michael S. Lewis-Beck and Peverill Squire, "Iowa: The Most Representative State?" *PS: Political Science and Politics* 42 (2009): 39–44.

27. For a description of the three ideal types of state political culture, see Elazar, *American Federalism: A View from the States*.

28. Bishop, *The Big Sort*, 299

29. Bishop, *The Big Sort*, 222.

30. Karl Kurtz, "A Significant Decline in Divided Government," November 7, 2012 on the National Conference of State Legislatures' blog, *The Thicket*.

31. As quoted in Karl Kurtz, "These Unified States," *State Legislatures* (May 2013).

32. Kurtz, "These United States," op. cit.

33. Dylan Scott, "Could Gay Marriage, Marijuana and Guns Lead to a Fragmented United States of America?" *Governing* (June 2013): 44.

34. James Q. Wilson, John J. Dilulo, Jr., and Meena Bose, *American Government*, 13th ed. (Belmont, CA: Wadsworth, 2013), 63.

Chapter 2

1. Sixty-first Legislature of the State of Idaho, HB 117, p. 2, lines 39–44.

2. *Florida v. Sibelius (2010)*, No. 3:10-CV-91-RV-EMT (N.D. Fla. March 23, 2010).

3. Mahalley D. Allen, "Federalism," in Donald Haider-Markel, ed. *Political Encyclopedia of U.S. States and Regions* (Washington, DC: CQ Press, 2009), 766.

4. John D. Donahue, *Disunited States* (New York: Basic Books, 1997), 17.

5. For purposes of simplicity, we use the term "states" here as the conventional term for regional government, it is not necessarily the term used in some of the federal systems we have identified.

6. Nicole Bolleyer and Lori Thorlakson, "Beyond Decentralization—The Comparative Study of Interdependence in Federal Systems," *Publius: The Journal of Federalism* 42, no. 4 (2012): 576. The eleven countries that meet their criteria are Argentina, Australia, Austria, Belgium, Canada, Germany, India, South Africa, Spain, Switzerland, and the United States.

7. Ronald L. Watts, "Federalism, Federal Political Systems, and Federations," *Annual Review of Political Science* 1 (1998): 123–24.

8. The four are the United States, Switzerland, Canada, and Australia. David E. Smith, *Federalism and the Constitution of Canada* (Toronto: University of Toronto Press, 2010), 17.

9. Campbell Gibson and Kay Jung, "Historical Census Statistics on Population Totals By Race, 1790 to 1990," US Census Bureau: Working Paper #56 (September 2002).

10. The figure is from Russell Thornton, *American Indian Holocaust and Survival: A Population History Since 1492* (Norman: University of Oklahoma Press, 1987), 133.

11. Thomas S. Kidd, *Patrick Henry, First Among Patriots* (New York: Basic Books, 2011), 183.

12. This discussion relies, in part, on William J. Bennett, *American Theories of Federalism* (Tuscaloosa: The University of Alabama Press, 1964), 128, chap. 3.

13. The quote appears on p. 103 of Bennett, *American Theories of Federalism*, who cites H. V. Ames, ed., *State Documents on Federal Relations* (Philadelphia, 1911) as his source. Also see Thomas E. Woods, Jr., *Nullification* (Washington DC: Regnery Publishing, 2010), chap. 3.

14. Bennett, *American Theories of Federalism*, 92–100.

15. John Dinan, "Contemporary Assertions of State Sovereignty and the Safeguards of American Federalism," *Albany Law Review* 74, no. 4 (2011): 1665.

16. See Christian G. Fritz, "Interposition and the Heresy of Nullification: James Madison and the Exercise of Sovereign Constitutional Powers" (Washington DC: The Heritage Foundation, 2012). This is Number 41 of the "First Principles" series of the Heritage Foundation, and can be found at report.heritage.org/fp41. Also see Bennett, *American Theories of Federalism*, especially pp. 98–100. For a different view that supports the constitutionality of nullification see Woods, Jr., *Nullification*.

17. See, for example, Jack N. Rakove, *Original Meanings* (New York: Vintage Books, 1996), chap. 7.

18. Cecelia M. Kenyon, ed., *The Antifederalists* (Indianapolis: Bobbs-Merrill, 1966). See her introduction, pp. xxi–cxvi.

19. 17 U.S. 316.

20. Kenyon, ed., *The Antifederalists*, xliii.

21. There is also the issue of national supremacy in this case, but for our purposes the question of the meaning of the necessary and proper clause is most important.

22. *McCulloch v Maryland*, p. 405.

23. *McCulloch v. Maryland*, p. 406.

24. *McCulloch v. Maryland*, p. 421.

25. Martha Derthick, "Federalism," in Peter H. Schuck and James Q. Wilson, eds., *Understanding America* (New York: Public Affairs, 2008), 127.

26. Kenyon, ed., *The Antifederalists*, xliii

27. 317 US 111 (1942).

28. *United States v. Lopez* 514 US 549 (1995).

29. John Kincaid, "The Constitutional Frameworks of State and Local Government Finance," in Robert Ebel and John Petersen, eds., *The Oxford Handbook of State and Local Government Finance* (New York: Oxford University Press, 2012), 60.

30. John Kincaid reports that 45 percent of federal revenues come from the personal income tax, 12 percent from corporate income taxes, and 36 percent from Social Security and Medicare payroll

taxes. These sources constitute over 90 percent of federal revenues. See Kincaid, "The Constitutional Frameworks of State and Local Government Finance," 60.

31. Russell L. Hanson, "Intergovernmental Relations," in Virginia Gray, Russell Hanson, and Thad Kousser, eds., *Politics in the American States*, 10th ed. (Washington, DC: CQ Press, 2013), 39.

32. *The Federalist*, ed. Jacob E. Cooke (Cleveland, OH: The World Publishing Co., 1961), 417.

33. Kincaid, "The Constitutional Frameworks of State and Local Government Finance," 50–51.

34. The German federal system retains a system similar to that originally established in the US Senate. In the German instance, the upper chamber, the Federal Council, is comprised of members chosen by the legislatures of the Länder (the states).

35. Martha Derthick and John J. Dinan, ""Progressivism and Federalism," in Sidney M. Milkis and Jerome M. Mileur, eds., *Progressivism and the New Democracy* (Amherst: University of Massachusetts Press, 1999), 81.

36. William Riker, "The Senate and American Federalism," *American Political Science Review* 49 (1955): 455.

37. Alexander Heard, "Reform: Limits and Opportunities," in A. Heard, ed., *State Legislatures in America* (Englewood Cliffs, NJ: Prentice-Hall, 1966), 154.

38. L. Sandy Maisel and Mark Brewer, *Parties and Elections in America*, 5th ed. (Lanham, MD: Rowman & Littlefield, 2008), 47.

39. Derthick, "Federalism," 128.

40. As quoted in Christopher Sullivan, "1963 at 50: A Year's Tumult Echoes Still," Associated Press, January 14, 2013.

41. This was especially the case in Mississippi. For a history of the resistance to segregation in Mississippi, see Joseph Crespino, *In Search of Another Country: Mississippi and the Conservative Counterrevolution* (Princeton, NJ: Princeton University Press, 2007) or Neil McMillen, *The Citizens Council* (Champaign: University of Illinois Press, 1994).

42. Joseph F. Zimmerman, *Contemporary American Federalism: The Growth of National Power* (Westport, CT: Praeger, 1992), 11.

43. Derthick, "Federalism," 130.

44. While most Republican presidents at least pay some lip service to restoring the role of the states in the federal system, George W. Bush seemed reluctant to even make the symbolic gesture. As one observer noted, "He paid no honor to federalism." In addition to meeting substantial state resistance to his efforts to nationalize education policy and to create a national identification card, the cost of the expansion of prescription drug benefits to Medicare resulted in substantial cost increases to the states. Derthick, "Federalism," 136.

45. Derthick, "Federalism," 123.

46. Larry N. Gerston, *American Federalism: A Concise Introduction* (Armonk, NY: M.E. Sharpe, 2007).

47. Gerston, *American Federalism*, 32.

48. Martha Derthick, *Keeping the Compound Republic* (Washington, DC: Brookings Institution Press, 2001), 140.

49. David Walker, *The Rebirth of Federalism* (Chatham, NJ: Chatham House Publishers, 1995), xii.

50. John D. Nugent, *Safeguarding Federalism: How States Protect Their Interests in National Policymaking* (Norman: University of Oklahoma Press, 2009).

51. Nugent, *Safeguarding Federalism*, 225.

52. Dylan Scott, "Medicaid: What Now?," in *Governing* (December 2012): 48.

53. Zimmerman, *Contemporary American Federalism*, 196.

54. These and other examples are discussed in Sean Nicholson-Crotty, "Leaving Money on the Table: Learning from Recent Refusals of Federal Grants in the American States," *Publius: The Journal of Federalism* 42 (2012): 449–66.

55. Derthick, "Federalism," 140.

56. James MacGregor Burns, J. W. Peltason, Thomas Cronin, David Magleby, and David M. O'Brien, *Government by the People* (Upper Saddle River, NJ: Prentice Hall, 2002), 61.

57. David M. Thomas, "Past Futures: The Development and Evolution of American and Canadian Federalism," in David M. Thomas and Barbara Boyle Torrey, eds., *Canada and the United States: Differences That Count*, 3rd ed. (Peterborough, Ontario: Broadview Press, 2008), 28.

58. Zimmerman, *Contemporary American Federalism*, 164.

59. Zimmerman, *Contemporary American Federalism*, 176, table 8.1. Also see chapter 7 of this book.

60. As discussed in Derthick, "Federalism," 125.

61. Derthick, "Federalism," 125, italics added.

62. Alice Rivlin, "Rethinking Federalism for More Effective Governance," *Publius: The Journal of Federalism* 42 (2012): 299.

63. See, for example, Erin Ryan, *Federalism and the Tug of War Within* (New York: Oxford University Press, 2011).

Chapter 3

1. See the discussion in Peverill Squire, *The Evolution of American Legislatures: Colonies, Territories, and States, 1619-2009* (Ann Arbor: University of Michigan Press, 2012), 72–83.

2. James Madison, Alexander Hamilton, and John Jay, *The Federalist Papers* (New York: New American Library, 1961), 303–4.

3. Horst Dippel, "The Changing Idea of Popular Sovereignty in Early America Constitutionalism: Breaking Away from European Patterns," *Journal of the Early Republic* 16 (1996): 21–45; Gordon S. Wood, *Creation of the American Republic 1776–1787* (Chapel Hill: University of North Carolina Press, 1969), 446–53.

4. John W. Burgess, "The American Commonwealth: Changes in its Relation to the Nation," *Political Science Quarterly* 1 (1886): 9–35.

5. Peverill Squire and Keith E. Hamm, *101 Chambers: Congress, State Legislatures, and the Future of Legislative Studies* (Columbus: Ohio State University Press, 2005), 68.

6. See the discussion in Squire, *The Evolution of American Legislatures*, 243–48.

7. Squire, *The Evolution of American Legislatures*, 271–73.

8. Jonathan Elliot, *Debates on the Adoption of the Federal Constitution, in the Convention Held at Philadelphia, in 1787; with a Diary of the Debates of the Congress of the Confederation; as Reported by James Madison, a Member and Deputy from Virginia* (Washington, DC: Jonathan Elliot, 1845), 327.

9. See the discussion in Leslie Lipson, *The American Governor from Figurehead to Leader* (Chicago: University of Chicago Press, 1939), 17–30.

10. The following discussion is drawn from Rui J. P. de Figueredo Jr., "Budget Institutions and Political Insulation: Why States Adopt the Item Veto," *Journal of Public Economics* 87 (2003): 2677–701; John A. Fairlie, "The Veto Power of the Governor," *American Political Science Review* 11 (1917): 473–93; National Conference of State Legislatures, *Inside the Legislative Process*, table 98-6.10, www.ncsl.org/documents/legismgt/ILP/98Tab6Pt3.pdf, and various state constitutions.

11. See the discussion in Peverill Squire and Gary Moncrief, *State Legislatures Today: Politics under the Domes* (Boston: Longman, 2010), 216–18.

12. See the discussion of gubernatorial power in Margaret Ferguson, "Governors and the Executive Branch," in Virginia Gray, Russell L. Hanson, and Thad Kousser, eds., *Politics in the American States*, 10th ed. (Thousand Oaks, CA: Sage, 2013).

13. This discussion was taken from Finla Goff Crawford, *State Government* (New York: Henry Holt and Company, 1931), 181–82. See also, Legislative Reference Bureau, *Constitutional*

Convention Bulletin No. 9, The Executive Department (Springfield, IL: Legislative Reference Bureau, 1920), 623–25.

14. This list is taken from *The Book of the States*, 2012 ed. (Lexington, KY: Council of State Governments, 2012), 231–33.

15. www.dpi.state.nd.us/dept/bio.shtm

16. Lawrence M. Friedman, *A History of American Law* (New York: Touchstone, 1973), 122–23.

17. Friedman, *A History of American Law*, 123–24.

18. Charts of current state court structures can be found at www.courtstatistics.org/Other-Pages/State_Court_Structure_Charts.aspx.

19. See G. Alan Tarr, "The Past and Future of the New Judicial Federalism," *Publius* 24 (1994): 63–79.

20. Robert W. Williams, "Introduction: The Third Stage of New Judicial Federalism," *NYU Annual Survey of American Law* 59 (2003): 211–19.

21. See Carl T. Bogus, "The Battle for Separation of Powers in Rhode Island," *Administrative Law Review* 56 (2004): 77–134.

22. William C. Dawson, *A Compilation of the Laws of the State of Georgia, Passed by the General Assembly, Since the Year 1819 to the Year 1829, Inclusive* (Milledgeville, GA: Grantland and Orme, 1831).

Chapter 4

1. See Larry Sabato, *Goodbye to Good-Time Charlie*, 2nd ed. (Washington, DC: CQ Press, 1983).

2. James Reston, "Boston: Big Problems and Little Men in State Capital," *New York Times*, October 5, 1962.

3. Martin F. Nolan, "The City Politic: Rocky's Road to Albany," *New York Magazine*, August 31, 1970.

4. Alan Rosenthal, *The Best Job in Politics* (Washington, DC: CQ Press, 2013).

5. Rosenthal, *The Best Job in Politics*, 3.

6. Rosenthal, *The Best Job in Politics*, 5.

7. Thad Kousser and Justin Phillips, *The Power of American Governors* (New York: Cambridge University Press, 2012).

8. See Adam Brown, "The Item Veto's Sting," *State Politics and Policy Quarterly* 12 (2012): 183–203.

9. See Thad Beyle and Margaret Ferguson, "Governors and the Executive Branch," in Virginia Gray and Russell L. Hanson, eds., *Politics in the American States*, 9th ed. (Washington, DC: CQ Press, 2008)

10. See John A. Hamman, "Career Experience and Performing Effectively as Governor," *American Review of Public Administration* 34 (2004): 151–63.

11. Margaret Ferguson, "Governors and the Executive Branch," in Virginia Gray, Russell Hanson and Thad Kousser, eds., *Politics in the American States*, 10th ed. (Washington, DC: CQ Press, 2012), 211.

12. These data were calculated by the authors from gubernatorial salary data found in various editions of the *Book of the States*.

13. John Mariani, "State's Highest-Paid Employee Made $958,000 for 2009; Gov. David Paterson No. 900 on Payroll," (Syracuse) *Post-Standard*, March 10, 2010.

14. Martin Finucane and Matt Carroll, "Gov. Patrick the 1,295th-Highest Earner in State Government," *Boston Globe*, February 19, 2010.

15. See Ann O'M. Bowman, Neal D. Woods, and Milton R. Stark II, "Governors Turn Pro: Separation of Powers and the Institutionalization of the American Governorship," *Political Research Quarterly* 63 (2010): 304–15.

16. These data are taken from the *Statistical Abstract of the United States, 1960*, 423; and the *State and Metropolitan Area Data Book: 2010*, 90.

17. These data are taken from Cynthia J. Bowling and Deil S. Wright, "Public Administration in the Fifty States: A Half-Century Administrative Revolution," *State and Local Government Review* 30 (1998): 52–64.

18. These data are taken from the American State Administrators Project, and can be found at www.auburn.edu/outreach/cgs/ASAP/index.htm.

19. See, for example, John D. Nugent, *Safeguarding Federalism: How States Protect Their Interests in National Policymaking* (Norman: University of Oklahoma Press, 2009) and Erin Ryan, *Federalism and The Tug of War Within* (New York: Oxford University Press, 2011).

20. Ryan, *Federalism and The Tug of War Within*, 271.

21. Ryan, *Federalism and The Tug of War Within*, 267–68.

22. Malcolm Jewell, "The Political Setting," in Alexander Heard, ed., *State Legislatures in American Politics* (Englewood Cliffs, NJ: Prentice-Hall, 1966), 71.

23. Stephen Ansolabehere and James Snyder, *The End of Inequality: One Person, One Vote and the Transformation of American Politics* (New York: Norton, 2008), 87–88.

24. Data from 1957 can be found in John C. Wahlke, Heinz Eulau, William Buchanan, and LeRoy C. Ferguson, *The Legislative System* (New York: Wiley, 1962), 489. Data for 2011 are from a survey conducted by the *Chronicle of Higher Education*, chronicle.com/article/Degrees-of-Leadership-/127797/.

25. These data are taken from the Center for American Women in Politics, www.cawp.rutgers.edu/fast_facts/levels_of_office/state_legislature.php.

26. Data on African American and Hispanic American state legislators over time can be found at www.ncsl.org/default.aspx?tabid=14850.

27. These figures are from table 1, p. 104 in Duane Lockard, "The State Legislator," in Heard, ed., *State Legislatures in American Politics*, op cit. The figures are for lower houses. Turnover was often even higher in state senates, but many of the "newcomers" in the senates had come over from the house, so it is difficult to get a good historical measure of true turnover in the upper chambers.

28. On turnover over the several decades, see Gary Moncrief, Richard G. Niemi, and Lynda W. Powell, "Time, Term Limits, and Turnover: Membership Stability in U.S. State Legislatures," *Legislative Studies Quarterly* 29 (2004): 357–81; Richard G. Niemi, and Laura R. Winsky, "Membership Turnover in U.S. State Legislatures: Trends and Effects of Districting," *Legislative Studies Quarterly* 12 (1987): 115–12, and Kwang S. Shin and John S. Jackson III, "Membership Turnover in U.S. State Legislatures: 1931–1976," *Legislative Studies Quarterly* 4 (1979): 95–114.

29. On turnover in recent years and the difference between states with term limits and states without term limits see Peverill Squire and Gary Moncrief, *State Legislatures Today: Politics under the Domes* (Boston: Longman, 2010), 63–66.

30. Marjorie Sarbaugh-Thompson, "Measuring 'Term-Limitedness' in U.S. Multi-State Research," *State Politics and Policy Quarterly* 10 (2010):199–217.

31. See Daniel C. Lewis, "Legislative Term Limits and Fiscal Policy Performance," *Legislative Studies Quarterly* 37 (2012): 307; David R. Berman, "Legislative Climate," in Karl Kurtz, Bruce Cain and Richard Niemi, eds., *Institutional Change in American Politics: The Case of Term Limits* (Ann Arbor: University of Michigan Press, 2007), 107–18 and Thad Kousser, *Term Limits and the Dismantling of State Legislative Professionalism* (Cambridge: Cambridge University Press, 2005).

32. Lewis, "Legislative Term Limits and Fiscal Policy Performance."

33. This discussion of legislative professionalization is derived from Peverill Squire, "Measuring Legislative Professionalism: The Squire Index Revisited," *State Politics and Policy Quarterly* 7 (2007): 211–27.

34. Jerrell D. Coggburn, "Exploring Differences in the American States' Procurement Practices," *Journal of Public Procurement* 3 (2003): 3–28.; Sangjoon Ka and Paul Teske, "Ideology and Professionalism—Electricity Regulation and Deregulation Over Time in the American States," *American Politics Research* 30 (2002): 323–43; J. E. Kellough and S. C. Selden, "The Reinvention of Public Personnel Administration: An Analysis of the Diffusion of Personnel Management Reforms in the States," *Public Administration Review* 63 (2003): 165–76; Edward Alan Miller, Lili Wang, Zhanlian Feng, and Vincent Mor, "Improving Direct-Care Compensation in Nursing Homes: Medicaid Wage Pass-through Adoption, 1999–2004," *Journal of Health Politics, Policy and Law* 37 (2012): 469–512; Mary Schmeida and Ramona McNeil, "Children's Mental-Health Language Access Laws: State Factors Influence Policy Adoption," *Administration and Policy in Mental Health and Mental Health Services Research* (2012); Joel Slemrod, "The Etiology of Tax Complexity: Evidence from U.S. State Income Tax Systems," *Public Finance Review* (2005) 33:279–99.

35. Vivian E. Thomson and Vicki Arroyo, "Upside-Down Cooperative Federalism: Climate Change Policymaking and the States," *Virginia Environmental Law Journal* 29 (2011): 3–61; Caroline J. Tolbert, Karen Mossberger, and Ramona McNeal, "Institutions, Policy Innovation, and E-Government in the American States," *Public Administration Review* 68 (2008): 549–63; Neal D. Woods, "The Policy Consequences of Political Corruption: Evidence from State Environmental Programs," *Social Science Quarterly* 89 (2008): 258–71.

36. Frederick J. Boehmke, "Sources of Variation in the Frequency of Statewide Initiatives: The Role of Interest Group Populations." *Political Research Quarterly* 58 (2005): 565–75.

37. Thad Kousser, *Term Limits and the Dismantling of State Legislative Professionalism* (New York: Cambridge University Press, 2005), 197–98.

38. See the discussions in Squire, "Measuring Legislative Professionalism" in Squire and Hamm, *101 Chambers.*

39. Melinda Gann Hall, "State Courts," in Virginia Gray, Russell Hanson, and Thad Kousser, eds., *Politics in the American States*, 10th ed. (Washington, DC: CQ Press, 2013), 255.

40. The federal court data were taken from Administrative Office of the United States Courts, *Federal Judicial Caseload Statistics: March 31, 2009*, Washington, DC, 2009. The state court data were taken from R. LaFountain, R. Schauffler, S. Strickland, S. Gibson, and A. Mason, *Examining the Work of State Courts: An Analysis of 2009 State Court Caseloads* (Williamsburg, VA: National Center for State Courts, 2011).

41. See Lawrence M. Friedman, *A History of American Law* (New York: Touchstone, 1973), 525–38; Robert A. Kagan, Bobby D. Infelise, and Robert R. Detlefsen, "American State Supreme Court Justices, 1900–1970," *American Bar Foundation Research Journal* (1984): 371–408.

42. These data are taken from National Center for State Courts, "Survey of Judicial Salaries," vol. 35, no. 2, as of July 1, 2010.

43. The chief justice is actually paid slightly more at about $151,000 annually.

44. See Stephen J. Choi, Mitu Gulati, and Eric A. Posner, "Are Judges Overpaid? A Skeptical Response to the Judicial Salary Debate," *Journal of Legal Analysis* 1 (Winter 2009): 47–117. For an example of a controversy, see Michael Cooper, "New York's Top Judge Threatens Suit to Get Raises for Bench," *New York Times*, April 10, 2007.

45. These data are from Center for Women in Government & Civil Society, *Women in Federal and State-level Judgeships* (Spring 2011).

46. These data are taken from Ciara Torres-Spelliscy, Monique Chase, and Emma Greenman, "Improving Judicial Diversity" (Brennan Center for Justice, 2010).

47. See Robert A. Kagan, Bliss Cartwright, Laurence M. Friedman, and Stanton Wheeler, "The Evolution of State Supreme Courts," *Michigan Law Review* 76 (1977): 961–1005.

48. See Peverill Squire, "Measuring the Professionalization of U.S. State Courts of Last Resort," *State Politics and Policy Quarterly* 8 (2008): 223–38.

49. These data were gathered from National Center for State Courts, Court Statistic Project, "State Court Caseload Statistics: An Analysis of 2008 State Court Caseloads," 2010.

50. Alan Rosenthal, *Engines of Democracy: Politics & Policymaking in State Legislatures* (Washington, DC: CQ Press, 2009), 8.

Chapter 5

1. Pamela Prah attributes this assessment to an analyst at the Cato Institute. See Pamela M. Prah, "Uncertainty from Washington Continues for States," Stateline.org, January 4, 2013, www.pewstates.org/projects/stateline/headlines/uncertainty-from-washington-continues-for -states-85899440207.

2. *Governing*, "Top Ten Issues to Watch in 2013," January 2013; *State Legislatures*, "Top 10 of 2013," January 2013.

3. Martha Derthick, *Keeping the Compound Republic* (Washington, DC: Brookings Institute, 2001), 28.

4. Virginia Gray, "The Socioeconomic and Political Context of States," in Virginia Gray, Russell Hanson, and Thad Kousser, eds., *Politics in the American States*, 10th ed. (Thousand Oaks, CA: CQ Press, 2013), 3.

5. This discussion is based in part on Todd Donovan, Christopher Mooney, and Daniel Smith, *State and Local Politics: Institutions and Reform*, 3rd ed. (Boston: Wadsworth/Cengage, 2013), chap. 13 ("Morality Policy") and Justin Phillips, "Public Opinion and Morality," in Gray, Hanson, and Kousser, eds., *Politics in the American States*, 440–58.

6. Gray, Hanson, and Kousser, eds., *Politics in the American States*, 6.

7. The policy diffusion literature is far too extensive to review here, but one must begin with Jack Walker's "The Diffusion of Innovation in the American States," *American Political Science Review* (1969) 63: 830–99 and Virginia Gray's "Innovation in the American States: A Diffusion Study," *American Political Science Review* 67 (1973): 1174–85. For recent treatments, see Andrew Karch, *Democratic Laboratories: Policy Diffusion among the States* (Ann Arbor: University of Michigan Press, 2007); Sean Nicholson-Crotty, "The Politics of Diffusion: Public Policy in the American States," *Journal of Politics* 71 (2009): 192–205; and Fred Boehmke and Paul Skinner, "State Policy Innovativeness Revisited," *State Politics and Policy Quarterly* 12 (2012): 304–30.

8. Graeme Boushey, *Policy Diffusion Dynamics in America* (New York: Cambridge University Press, 2010), 5.

9. Nicholson-Crotty, "The Politics of Diffusion," 199–200.

10. See Boehmke and Skinner, "State Policy Innovativeness Revisited," and Melissa Maynard, "Which States Are Most Innovative?," The Pew Center on the States, Stateline.org, www.pewstates .org/projects/stateline/headlines/which-states-are-most-innovative-858994.

11. Italics added by authors to emphasize relevant phrases.

12. Center on Budget and Policy Priorities, "Policy Basics: Where Do Our State Tax Dollars Go?," March 28, 2012, www.cbpp.org/cms/index.cfm?fa=view&id=2783.

13. Doris Nhan, "Analysis: How Much States Spend on Their Kids Really Does Matter," *National Journal*, October 23, 2012, www.nationaljournal.com/thenextamerica/education/analysis -how-much-states-spend-on-their-kids-really-does-matter-20121016. The article is based on data from the Annie E. Casey Foundation.

14. Nhan, "Analysis: How Much States Spend on Their Kids Really Does Matter."

15. National Education Access Network, www.schoolfunding.info/.

16. Michael Berkman and Eric Plutzer, "The Politics of Education," in Virginia Gray, Russell Hanson, and Thad Kousser, eds., *Politics in the American States*, 10th ed. (Thousand Oaks, CA: CQ Press, 2013), 388.

17. These figures are from 2008 and appear in table 12-5 of Berkman and Plutzer, "The Politics of Education," 393.

18. The Council of Governments, "2010-11 Four Year Regulatory Adjusted Cohort Graduation Rates," *The Book of the States, 2012*.

19. Tufts University, The Center for Information on Civic Learning and Engagement, "Fact Sheet," October 19, 2012, www.civicyouth.org.

20. University of Pennsylvania Graduate School of Education, "Is There an NCLB Curriculum?," www.gse.upenn.edu/features/research/de_facto. The article cites work by Andy Porter, Morgan Polikoff, and John Smithson in mapping curriculum content from state to state.

21. "Anti-Evolution Movement," *Oklahoma Historical Society's Encyclopedia of Oklahoma History and Culture*, digital.library.okstate.edu/encyclopedia/entries/A/AN011.html.

22. Pew Research Center for the People and the Press, "Reading the Polls on Evolution and Creationism," September 28, 2005.

23. Michael Berkman, Eric Plutzer, and Nicholas Stark, "Teaching Evolution: State Institutions, Public Opinion and Science Curriculums," paper presented at the 2006 State Politics and Public Conference, Texas Tech University, May 2006.

24. Berkman and Plutzer, "The Politics of Education," 399.

25. Phi Delta Kappa, "Highlights of the PDK/Gallup Poll." See table 39. www.pdkintl.org/poll/docs/2012-Gallup-poll-full-report.pdf.

26. Jack Nicas, "Indiana's Law on Vouchers is Upheld," *Wall Street Journal*, March 27, 2013; Ben Wolfgang, "Funding for La. Governor Jindal's Voucher Program Struck Down by Court," *Washington Times*, May 7, 2013.

27. National Conference of State Legislatures, www.ncsl.org/issues-research/educ/school-choice-scholarship-tax-credits.aspx.

28. Stephanie Saul, "Public Money Finds Backdoor to Private Schools," *New York Times*, May 21, 2012.

29. *Education Week*, "Home Schooling," www.edweek.org/ew/issues/home-schooling/; Brian Ray, "2.04 Million Homeschooled Students in the United States in 2010," National Home Education Research Institute, January 2011.

30. Berkman and Plutzer, "The Politics of Education," 396.

31. Home School Legal Defense Association, 2013, "State Laws," www.HSLDA.org/laws/.

32. Home School Legal Defense Association, "State Laws," 2013.

33. On the other hand, more than half the research funds for universities in the United States are from the national government. Congressional Research Service, "Federal Support for Academic Research," report 7-5700, October 18, 2012.

34. Jung-cheol Shin and Sande Milton, "Rethinking Tuition Effects on Enrollment in Public Four-Year Colleges and Universities," *The Review of Higher Education*, 29 (2006): 213–37; James Hearn, Carolyn Griswold, and Ginger Marine, "Region, Resource, and Reason: A Contextual Analysis of State Tuition and Student Aid Policies," *Research in Higher Education* 37 (1996): 241–78.

35. The relative importance of these revenue streams varies within states as well. For example, North Carolina State University recently reported that almost 40 percent of its budget was from state-appropriated funds, while the University of North Carolina reported that 20 percent of its budget was from the same source. See www.ncsu.edu/budget/faq/ and universityrelations.unc.edu/budget/content/FAQ.php#statefundingfactor.

36. College Board Advocacy & Policy Center, "Trends in Tuition and Fees, Enrollment, and State Appropriations for Higher Education by State," July 2012. See pp. 4–6.

37. Kevin Dougherty, "Financing Higher Education in the United States," address to the Institute for Economics of Education, Peking University, Peking, China, 2004, p. 10.

38. University of Michigan Office of the Vice President for Communications, "Understanding Tuition" (August 2012), www.vpcomm.umich.edu/pa/key/understandingtuition.html.

39. College Board Advocacy Center, "Trends in Tuition and Fees," op. cit., table 2, p. 9.

40. This assessment is based on data from the Brady Campaign to Prevent Gun Violence, "2011 Brady State Scorecard," www.bradycampaign.org/stategunlaws/scorecard/.

41. Lynn Bartels and Kurtis Lee, "3 New Gun Bills on the Books in Colorado Despite Its Wild West Image," *Denver Post*, March 21, 2013; Ron Scherer, "Connecticut Responds to Newtown with Groundbreaking Gun Control Laws," *Christian Science Monitor*, April 2, 2013.

42. Jason Clayworth, "Register Investigation: 99.6% of Iowa Gun Permits Approved," *Des Moines Register*, March 10, 2013.

43. See Cheng Cheng and Mark Hoekstra, "Does Strengthening Self-Defense Law Deter Crime or Escalate Violence? Evidence from the Expansions to Castle Doctrine," *Journal of Human Resources*, forthcoming.

44. Adam Cohen, "Will States Lead the Way to Legalizing Marijuana Nationwide?," *Time Magazine*, January 28, 2013, ideas.time.com/2013/01/28/will-states-lead-the-way-to-legalizing -marijuana-nationwide/.

45. Centers for Disease Control and Prevention, "State Smoke Free Laws for Workshops, Restaurants and Bars—United States, 2000–2010," vol. 60, no. 15 (April 22, 2011), www.cdc.gov/ tobacco/data_statistics/mmwrs/byyear/2011/mm6015a2/highlights.htm. This is not to say that there weren't bans on one or more of the three sites as imposed by some southern states. North Carolina, for example, did outlaw smoking in bars and restaurants, but not in workplace sites.

46. Based on US Bureau of Justice Statistics, "Correctional Populations in the United States, 2010."

47. From table 9.2 in John Wooldredge, "State Corrections Policy," in Gray, Hanson, and Kousser, eds., *Politics in the American States*, 289.

48. www.washingtonpost.com/wp-dyn/content/story/2008/02/28/ST2008022803016.html.

49. Legislative Analyst's Office, "A Primer: Three Strikes—The Impact after More Than a Decade," October 7, 2005, www.lao.ca.gov/2005/3_strikes/3_strikes_102005.htm.

50. Calculated by the authors from data in Erica E. Phillips, "'Three-Strikes' Prisoners Drawing a Walk," *Wall Street Journal*, March 30–31, 2013.

51. John Wooldredge, "State Corrections Policy," in Gray, Hanson, and Kousser, eds., *Politics in the American States*. See table 9-1.

52. Wooldredge, "State Corrections Policy," 283.

53. Statistics are from the Death Penalty Information Center, www.deathpenaltyinfo.org/ number-executions-state-and-region-1976.

54. Cody Mason, "Too Good to Be True: Private Prisons in America," The Sentencing Project: Washington, DC 2012. Figures are from 2010. State figures are found on pp. 4–5.

55. 32 Cal. 2 711. See the discussion in R. A. Lenhardt, "Beyond Analogy: Perez V. Sharp, Antimiscegenation Law, and the Fight for Same-Sex Marriage," *California Law Review* 96 (2008): 839–900.

56. 388 U.S. 1

57. *New York Times*, "President Bush's Remarks on Same-Sex Marriage," February 24, 2004.

58. 410 U.S. 113 (1973).

59. See Barbara Hinkson Craig and David M. O'Brien, *Abortion and American Politics* (Chatham, NJ: Chatham House, 1996), 74–75; Roy Lucas, "Federal Constitutional Limitations on the Enforcement and Administration of State Abortion Statutes," *North Carolina Law Review* 46 (1967–1968): 730–78; Karen O'Connor, *No Neutral Ground?* (Boulder, CO: Westview Press, 1996), 46–47; A. A. Smyser, "Hawaii's Abortion Law 30 Years Old," *Hawaii Star-Bulletin*, March 21, 2000.

60. Craig and O'Brien, *Abortion and American Politics*, 75.

61. *Planned Parenthood of Southeastern Pennsylvania v. Casey*, 505 U.S. 833.

62. *St Louis Post Dispatch*, "North Dakota Governor Approves 6-Week Abortion Ban," March 26, 2013.

63. The Guttmacher Institute provides a useful compendium of state abortion laws: www.guttmacher.org/statecenter/spibs/spib_OAL.pdf.

64. Gardiner Harris, "In Hawaii's Heath System, Lessons for Lawmakers," *New York Times*, October 16, 2009.

65. Christine Vestal, "Utah's Health Insurance Exchange in Limbo," *Stateline*, January 11, 2013.

66. See the data presented at statehealthfacts.org: www.statehealthfacts.org/comparecat.jsp?cat=3.

67. Congressional Research Service, "Medicaid's Federal Medical Assistance Percentage (FMAP) FY2014," January 30, 2013.

68. These figures were taken from the Kaiser Commission on Key Facts, "Where Are the States Today? Medicaid and CHIP Eligibility Levels for Children and Non-Disabled Adults," updated July 2012.

69. See the excellent map at www.advisory.com/Daily-Briefing/2012/11/09/MedicaidMap.

70. Rick Pluta, "A Michigan State-Federal Health Care Exchange Killed by Senate Republicans," March 22, 2013, www.michiganradio.org/post/michigan-state-federal-health-care-exchange-killed-senate-republicans.

71. See www.ncsl.org/issues-research/health/state-actions-to-implement-the-health-benefit-exch.aspx.

72. These data were taken from David Kassabian, Anne Whitesell, and Erika Huber, *Welfare Rules Databook: State TANF Policies as of July 2011*, OPRE Report #2012-57, Washington, DC: Office of Planning, Research and Evaluation, Administration for Children and Families, US Department of Health and Human Services, 2012, pp. 72–73, 90–91.

73. See Heather Hahn, David Kassabian, and Sheila Zedlewski, *TANF Work Requirements and State Strategies to Fulfill Them*, Urban Institute, Brief #05, March 2012.

74. See the NCSL compilation of these laws: www.ncsl.org/issues-research/human-services/drug-testing-and-public-assistance.aspx.

75. Mark Carl Rom, "State Health and Welfare Programs," in Gray, Hanson, and Kousser, eds., *Politics in the American States*.

76. See Jacquelyn Pless, *Natural Gas Development and Hydraulic Fracturing. A Policymaker's Guide*, National Conference of State Legislatures, revised June 2012.

77. Ryan Tracy, "States Cooling to Renewable Energy," *Wall Street Journal*, March 29, 2013. See also the Database of State Incentives for Renewables and Efficiency, www.dsireusa.org/.

78. See the list of legislation compiled by the National Conference of State Legislatures, www.ncsl.org/issues-research/educ/bullying-legislation-since-2008.aspx.

79. See www.ncsl.org/issues-research/justice/caylees-law.aspx.

80. See www.ncsl.org/issues-research/human-services/mandatory-rprtg-of-child-abuse-and-neglect-2013.aspx.

81. Jack Nicas and Joe Palazzolo, "Pro-Gun Laws Gain Ground," *Wall Street Journal*, April 4, 2013; www.governing.com/blogs/view/gov-advancing-the-debate-guns-teachers-and-classrooms-in-south-dakota.html.

82. Louise Radnofsky, "States Harden Views Over Laws Governing Abortion," *Wall Street Journal*, April 1, 2013.

83. See www.thedailyshow.com/watch/mon-april-26-2010/law---border. The comment comes at 1:14.

84. Malcolm Gay, "The Catfish are Biting (and It Hurts)," *New York Times*, July 28, 2007; Missouri Department of Conservation, "Why 'No' to Noodling," mdc.mo.gov/fishing/regulations/why-no-noodling.

85. See "Charges Filed against Men for 'Noodling' Catfish," www.wowt.com/news/headlines/160367085.html.

Chapter 6

1. *USA Today*, "Unbelievable Sum of Money in Ga. Runoff," November 27, 2008.

2. Louisiana now has a similar requirement.

3. While Cruz had never run for office before, it would be inaccurate to describe him as a political novice. A Harvard-educated lawyer, he had clerked for former US Supreme Court Chief Justice Rehnquist and had been appointed Solicitor General of Texas.

4. Nathan Koppell and Naftali Bendavid, "A Tea-Party Favorite Wins Texas GOP Race," *Wall Street Journal*, August 1, 2012.

5. The twelve were former House members Neal Abercrombie (Hawaii), Nathan Deal (Georgia), Mary Fallin (Oklahoma), Jay Inslee (Washington), Bobby Jindal (Louisiana), John Kasich (Ohio), Butch Otter (Idaho), Mike Pence (Indiana), and Bob Riley (Alabama). Former Senate members were Lincoln Chafee (Rhode Island) and Mark Dayton (Minnesota). Kansas governor Sam Brownback served in both the House and Senate.

6. One source determined that by 1992 there were 510,497 elected officials, a figure that almost certainly has increased over the years. The figure is reported in Frank Shelly, J. C. Archer, F. M. Davidson, and S. D. Brunn, *Political Geography of the United States* (New York: Guilford Press, 1996), 123.

7. There are some excellent discussions of these matters, however. The reader is directed to Douglas Rae, *The Political Consequences of Electoral Laws* (New Haven, CT: Yale University Press, 1967). Also see David M. Farrell, *Electoral Systems: A Comparative Introduction*, 2nd ed. (New York: Palgrave, 2011); Pippa Norris, *Electoral Engineering: Voting Rules and Political Behavior* (New York: Cambridge University Press, 2004); and Michael Gallagher and Paul Mitchell, eds., *The Politics of Electoral Systems* (New York: Oxford University Press, 2005).

8. Richard G. Niemi, Jeffrey S. Hill, and Bernard Grofman, "The Impact of Multimember Districts on Party Representation in U.S. State Legislatures," *Legislative Studies Quarterly* 10 (1985): 441–55.

9. ncsl.typepad.com/the_thicket/2012/09/a-slight-decline-in-legislatures-using-multimember-districts-after-redistricting.html.

10. Stephen Calabrese, "Multimember District Congressional Elections," *Legislative Studies Quarterly* 25 (2000): 611–43.

11. L. Sandy Maisel and Mark D. Brewer, *Parties and Elections in America*, 5th ed. (Lanham, MD: Rowman & Littlefield, 2010), 199.

12. That is, nine states have four-year electoral cycles that are held at the same time as the presidential election. But since New Hampshire and Vermont have elections every two years, there are actually eleven states holding gubernatorial elections during the presidential election year.

13. In Alabama, the number of seats flipping from the Democrats to the Republicans was sufficient to give the GOP a legislative majority for the first time in 130 years.

14. There were no regularly scheduled state legislative elections in Louisiana either. There were, however, several special elections to fill vacant seats.

15. Ultimately, the one-year "electoral reprieve" did not help Democratic legislators in Mississippi and Virginia, where Republicans gained thirteen and eleven seats, respectively, in 2011. Only in Louisiana did the Democrats stave off the effects of the Republican "wave"; the Democrats lost but one seat in the Louisiana House and two in the Senate in 2011.

16. One expert finds that 87 percent of judges in state court systems face the electorate in one way or another. See Roy A. Schotland, "Judicial Elections," in Paul Herrnson, ed., *Guide to Political Campaigns in America* (Washington, DC: CQ Press, 2005), 391.

17. www.opensecrets.org/news/2011/04/wisconsin-supreme-court-elections-b.html.

18. Schotland, "Judicial Elections," 393.

19. Schotland, "Judicial Elections," 394.

20. David Rottman, "Judicial Elections in 2008," Council of State Governments, *Book of the States 2009* 41:291.

21. Rottman, p. 391.

22. "2010 Judicial Elections Increase Pressure on Courts, Reform Groups Say Michigan Saw the Highest Overall Spending on Supreme Courts TV Ads, legalnews.com, November 9, 2010, www.legalnews.com/detroit/776290 .

23. See Todd Donovan, Christoper Z. Mooney, and Daniel A. Smith, *State and Local Politics: Institutions and Reform*, 2nd ed. (Stamford, CT: Wadsworth, Cengage Learning, 2011), 335–37.

24. Melinda Gann Hall, "State Courts: Politics and the Judicial Process," in Virginia Gray and Russell Hanson, eds., *Politics in the American States*, 9th ed. (Washington, DC: CQ Press, 2008), 245.

25. *Caperton v. A.T. Massey Co, Inc.* 129 S.Ct 2252 (2009). The case was decided on a 5-4 opinion.

26. Maisel and Brewer, *Parties and Elections in America*, 211–12.

27. The quote is from Norimitsu Onishi, "New Rules Upend House Re-Election Races in California," *New York Times*, September 24, 2012. www.nytimes.com/2012/09/25/us/politics/new-rules-upend-house-re-election-races-in-california.html?pagewanted=all&_r=0.

28. www.ncsl.org/legislatures-elections/elections/absentee-and-early-voting.aspx.

29. See Michael McDonald's website at elections.gmu.edu/early_vote_2010.html.

30. To be completely accurate, only 428 districts are currently redrawn by the states because seven states have only one congressional district each. In those instances the congressional district is the entire state, and does not have to be redrawn.

31. This includes states in which there is a "backup commission" that takes over the process if the legislature does not complete the redistricting task by a specific date. Moreover, there are some states in which a commission is used to draw state legislative lines but in which the legislature has responsibility for drawing congressional districts within the state.

32. While this is generally true, it is possible for redistricting to be done more than once every decade. Perhaps the best known instance of this was when the Republican Party won majority control of the Texas Legislature in 2003 and moved to redistrict despite the fact that the legislature had just effected a new redistricting plan (under the then-majority Democrats) in 2002.

33. There is some latitude for interpretation of the phrase "outside the control over the legislature." For example, in Maine and Vermont the redistricting commissions are advisory; they recommend plans but the legislature has the authority to reject the recommendation and adopt a different plan.

34. See, for example, Sam Wang, "The Great Gerrymander of 2012," *New York Times*, February 2, 2013, www.nytimes.com/2013/02/03/opinion/sunday/the-great-gerrymander-of-2012.html?pagewanted=all.

35. See "Not Gerrymandering, but Districting: More Evidence on How Democrats Won the Popular Vote but Lost the Congress," in the blog, "The Monkey Cage," themonkeycage.org/2012/11/15/not-gerrymandering-but-districting-more-evidence-on-how-democrats-won-the-popular-vote-but-lost-the-congress/.

36. Jeff Mayers, "Democrats Flee Wisconsin to Protest Union Curbs," *Reuters*, February 17, 2011.

37. For a list of recalled state legislators, see www.ncsl.org/legislatures-elections/elections/recall-of-state-officials.aspx.

38. Pete Nichols, "Tax Hike Opponents Lecture on Recall Rights," *The State News*, July 20, 2007.

39. According to Jennie Drage Boweser of the National Conference of State Legislatures, Delaware's referendum authority is extremely limited, applying only to the question of whether or not "Bingo" should be licensed or prohibited. See "NCSL, Legislative Referendum: Constitutional Provisions," information sheet dated January 2012.

40. Todd Donovan, Christopher Z. Mooney, and Daniel A. Smith, *State and Local Politics*, 2nd ed. (Stamford, CT: Wadsworth Cengage Learning, 2011), 114–15.

41. Initiative & Referendum Institute, *Ballotwatch* 2011, no. 2 (December), 1.

42. Unlike Wisconsin, where the prounion forces were outspent in the effort to recall Governor Walker, in Ohio they held a commanding advantage in campaign expenditures. The prounion groups outspent the antiunion coalition by more than 3:1.

43. Initiative and Referendum Institute, www.iandrinstitute.org/BW%202008-3%20Results%20v4.pdf.

44. Elizabeth Garrett, "Hybrid Democracy," *George Washington University Law Review* 73 (2005): 1096–130.

45. Shaun Bowler and Todd Donovan, "Measuring the Effect of Direct Democracy on State Policy: Not All Initiatives Are Created Equal," *State Politics and Policy Quarterly* 4 (2004): 345–63.

46. Peverill Squire and Gary Moncrief, *State Legislatures Today: Politics under the Domes* (Boston: Longman, 2010), 212.

47. Donovan, Mooney, and Smith, *State and Local Politics*, 148.

48. *U.S. Term Limits, Inv. v. Thornton* 514 U.S. 779 (1995).

49. Karl T. Kurtz, "An Unexpected Benefit of Term Limits," entry on the National Conference of State Legislature's blog, "The Thicket," April 23, 2009, ncsl.typepad.com/the_thicket/2009/04/an-unexpected-benefit-of-term-limits.html.

50. Marjorie Sarbaugh-Thompson, "Measuring 'Term-Limitedness' in U.S. Multi-State Research," *State Politics and Policy Quarterly* 10 (2010): 199–217.

51. Information on the poll was accessed from www.gallup.com/poll/141548/states-competitive-terms-party-identification.aspx.

52. The Pearson correlation between Republican Party identification and percent seats held by the Republicans in the state legislature is r = .81.

53. "Wyoming, Mississippi, Utah Rank as Most Conservative States," August 2, 2010, www.gallup.com.

54. Thomas Holbrook and Ray LaRaja, "Parties and Elections" in Gray, Hansen, and Kousser, eds., *Politics in the American States*, 10th ed. (Thousand Oaks, CA: CQ Press: 2013), table 3–4, p. 88.

55. Some of these are statewide winner-take-all (whoever receives the most votes statewide receives all the delegates); some of these are district winner-take-all (whomever gets the most votes in each congressional district gets all 3 district votes). About half of the GOP delegates at the 2008 convention were selected through some form of winner-take-all rule. See table 2, p. 13 in Justin Sizemore, "Political Conventions in 2008," in Larry Sabato, ed., *The Year of Obama* (Boston: Longman/Pearson, 2010).

56. In fact, in 2008 Obama actually received a lower percentage of the pledged delegates than his popular vote would anticipate. This is partly due to the mechanics of delegate distribution and partly due to the fact that there were a number of unpledged "Super-delegates." These "Super-delegates" are individuals who are accorded seats at the national convention by virtue of their positions as elected or party officials. These "ex-officio" delegates comprised almost 20 percent of the delegates at the Democratic National Convention in 2008.

57. Stephen Wayne, *Is This Any Way to Run a Democratic Election?*, 4th ed. (Washington, DC: CQ Press, 2011), 179.

58. Barry Burden, "The Nominations: Rules, Strategies, and Uncertainty," in Michael Nelson, ed., *The Elections of 2008* (Washington, DC: CQ Press, 2010), 25.

59. L. Sandy Maisel and Mark D. Brewer, *Parties and Elections in America*, 5th ed. (Lanham, MD: Rowman & Littlefield, 2008), 292.

60. Maisel and Brewer, *Parties and Elections in America*, 319.

61. Darrell West, *Air Wars*, 5th ed. (Washington, DC: CQ Press, 2010), 19.

62. The figures represent the number of electors in each of these states in 2008. The new census figures will result in Nevada (+1) and Texas (+4) picking up additional congressional seats and, consequently, additional electors.

63. The two states are Maine and Nebraska.

64. "Presidential Campaign Stops: Who's Going Where," *Washington Post*, www.washington post.com/wp-srv/special/politics/2012-presidential-campaign-visits/.

65. The elections of 1824, 1876, and 1888 all resulted in the selection of a president who had not won the popular vote. While the evidence is not definitive, the 1960 election may also fall into this category. See, for example, Stephen Medvic, *Campaigns and Elections* (Boston: Wadsworth/Cengage, 2010), 48.

66. Martin Diamond, *The Electoral College and the American Idea of Democracy* (Washington, DC: American Enterprise Institute, 1977).

Chapter 7

1. www.usatoday.com/news/nation/2009-05-04-fed-states-revenue_N.htm.

2. Government Accountability Office, www.gao.gov/special.pubs/longterm/state/fiscalconditionsfaq.html.

3. Another way to think about this is that the calendar year is divided into four quarters and these quarters are often important reporting periods for businesses and economic analysis (e.g., "second quarter sales were up by 5 percent"). The New York state government operates on a fiscal year that begins on the first day of the second quarter (April 1). Forty-six states operate on a fiscal year that begins on the first day of the third quarter (July 1). Alabama, Michigan, and the federal government begin their fiscal year on the first day of the fourth quarter (October 1). Only Texas does not operate off of one of the four economic quarters.

4. The National Bureau of Economic Research (NBER) has determined that the recession actually began in December of 2007 and bottomed out in June of 2009.

5. National Conference of State Legislatures (NCSL), *Update on State Budget Gaps: FY 2009 & FY 2010* (Denver: National Conference of State Legislatures, February 20, 2009), 2.

6. These and subsequent figures are from the Center on Budget and Policy Priorities, "Largest State Budget Shortfalls on Record."

7. NCSL, *Update on State Budget Gaps: FY 2009 & FY 2010*.

8. Pamela Prah, "States Balance Budgets with Cuts, Not Taxes," Stateline.org, June 15, 2011, www.pewstates.org/projects/stateline/headlines/states-balance-budgets-with-cuts-not-taxes-85899375037.

9. With the exception of the last four years of the Clinton administration, the federal government spent more than it received in every year since at least 1971. In other words, the federal government has run a deficit in 90 percent of its budgets over the past forty years.

10. John Kincaid, "The Constitutional Frameworks of State and Local Government Finance," in Robert D. Ebel and John E. Petersen, eds., *The Oxford Handbook of State and Local Government Finance* (New York: Oxford University Press, 2012), 62–63.

11. See David M. Primo, *Rules and Restraint: Government Spending and the Design of Institutions* (Chicago: University of Chicago Press 2008), chap. 5.

12. See Carl E. Klarner, Justin H. Phillips, and Matt Muckler, "Overcoming Fiscal Gridlock: Institutions and Budget Bargaining," *Journal of Politics* 74 (2012): 992–1009.

13. "What's Open, What's Closed: Your Guide to the Shutdown," Minneapolis *Star-Tribune*, July 12, 2011, www.startribune.com/politics/statelocal/124952649.html.

14. See W. Mark Crain, *Volatile States*. (Ann Arbor: University of Michigan Press, 2003), especially chapter 8. For an alternative point of view, see Thad Kousser, Mathew D. McCubbins, and Ellen Moule, "For Whom the TEL Tolls: Can State Tax and Expenditure Limits Effectively Reduce Spending?," *State Politics and Policy Quarterly* 8 (2008): 331–61.

15. Katharine Bradbury, "State Government Budgets and the Recovery Act," Public Policy Briefs, No.10-1 (February 17, 2010), Federal Reserve Bank of Boston, 3.

16. Tax rates for income, general sales, and excise taxes are from the January 2012 report of the Federation of Tax Administrators, www.taxadmin.org/fta/rate/.

17. David Brunori, *State Tax Policy: A Political Perspective*, 2nd ed. (Washington, DC: Urban Institute Press, 2005), 53.

18. Brunori, *State Tax Policy: A Political Perspective*, 54.

19. The median state tobacco tax rate was $1.25 per pack (Ohio), while five states (Connecticut, Hawaii, New York, Rhode Island, and Washington) taxed at a rate of more than $3.00 per pack. See Federation of Tax Administrators, "State Excise Tax Rates on Cigarettes, January 1, 2012."

20. Prah, "States Balance Budgets with Cuts, Not Taxes."

21. www.statejournal.com/story/16933140/long-term-growth-of-severance-tax-unlikely.

22. Source: NCSL, "Registration and Title Fees by State," www.ncsl.org/issues-research/transport/registration-and-title-fees-by-state.aspx.

23. Governors' Highway Safety Association, "Seat Belt Laws, July 2012," www.ghsa.org/html/stateinfo/laws/seatbelt_laws.html accessed.

24. Donna Leinwand, "Cities, States Tack on More User Fees," *USA Today*, March 18, 2009 www.usatoday.com/news/nation/2009-03-17-user-fees_N.htm.

25. Cletus C. Couglin, Thomas A. Garrett, and Ruben Hernandez-Murillo, "The Geography, Economics, and Politics of Lottery Adoption," *Federal Reserve Bank of St. Louis Review* (May/June 2006). Also see Frances S. Berry and William D. Berry, "State Lottery Adoptions as Policy Innovations: An Event History Analysis," *American Political Science Review* 84 (1990): 395–414.

26. Lee Davidson, "Utahns Buy 19% of Idaho's Lottery Tickets," *Salt Lake City Tribune*, April 6, 2012, www.sltrib.com/sltrib/news/53862915-78/lottery-idaho-utah-sales.html.csp.

27. These figures, as well as state-specific figures discussed in the text, are based on information from the National Conference of State Legislatures, "Chart of Lottery Payouts and Revenue, By State," www.ncsl.org/issues-research/econ/lottery-payouts-and-state-revenue-2010.aspx.

28. See www.americangaming.org/sites/default/files/uploads/docs/sos/aga_sos_2012_web.pdf.

29. See www.indiangaming.org/info/NIGA_2009_Economic_Impact_Report.pdf.

30. The Morrill Land Grant Act (1862) is usually noted as the first actual example of fiscal federalism, transferring federal lands to states for the establishment of land grant colleges.

31. Another six states adopted lotteries between 2000 and 2009.

32. See Donald Bruce, William F. Fox, and LeAnn Luna, "State and Local Government Sales Tax Revenue Losses from Electronic Commerce," The University of Tennessee, April 13, 2009. Also see Penelope Lemov, "Checking in on the Amazon Tax Battle." Governing.com, August 2, 2012, at www.governing.com/columns/public-finance/col-checking-in-amazon-tax-battle.html.

33. California has since struck a deal with one very large online enterprise, Amazon, to begin collecting the tax on sales to California consumers in exchange for certain concessions. At least eight other states that have recently made similar arrangements with Amazon, among them Virginia, Texas,

and New Jersey. See Penelope Lemov, "Checkin in On the Amazon Battle," at governing.com, www.governing.com/columns/public-finance/col-checking-in-amazon-tax-battle.html.

34. See State & Local Government Finance Data Query System, The Urban Institute-Brookings Institution Tax Policy Center, www.taxpolicycenter.org/taxfacts/displayafact.cfm?DocID=528&Topic2id=90&Topic3id=92.

35. See Ronald Fisher and Andrew Bristle, "State Intergovernmental Grant Programs," in Robert Ebel and John Petersen, eds., *The Oxford Handbook of State and Local Government Finance* (New York: Oxford University Press, 2012), see especially table 9.2, pp. 218–20.

36. This summary is based on data in table 8-15, "Variations in Local Dependency on State Aid, 2007–2008," in Harold Stanley and Richard Niemi, *Vital Statistics on American Politics 2011–2012* (Washington, DC: CQ Press, 2011), 322.

37. "Property Taxes on Owner-Occupied Housing, by State, 2009." See Taxfoundation.org at taxfoundation.org/article/property-taxes-owner-occupied-housing-state-2004-2009.

38. The Tax Foundation also measures property taxes as a percent of income, and arrives at similar figures. For example, the median property tax of $398 in Alabama is about 0.8 percent of the $51,000 median homeowner income; in Jersey, where the median property tax is $6579, which is 7.45 percent of the median homeowner income of $88,343 in that state. All figures are from 2009 data. See taxfoundation.org/article/property-taxes-owner-occupied-housing-state-2004-2009.

39. The Pew Charitable Trusts, "The Local Squeeze" (Washington, DC, 2012), 8. www.pewstates.org/research/reports/the-local-squeeze-85899388655. Also see Federal Funds Information for the States, "State Policy Reports," vol. 30, no. 10 (July 2012) and Lucy Dadayan, "The Impact of the Great Recession on Local Property Taxes," State University of New York at Albany, The Rockefeller Institute, July 2012.

40. Susan Landes, "Financing Recreations and Parks," Commonwealth of Pennsylvania (2005), 10, www.dcnr.state.pa.us/brc/publications/Pubs/Finance_Handbook.pdf.

41. Perhaps our favorite such case is from the State of Washington. State law (chapter 36.95 of the Revised Code of Washington) allows for the creation of "Television Reception Improvement Districts," which may be financed by the imposition of an annual fee of up to $60 per television on households and hotels/motels. See RCW 36.95.100. There is at least one such district in operation, in the municipality of Okanogan.

42. See www.ncsl.org/issues-research/budget/local-option-taxes.aspx.

43. Tennessee does tax income on dividends, however.

44. See Congressional Budget Office, "Actual ARRA Spending Over the 2009–2011 Period Quite Close to the CBO's Original Estimate," www.cbo.gov/publication/42682.

45. Not all these funds went directly to state and local governments, as some were directed to small businesses and qualifying individuals. Moreover, ARRA yielded at least an additional $200 billion in tax reductions to individuals and corporations, making the "value" of the total stimulus package in excess of $700 billion.

46. There were at least half a dozen governors (all Republicans) who announced they would refuse ARRA funds that extended unemployment benefits, arguing that certain strings attached to these funds would obligate their state to offer extended benefits in the future. Ultimately, the funds were accepted in most of these states.

47. But it does happen from time to time. For an explanation of the causes of such refusals to accept the federal funds, see Sean Nicholson-Crotty, "Leaving Money on the Table: Learning from Recent Refusals of Federal Grants in the American States," *Publius* 42 (2012): 449–66.

48. Brunori, *State Tax Policy: A Political Perspective*, 116.

49. The remainder (17 percent) is categorized as "other." See OMB, "Fiscal Year 2013 Analytical Perspectives," Table 18-2, "Trends in Federal Grants to State and Local Governments," www.whitehouse.gov/sites/default/files/omb/budget/fy2013/assets/spec.pdf.

50. See The Pew Center for the States, "The Impact of the Fiscal Cliff on the States," November 2012.

51. Josh Goodman, "The Year School Budget Cuts Went Straight to the Classroom," Stateline. org, June 14, 2011, www.pewstates.org/projects/stateline/headlines/the-year-school-budget-cuts -went-straight-to-the-classroom-85899375039.

52. Peter Harkness, "Public Universities Reach Tipping Point after Years of Decreased Education Funding," *Governing*, June 12, 2012. www.governing.com/topics/education/gov-public -universities-reach-tipping-point.html

53. Note that we refer to state spending, not state and local combined. Medicaid funds are part of the state appropriations process.

54. Rachel Brand, "Medicaid: The 800-Pound Gorilla," *State Legislatures* (October/November 2011): 15.

55. The National Association of State Budget Officers (NASBO), "Summary: NASBO State Expenditure Report," December 13, 2011 (Washington, DC: NASBO).

56. Center for Colorado's Economic Future, "Issue Brief: Colorado's State Budget Tsunami," University of Denver, July 2009, p. 6.

57. NCSL, www.ncsl.org/issues-research.aspx?tabs=951,69,140.

58. Timothy Conlan and Paul Posner, "Federalism Trends, Tensions and Outlook," in Robert Ebel and John Petersen, eds., *The Oxford Handbook of State and Local Government Finance* (New York: Oxford University Press, 2012), 98.

59. David Eggert, "In Michigan, GOP Governor Finds a Tax to Like," The Associated Press, news.yahoo.com/michigan-gop-governor-finds-tax-220952571.html.

Chapter 8

1. "Institute Q&A," The Nelson Rockefeller Institute of Government, University of Albany, New York (September 2010).

2. Anne Leland and M-J Oboroceanu, "American War and Military Operations Casualties: Lists and Statistics," Washington, DC: Congressional Research Service Report 7-5700 (February 26, 2010).

3. Robert S. Allen, "The Shame of the States," in Robert S. Allen, ed., *Our Sovereign State* (New York: Vanguard Press, 1949), xiii.

4. Alexander Heard, "Introduction-Old Problem, New Context." In Heard, *Our Sovereign State*, 3

5. Stephen Ansolabehere and James Snyder, *The End of Inequality: One Person, One Vote and the Transformation of American Politics* (New York: Norton, 2008), 88.

6. As quoted in Robert S. Allen, "The Shame of the States," xxii.

7. See the discussion in Peverill Squire, *The Evolution of American Legislatures, Colonies, Territories, and States, 1619–2009* (Ann Arbor: University of Michigan Press, 2012), 291–97; and Belle Zeller, *American State Legislatures* (New York: Thomas Y. Crowell, 1954).

8. Jon C. Teaford, *The Rise of the States* (Baltimore: The Johns Hopkins University Press, 2002), 199–200; Squire, *The Evolution of American Legislatures*, 297–307.

9. Carl Van Horn, ed., *The State of the States* (Washington, DC: CQ Press, 1989), 1–12; Teaford, *The Rise of the States*, op. cit.; see, in particular, chapter 8: "Reform and Recognition."

10. Alison LaCroix, "How the Noisy Debate Over States' Rights Distorts History and the Intent of Federalism," *Washington Post*, March 25, 2010, voices.washingtonpost.com/political -bookworm/2010/03/how_the_noisy_debate_over_stat.html accessed. Also see Alison LaCroix, *The Ideological Origins of American Federalism* (Cambridge, MA: Harvard University Press, 2010).

11. There are numerous references to the "Alabama syndrome," but it is generally attributed to James L. Sundquist, *Making Federalism Work* (Washington, DC: The Brookings Institution, 1969), 271. Also see Ira Sharkansky, *The Maligned States*, 2nd ed. (New York: McGraw-Hill, 1978), 7; Kimberly Johnson, *Governing the American State*, 159 (Princeton, NJ: Princeton University Press, 2006) and John D. Nugent, *Safeguarding Federalism: How States Protect Their Interests in National Policymaking* (Norman: University of Oklahoma Press, 2009), 221.

12. Martha Derthick, *Keeping the Compound Republic* (Washington, DC: Brookings Institute, 2001), 148

13. David Brian Robertson, *Federalism and the Making of America* (New York: Routledge, 2011), 9.

14. Ann Althouse, "Vanguard States, Laggard States, Federalism and Constitutional Rights," *University of Pennsylvania Law Review* 152 (June 2004): 1745–827.

15. Ann Althouse, "Vanguard States, Laggard States," 1746.

16. *The Economist* 406, no. 8827 (March 16–22, 2013): 16.

17. Virginia Gray, "The Socioeconomic and Political Context of States," in Virginia Gray, Russell Hanson, and Thad Kousser, eds., *Politics in the American States*, 10th ed. (Thousand Oaks, CA: CQ Press, 2013), 26.

18. Alice Rivlin, "Rethinking Federalism for More Effective Governance," *Publius* 42 (2012): 390.

19. Shama Gamkhar and J. Mitchell Pickerill, "The State of American Federalism 2011–2012: A Fend for Yourself and Activist Form of Bottom-up Federalism," *Publius* 42 (2012): 378.

20. John D. Nugent, *Safeguarding Federalism*, 215–16.

21. Alan Rosenthal, *The Decline of Representative Democracy* (Washington DC: CQ Press, 1997), Peverill Squire and Gary Moncrief, *State Legislatures Today: Politics Under the Domes* (Boston: Longman, 2010), 241–44.

22. Jennifer Dorrah, "Statehouse Exodus," *American Journalism Review* (April/May 2009), www.ajr.org/article.asp?id=4721.

23. Nugent, *Safeguarding Federalism*, 216.

Index

About the Authors

Gary Moncrief is University Distinguished Professor of Political Science and University Foundation Research Scholar at Boise State University. He is the editor of *Reapportionment and Redistricting in the West* and coauthor of *State Legislatures Today: Politics Under the Domes* and *Who Runs for the Legislature?* Professor Moncrief has published more than sixty book chapters and research journal articles. He is a frequent speaker at training workshops for state legislators and staff.

Peverill Squire holds the Hicks and Martha Griffiths Chair in American Political Institutions and the Frederick A. Middlebush Chair in Political Science at the University of Missouri. He is the author of *The Evolution of American Legislatures: Colonies, Territories and States, 1619-2009*; coauthor of *State Legislatures Today: Politics Under the Domes*; *101 Chambers: Congress, State Legislatures, and the Future of Legislative Studies*; and *Who Runs for the Legislature?*, and coeditor of *Legislatures: Comparative Perspectives on Representative Assemblies*. Professor Squire is the senior editor of *Legislative Studies Quarterly*.